SKETCHING
IN THE CITY

TOBY HASELER

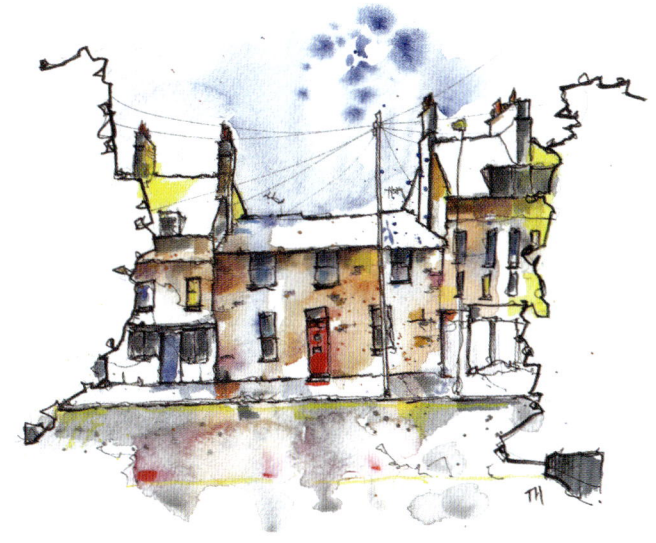

TOOLS AND TECHNIQUES FOR THE URBAN ARTIST

DAVID & CHARLES
—PUBLISHING—

www.davidandcharles.com

CONTENTS

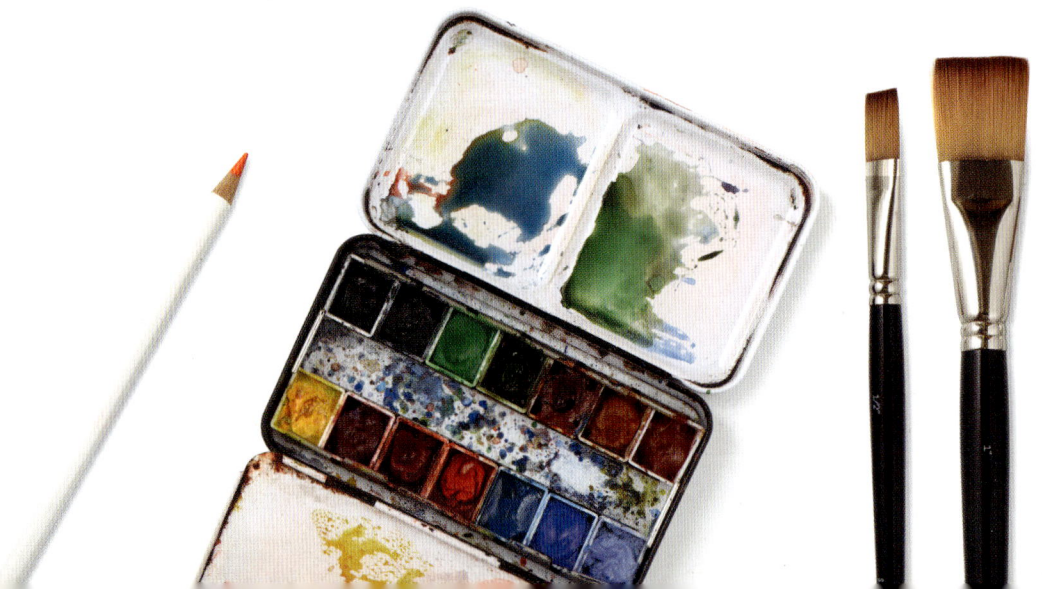

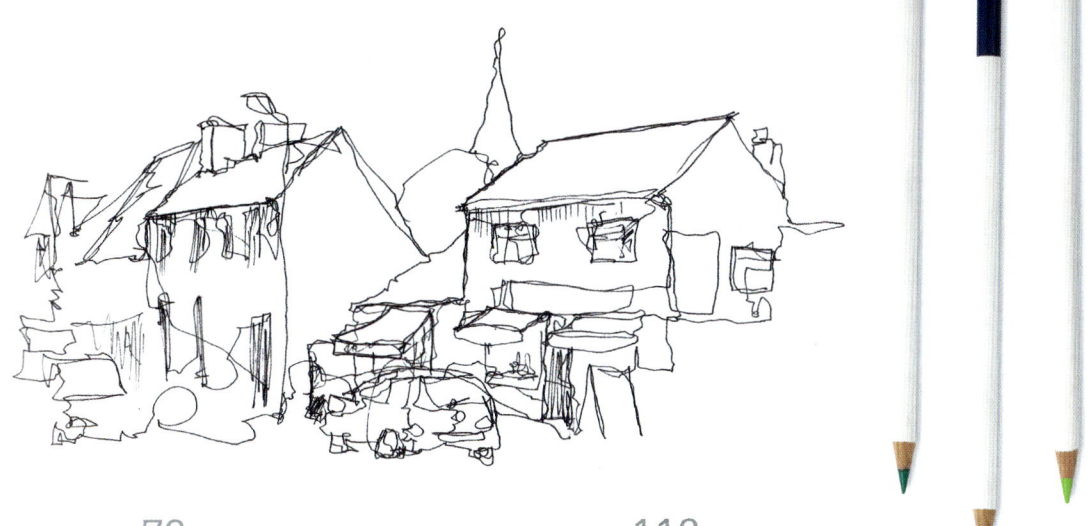

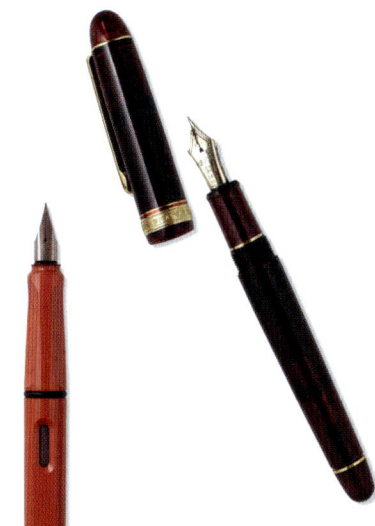

INTRODUCTION

Hello and welcome to *Sketching in the City*. In this book, my goal is to make urban sketching feel achievable. We will use the vibrant bustling environment of the city to break free from the pressure of perfection, and lose the 'I'm not good enough' mindset. Through encouraging experimentation, and a focus on fundamentals, you'll find moments of magic to liberate your artistic style. Packed with diverse ideas and techniques, it's a guide to finding joy, confidence, and creativity in capturing the energy of city life.

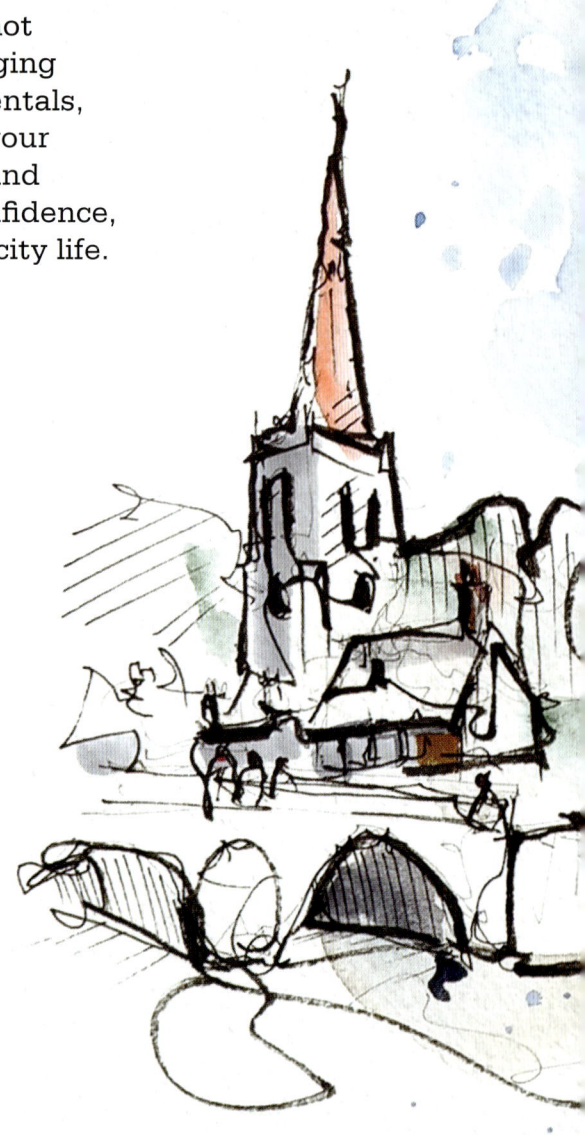

SKETCHING AS ART

'To sketch' is traditionally defined as 'making a rough draft or outline'. This makes sketching sound like an incomplete art form. However, in recent years, sketching has taken on a contemporary twist and become something more. Much more. Sketching is a celebration of observation, imagination, and spontaneity. It combines elements of drawing, mark-making, painting, and mixed media to capture the essence of a moment, place, or idea in its raw, unpolished form.

A BRAVE MINDSET

Expression is at the heart of sketching. It's not about perfection but about discovering and embracing your unique style. Being confident and brave means accepting what happens on the page, whether it's a happy accident or a learning opportunity. Each sketch is a step forward – a chance to grow, explore, and refine your approach.

Use every sketch as a chance to identify small improvements, but remember that the most important thing is to enjoy the process. When you focus on the joy of creating, you'll naturally feel more confident and inspired to keep going. With time and practice, you'll find that your sketches not only improve but will also carry the energy and personality of your own expressive style.

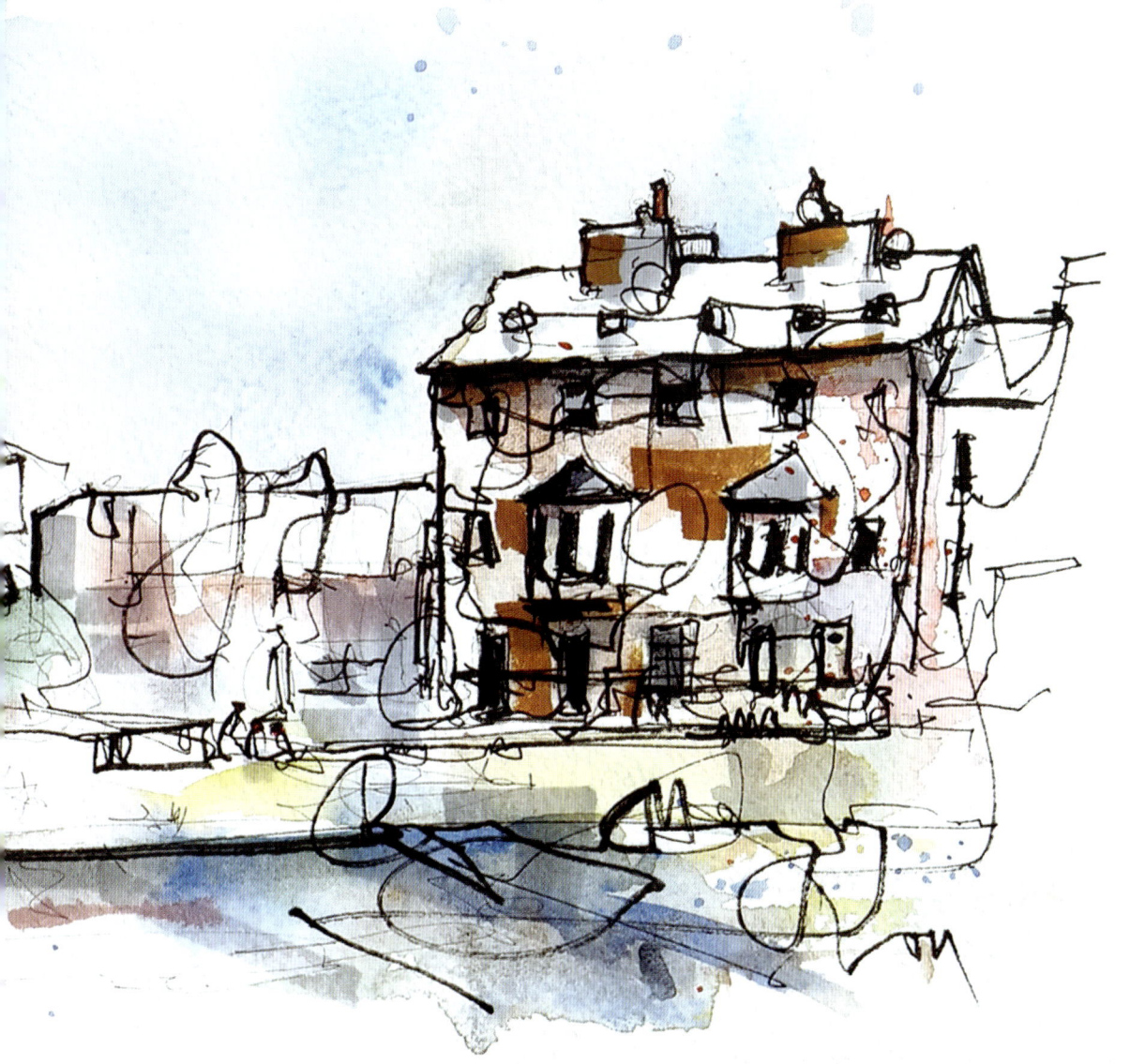

TOOLS AND TECHNIQUES

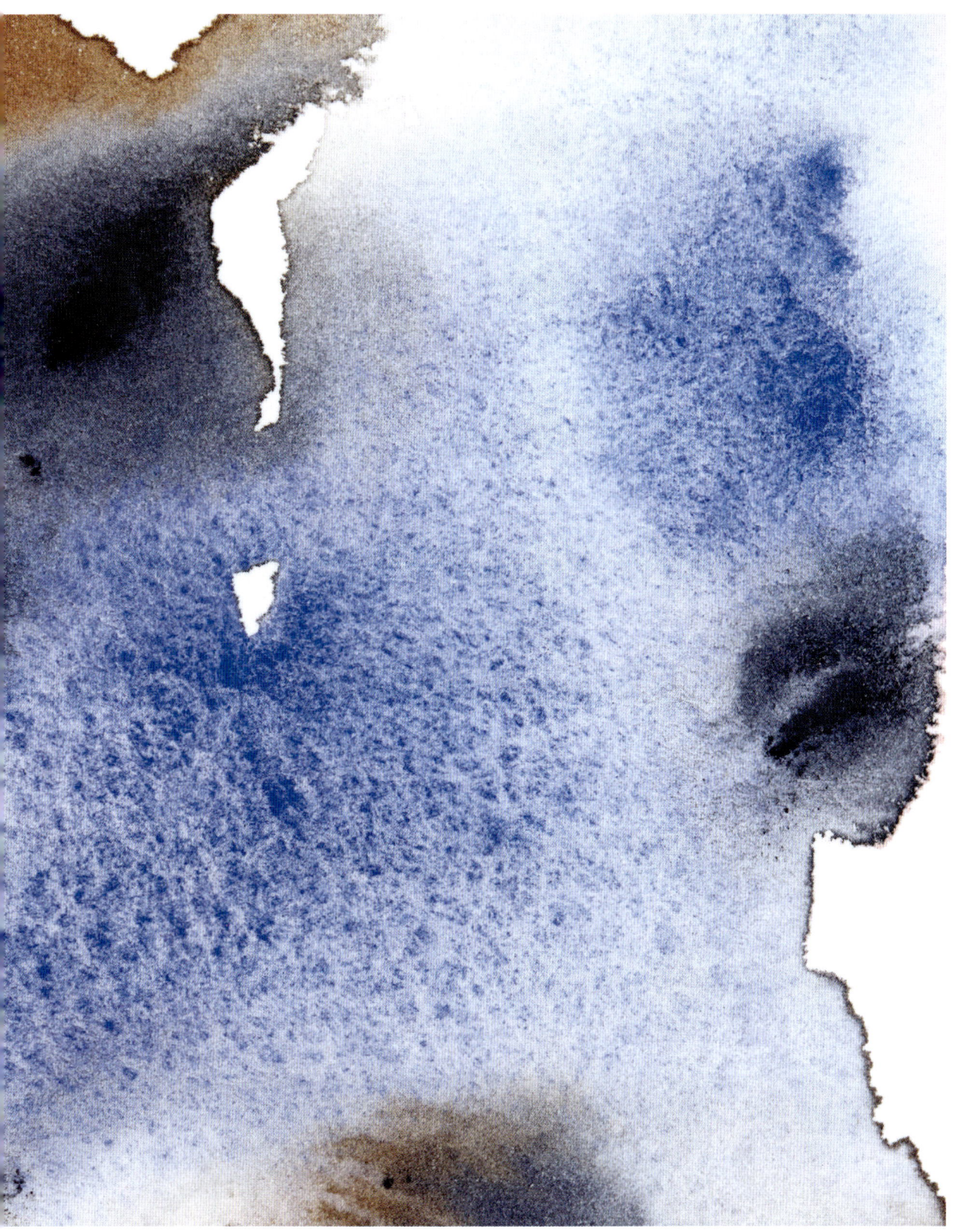

ESSENTIAL TOOLS

Sketching doesn't require fancy equipment; simplicity is key. Here are the basics that you'll need to complete the projects in this book, along with some of my favourite items and additional supplies to broaden your practice.

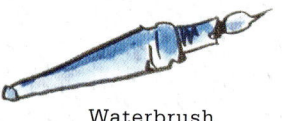

Waterbrush

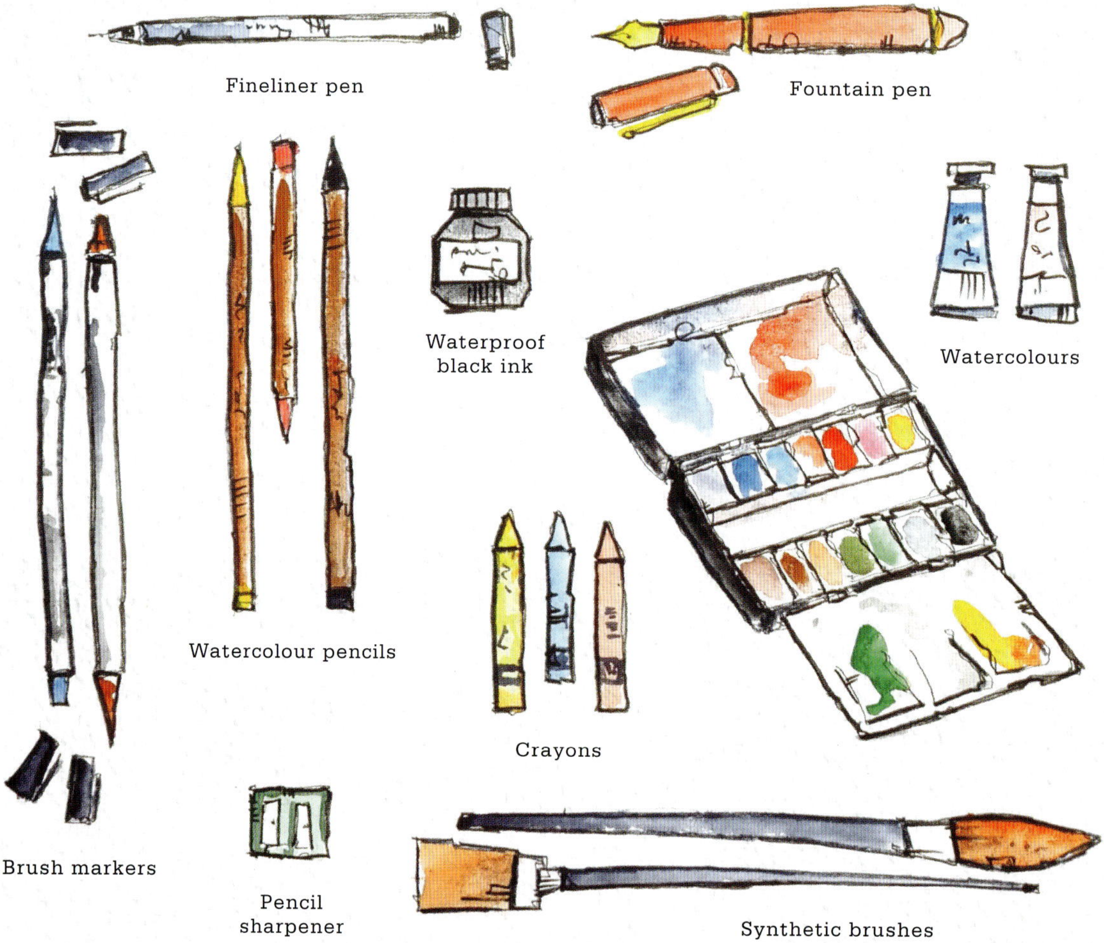

Fineliner pen

Fountain pen

Waterproof black ink

Watercolours

Watercolour pencils

Crayons

Brush markers

Pencil sharpener

Synthetic brushes

FOUNTAIN PENS

I prefer a fountain pen as my main sketching implement. The nib of a fountain pen is flexible, providing a wide range of line widths and characters. The reverse of the nib can also be used to create an ultra-fine line. A terrific starting point is a Platinum Preppy with a fine or extra-fine nib, while my favourite pen is the Platinum 3776 with an ultra-extra-fine nib.

FINELINER PENS

Fineliners have a more controlled line, and tend to be defined by the width of the line they produce. They range from 0.03mm all the way up to 1.0mm or bolder. With a number of different fineliners, you can therefore achieve a range of line widths similar to a fountain pen.

FUDE PENS

These pens are designed to mimic the expressiveness of traditional calligraphy brushes. They can be soft-nibbed fineliners or fountain pens with a bent nib.

INK

Most fineliners are waterproof, which is important for the 'line and wash' techniques used in the book, where we add watercolour after our ink marks. With fountain pens, be careful when selecting a waterproof ink to ensure it is fountain-pen safe. Pigment inks like Platinum's carbon black are waterproof when dry and designed specifically for fountain pens. Inks such as India ink, acrylic ink, or iron gall ink are not safe for fountain pens and can permanently block them.

WATERCOLOURS

A small palette of vibrant hues adds depth and energy to your sketches. I personally use 12 to 14 pigments in my palette, but rarely more than 5 or 6 in each sketch. Start with primary colours and build your collection as you go. Artist-quality paints usually offer superior transparency and vibrancy, but student-quality paints are also more than adequate for producing beautiful art.

BRUSHES

A few versatile synthetic brushes – such as a round brush for details and a flat or mop brush for washes – are all you need to begin. Don't be tempted to go too small – a bigger brush holds more water, creates more transparent colours, and prevents you overworking.

OTHER SUPPLIES

Low tack masking tape or painter's tape can be used to hold down loose sheets of paper and create lovely frames on your page. There is also a diverse range of mixed media: pastels, pencils, crayons, acrylic markers, and brush pens are amongst the most common you might employ. See the Mixed Media section later in this chapter for more details.

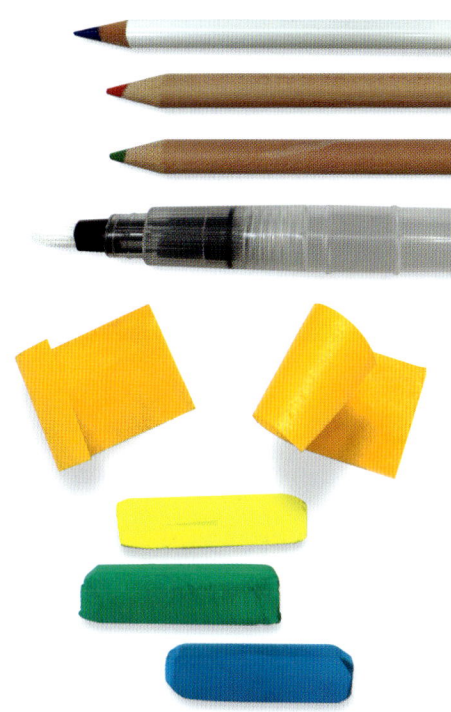

SKETCHING SURFACES

Every great sketch begins with the surface. The type and quality of paper you choose plays a crucial role in shaping your art. We are often all too keen to invest in new paints and pens, but don't underestimate the importance of finding the right surface for your style.

THE CASE FOR SKETCHBOOKS

A well-used sketchbook can become a work of art. The individual sketches within might be imperfect, but as a collection, they show your journey as an artist. They might be memories from a holiday, or a certain phase of experimentation and style.

Add personal touches swatches – or even physical elements such as pressed leaves or tickets – to create a layered, immersive experience. Allow your scenes to spill across pages, incorporating the physical structure of the page into your art.

THE CASE FOR BLOCKS OR SHEETS

The highest quality paper, ideal for handling heavy use of water and watercolours, is typically available loose or in blocks rather than in sketchbooks. This makes it perfect for projects you may want to frame or share.

For the best results, choose paper that is 300gsm (140lb) or heavier, as it provides the durability needed for wet techniques without warping. Cotton paper, made from 100 per cent cotton fibres, is superior for watercolour work, offering excellent absorption, smooth blending, and vibrant colour retention.

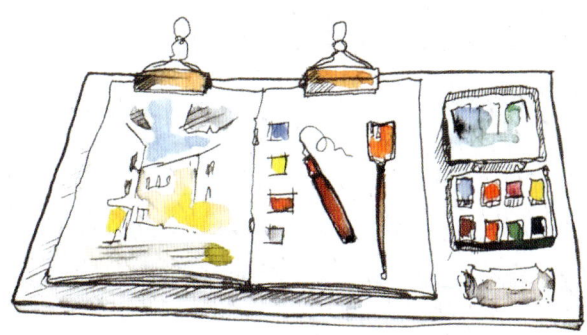

If you plan to use a lot of water or create multiple layers, consider 450gsm (210lb) paper, which can withstand even the heaviest washes, while maintaining its texture and integrity.

A PORTABLE STUDIO

For ultimate portability, a simple piece of foam board can transform your set-up into a flexible studio. With a few clips (you'll spot these in some of my sketches), you can secure your chosen surface to your board. Foam board is lightweight, durable, and inexpensive. It's also easy to cut to a size that suits your style, making it a practical choice.

While foam board is an excellent and affordable option, there are many other tools available. You can explore specialized sketching boards, easels, or bags with built-in storage and tripod attachments. Starting simple is key – a basic set-up allows you to focus on your art and discover what's truly needed. Over time, you can identify what might enhance your experience and invest in tools that fit your workflow.

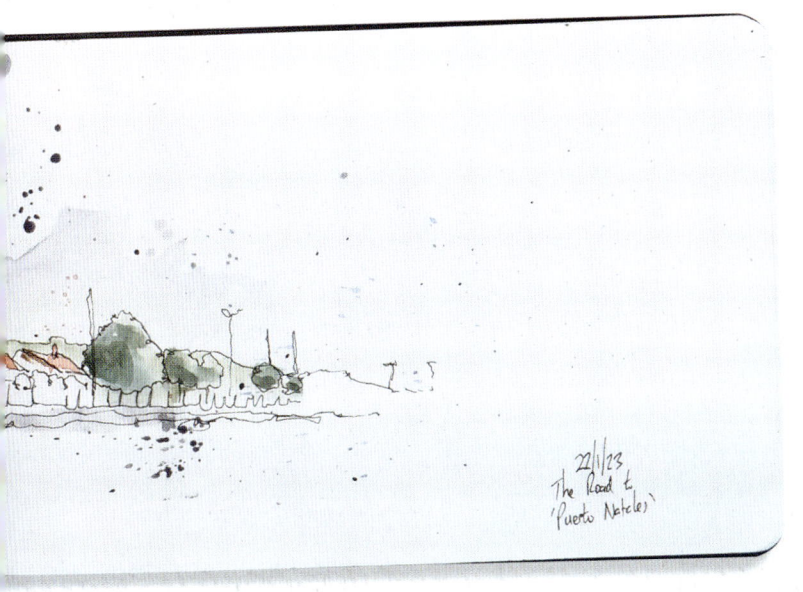

LINE WORK AND MARK-MAKING

Line art, most commonly in ink, is the starting point for many sketchers. Learning to wield your ink lines with confidence and variety is a fundamental skill that might even define your style.

LINES, CONTOURS, AND SHAPES

Lines can build the contour of an object or scene. That contour provides a silhouette that often describes a scene remarkably well without the need for further detail. Lines can also build shapes on a page. Describing the various parts of, for example, a building in terms of circles, squares, and triangles simplifies the process of capturing complex objects with relative ease (**A**).

TEXTURE

We use the word 'texture' to describe the way we create a visual representation of the tactile quality of a surface, for example in this delicate stonework (**B**).

The textures we create can be completely abstract. Scribbles on a page build up to represent the tones, values, and shapes of this modernist architecture (**C**). And for any given scene or object, there will be myriad ways of representing the textures.

A

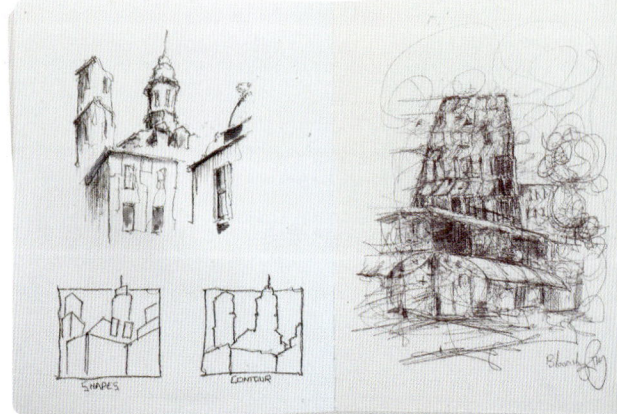

C

B

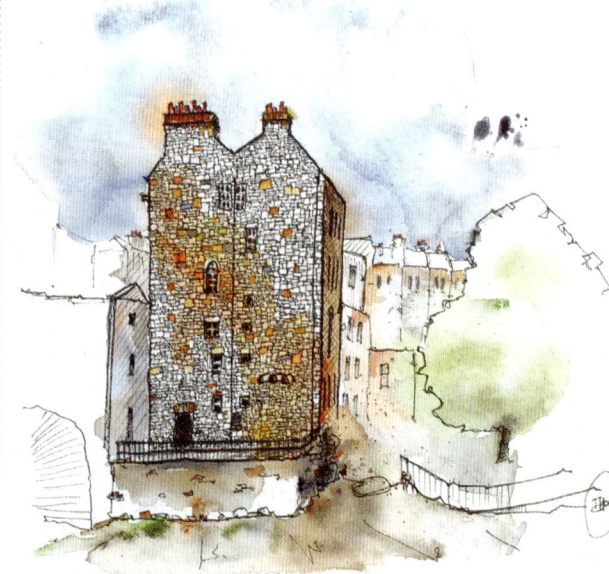

HATCHING IN INK

Hatching is a fundamental ink technique that adds depth, value, and texture. You can explore hatching by filling abstract squares (D) with varied marks, or creating small thumbnail scenes (E). As you experiment, consider the following to create variety.

Density: closer lines create darker values, while more spaced lines suggest lighter areas.

Direction: changing the direction of your hatching can define the shape and flow of a surface.

Layering: build layers of hatching to deepen shadows and add complexity to textures.

Varied marks: strict linear marks are often used, but stippling, scribbling, or other repetitive shapes are among many other possibilities.

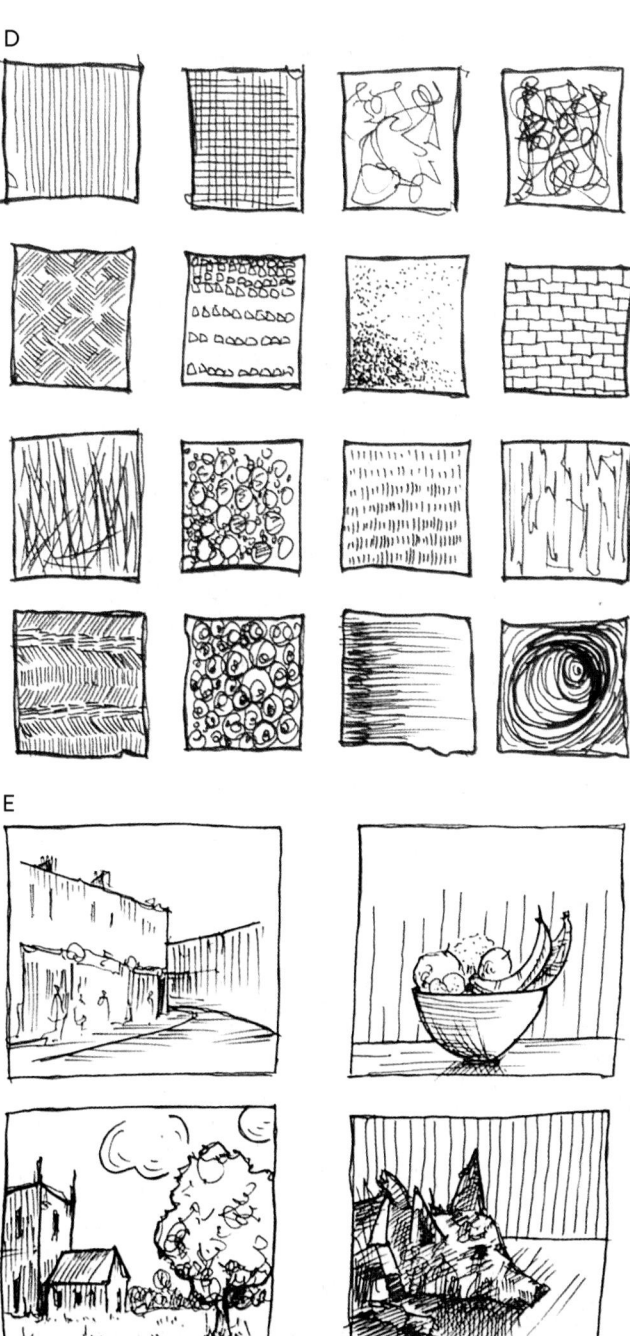

An interesting experiment is to head outside, find a heavily textured wall, and recreate that texture while exploring the marks your pen is capable of. My fude pen (**F**) and fountain pen (**G**), despite having many similarities, can also produce remarkably different marks and lines.

F

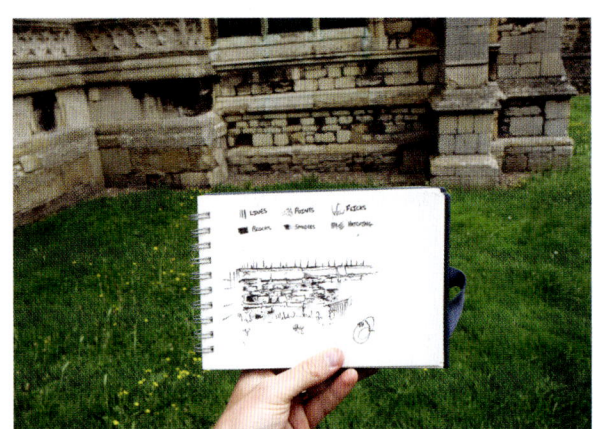

G

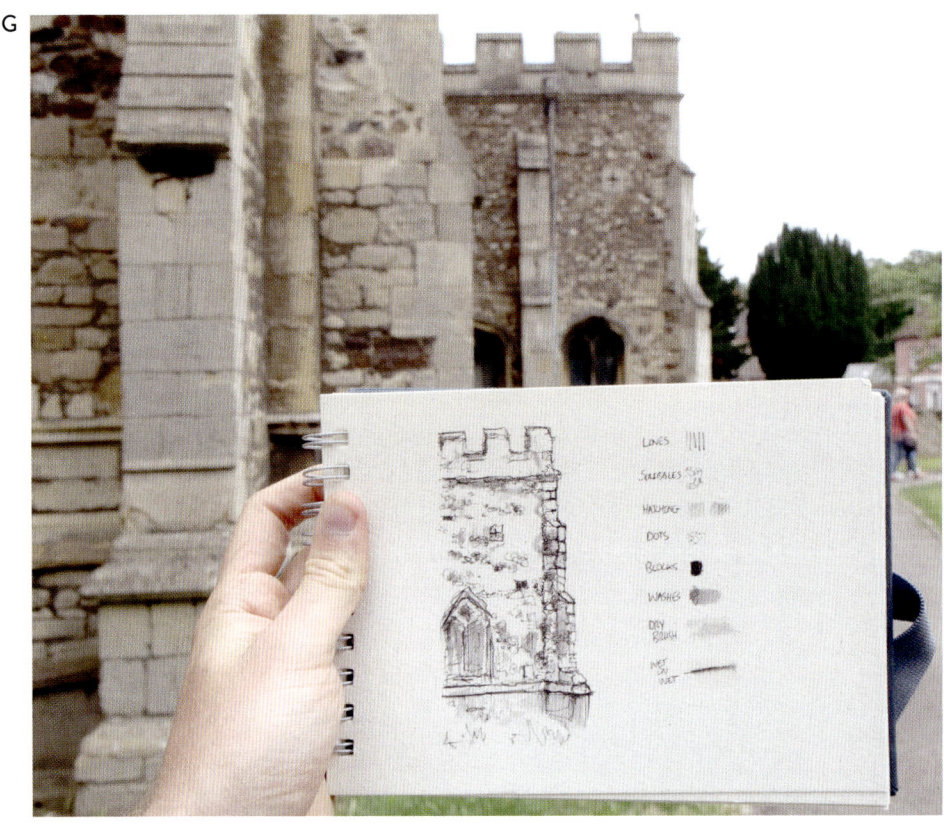

VALUE STUDIES

Use the following exercises to develop a deeper understanding of texture and value, enhancing your ability to bring life to your art.

Linear Hatching

A household object like a packet of crisps offers a multitude of shadows and reflections so serves as a fascinating study.

1 Start with a simple contour drawing of the packet, with interior lines to show key folds.

2 Squinting at the packet will help simplify the shadows. Add hatching to everywhere you see shadow, making sure to leave the lightest areas white.

3 Slowly build up the hatching in the areas of darkest shadow. It can be helpful to build a value scale as a reference at the side of your page.

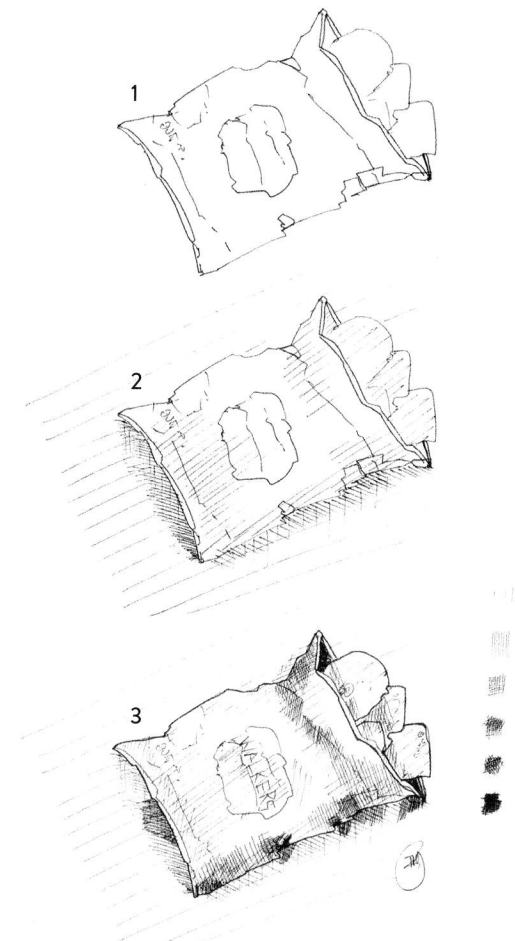

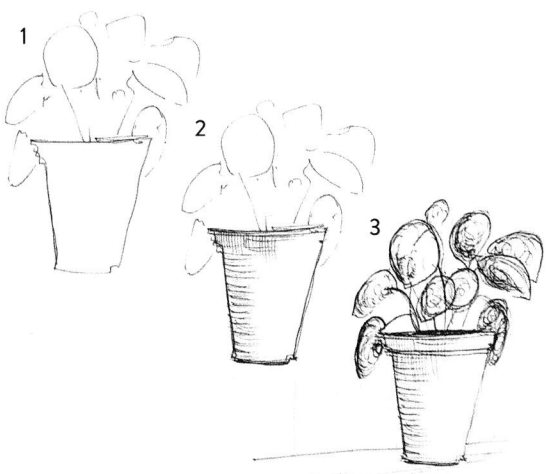

Naturalistic Hatching

A house plant offers a different challenge, with fewer angles and more flowing shapes.

1 Again, start with a simple contour drawing of the pot and the shapes of the leaves.

2 Paying attention to the form of the objects, you can use curved hatching on the pot to accentuate the cylindrical dimensions.

3 Similarly, looping lines that mimic the shapes of the leaves can be used to add value to the key shadows of the plant itself.

SOLUBLE INK

Soluble ink offers a unique opportunity to create expressive, moody artwork. Unlike permanent ink, soluble ink reacts with water, allowing you to blur, soften, and blend your lines into captivating washes.

TOOLS

To create these effects, you'll need some specific tools.

Soluble ink pens: fountain pens or rollerball pens with water-soluble ink.

Waterbrush: a simple tool with a reservoir for water, perfect for softening lines and blending ink on the go.

Paper: use watercolour or mixed-media paper to handle the added moisture.

THE PROCESS

Once you've sketched your image with soluble ink lines, use a waterbrush to move the ink around the image (A and B). Repeat the process to create deeper shadows and to create mood (C) – this interplay of defined lines and fluid gradients lends itself to atmospheric sketches and dynamic compositions.

ADDING COLOUR

The additional technique of pairing two soluble inks can produce fantastic effects, with a simple line drawing suddenly coming to life when activated by water (D).

You can paint directly with your ink too, lifting it from your fountain pen with a brush to create much bolder marks (E).

Flicks or splatters of ink, wet-on-wet lines, and far more besides are all possible. And all that this requires is a pen and a brush, making it an accessible tool for sketching outside, on location (F).

EXPERIMENT AND EXPLORE

The beauty of soluble ink lies in its unpredictability and fluidity. The number of inks available are vast, and soluble ink sketching and ink painting is a whole artform in itself. Take time to explore this medium, and let the interplay of line and wash inspire your work.

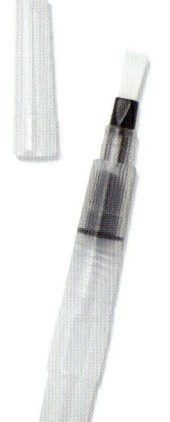
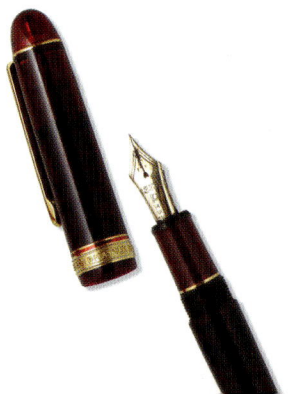

A

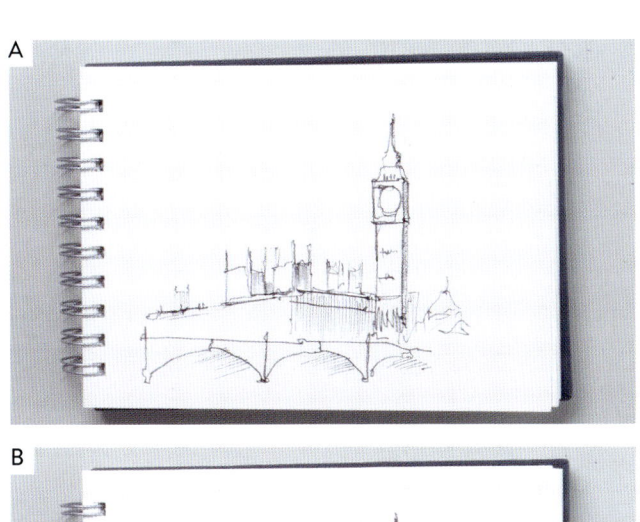

B

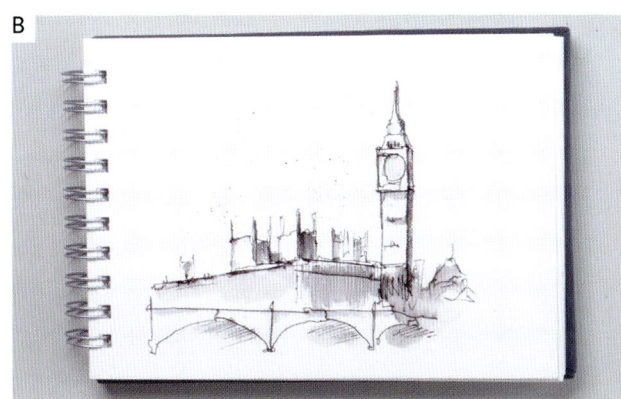

C

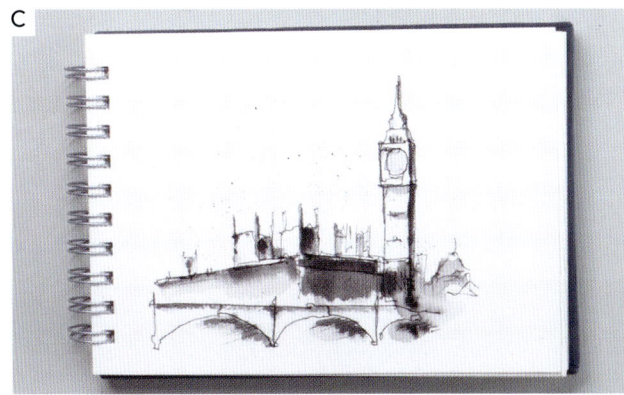

D

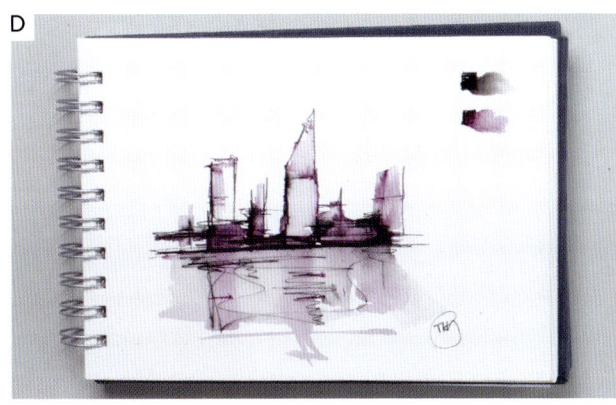

E

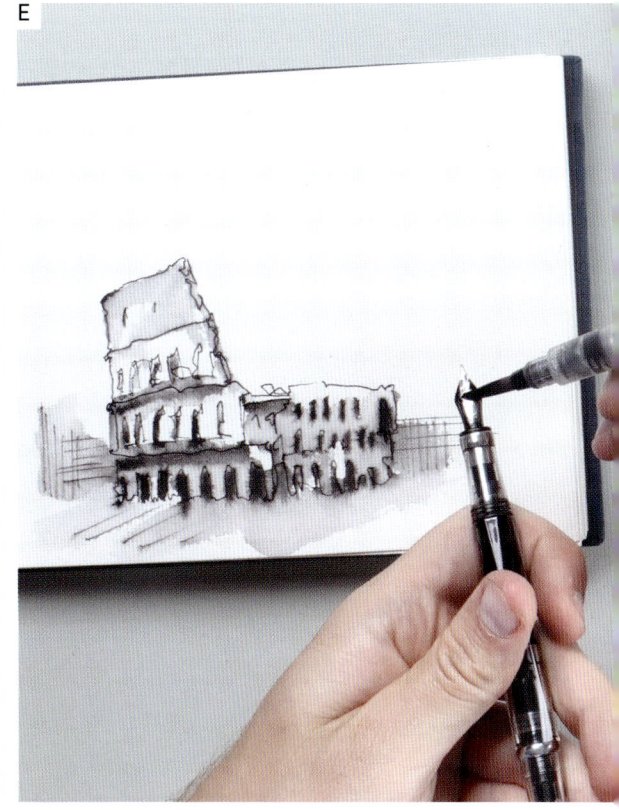

F

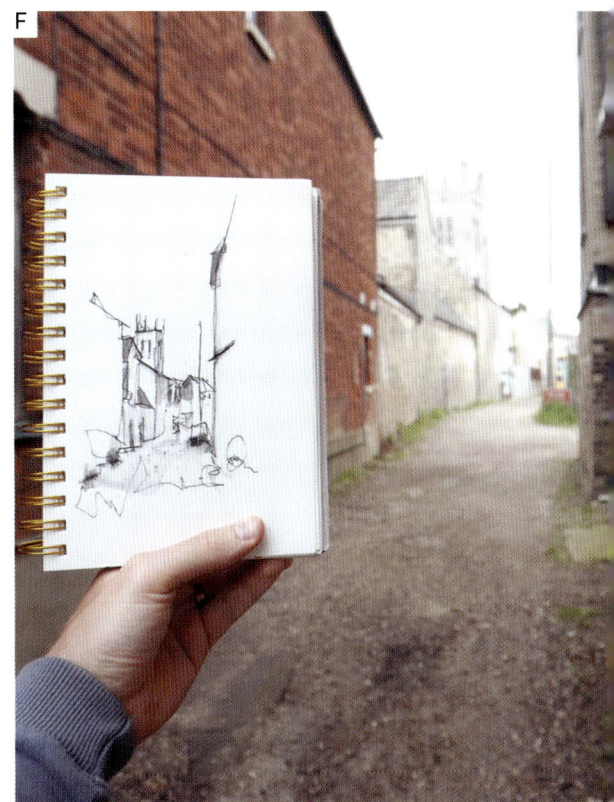

PERSPECTIVE

Perspective can feel intimidating, with whole books written about the subject. While major inaccuracies can feel 'off', overly precise perspective can be rigid and dull. As observational sketchers, however, approaching perspective without rigid rules can actually improve your sketches and create a livelier image.

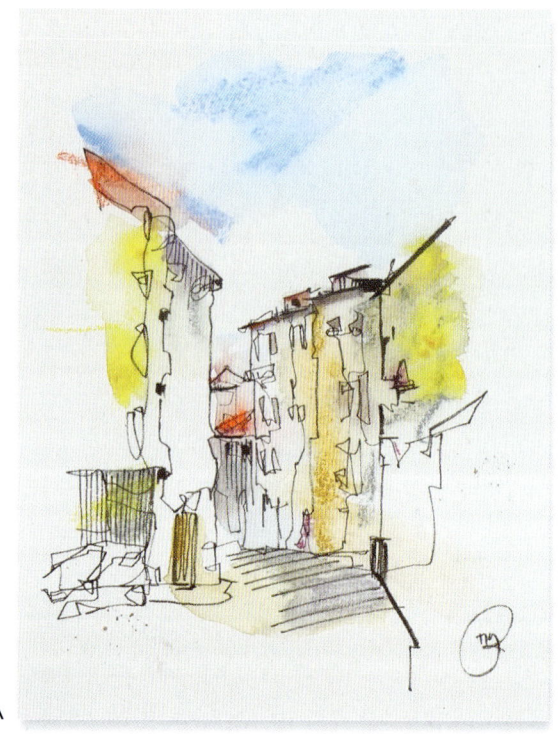

A

WHAT IS PERSPECTIVE?

Perspective in sketching is the technique used to represent three-dimensional objects and scenes on our two-dimensional surface, such as on paper, helping to bring them to life. Capturing the perspective of a city street can be engaging, drawing you down into the scene (A), as well as helping make tricky subjects like long trains believable (B).

B

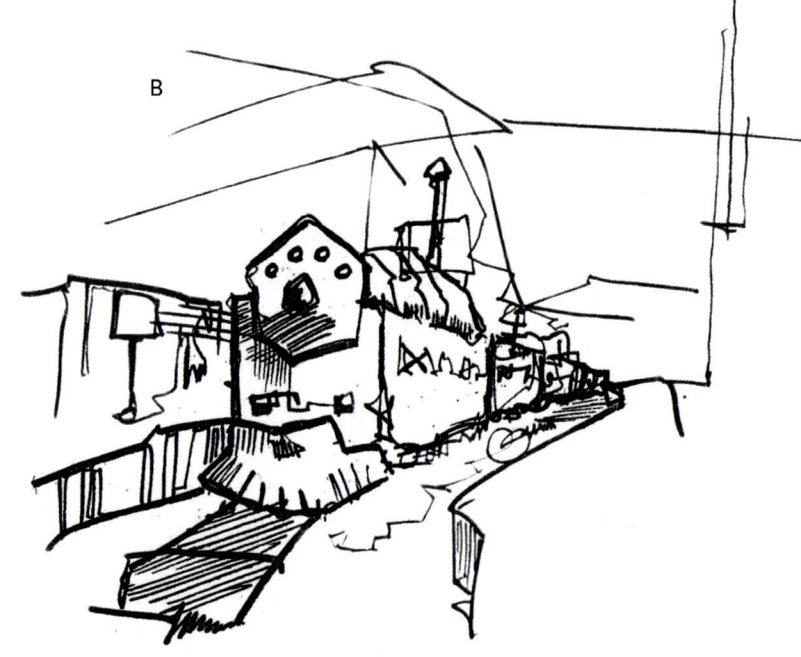

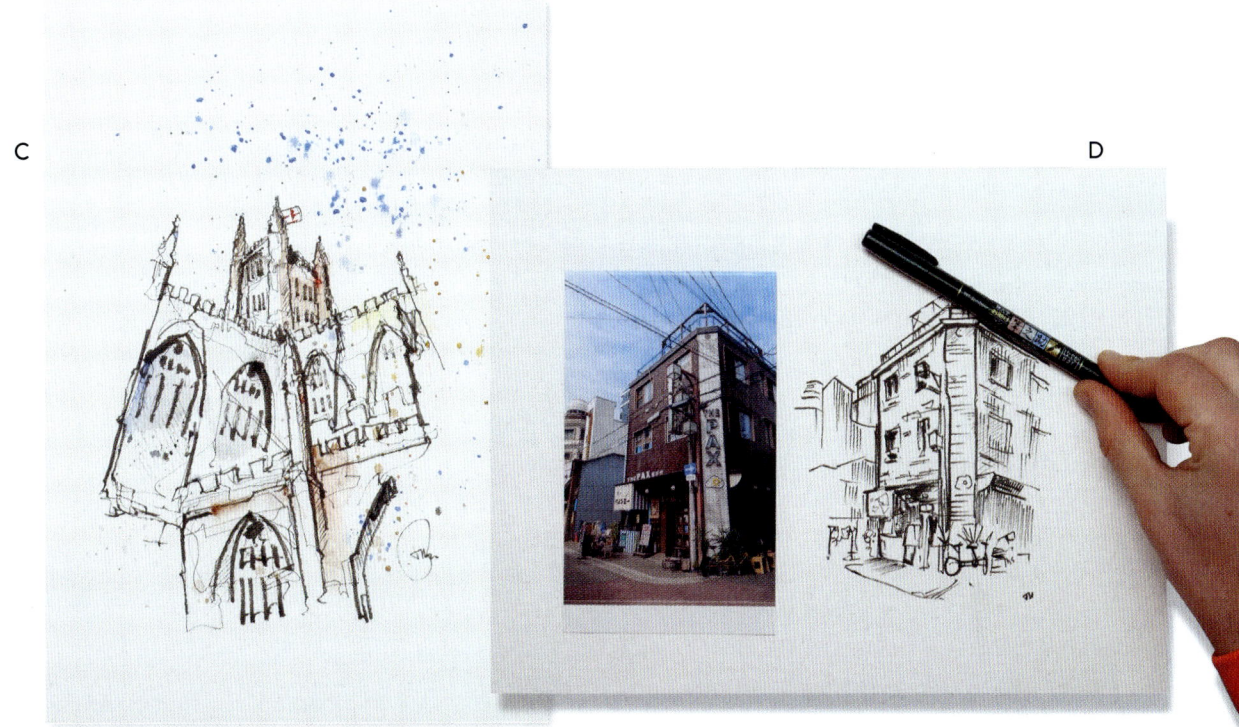

C

D

EMBRACE IMPERFECTION

Perspective doesn't need to be precise – small inaccuracies add character to your work (**C**). The real world is messy, with lines that rarely align perfectly. Your sketches should feel believable, not technical.

SIGHTING YOUR PERSPECTIVE

There is a bamboozling array of terms that are used to describe perspective, but the reality is that observation (referred to as sighting your perspective) is often far more practical and effective.

I suggest the following as a useful framework for approaching perspective both from reference photos and on location sketching (**D**). Over time, observational practice will refine your intuitive sense of perspective, making your drawings more natural and dynamic.

Look closely: notice how lines converge in roads, railways, and buildings.

Trust your instincts: sketch what feels right instead of overthinking perspective rules.

Use your pen: align it with an angle in your scene, then replicate it on paper.

Find key lines: use dominant lines like rooflines or windows as guides.

Compare proportions: check the relative sizes of objects in your sketch to ensure they are approximately correct in relation to one another.

Focus on overlaps: overlapping objects create a stronger sense of depth.

Be playful: experiment with exaggerating, reversing, or ignoring perspective.

WATERCOLOURS

Watercolour is a versatile and expressive medium that can produce delicate washes through to bold, opaque, and painterly brushstrokes. They also have a key advantage to sketchers that they are portable and can be used anywhere, are quick to paint with, and require little cleaning. Most surfaces can simply be wiped clean if any paint does go astray.

CHOOSING YOUR PALETTE

The right watercolour palette cannot be scientifically chosen. Every set-up will have pros and cons, and what works for you should reflect your personal style and preferences. Our style tends to develop over time, which means our palette and taste in colours tends to change as well.

Many of the basic sets by well-known brands are well-thought through, provide a wide range of pigments without being overwhelming, and are an excellent place to start.

As your style develops, you may wish to build your own palette. The core of my palette is usually five to seven primary colours, including both cool and warm tones to maximise versatility. For example, rhodonite in my palette is a very cool red, while pyrrol scarlet is warm. But you can take personal preference into account too – for example, I have three blues, but only one yellow.

Next, I add two to four earth tones. These are atmospheric colours, browns and neutrals that add depth and mood.

Finally, consider some speciality or convenience colours. These are colours or pigments that you find especially interesting to use, or convenient to have pre-mixed. For example, I usually have pre-mixed greens in my palette as it is convenient to paint with them even though they are easily mixed. I also include colours with special properties such as granulation or opacity to add extra texture.

CREATE A COLOUR CHART

Swatch each colour in your palette onto a piece of paper. This is a useful reference when getting to know your palette.

As you paint, you'll also learn a little about each of the colours – from how well it re-wets in your palette, to its texture when you paint.

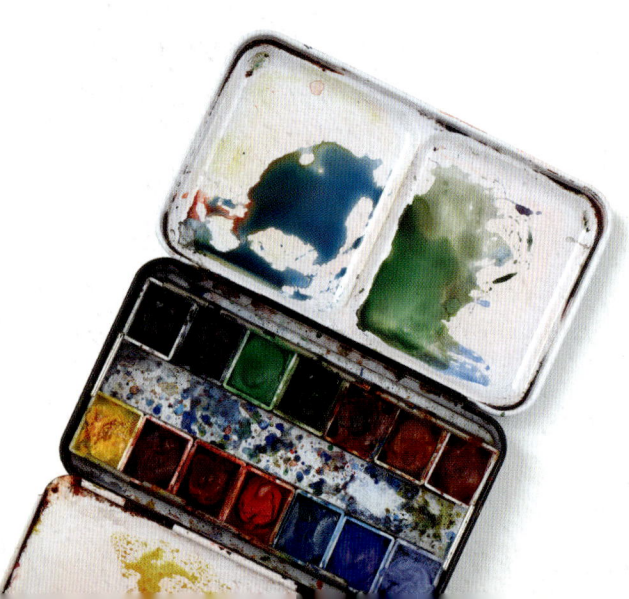

PRIMARY COLOURS

Lavender

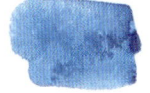

Cobalt blue

Cerulean blue

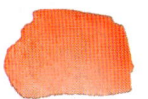

Organic vermilion

Pyrrol scarlet

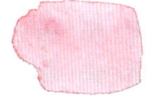

Rhodonite

Hansa yellow medium

EARTH TONES

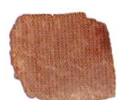

Indian red

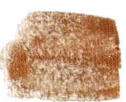

Lunar earth

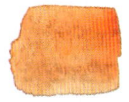

Quinacridone sienna

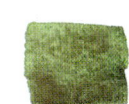

Green apatite

Cobalt green

Indigo

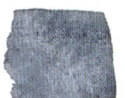

Payne's grey

FOCUSSED SWATCHES

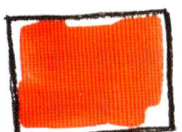

Masstone

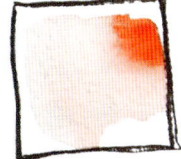

Wet-on-wet

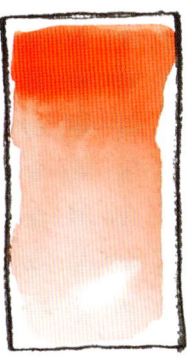

Gradient

CREATE FOCUSSED SWATCHES

To learn more about the colours in your palette, you can make specific swatches for each.

Start by painting a square of a flat strong wash – this is the 'masstone' of a colour.

Next, create a gradient. Start with the bold masstone and gradually add more water to appreciate the full range achievable with your pigment.

Finally, pre-wet a square on your page and then touch in a bit of pigment to the corner with your brush. Notice how the pigment moves with the water and the textures it creates when it settles. This is the wet-on-wet technique.

MY FIVE-STEP PROCESS

Now that we've looked at various tools and techniques, it's time to bring ink and watercolour together to create your sketches. The process outlined here forms the foundation of my sketching and style. It's not a set of strict rules, but rather a way of thinking and approaching your art.

WHY HAVING A PROCESS MATTERS

Having a process is like having a reliable framework to support your creativity. It may sound counter-intuitive, but a strong process is liberating, not restrictive. By breaking your sketching into steps, it prevents the whole process feeling overwhelming. And when you know what works, you can confidently experiment and take risks, knowing there's an underlying structure to guide you.

A GUIDE, NOT RULES

This process is not a set of rules. Over time, you will find your personal style and the processes that you enjoy and trust the most. To find that place, experimenting and breaking the rules a little is necessary. In the meantime, this process forms the backbone of all the art in this book so take time to get to know it.

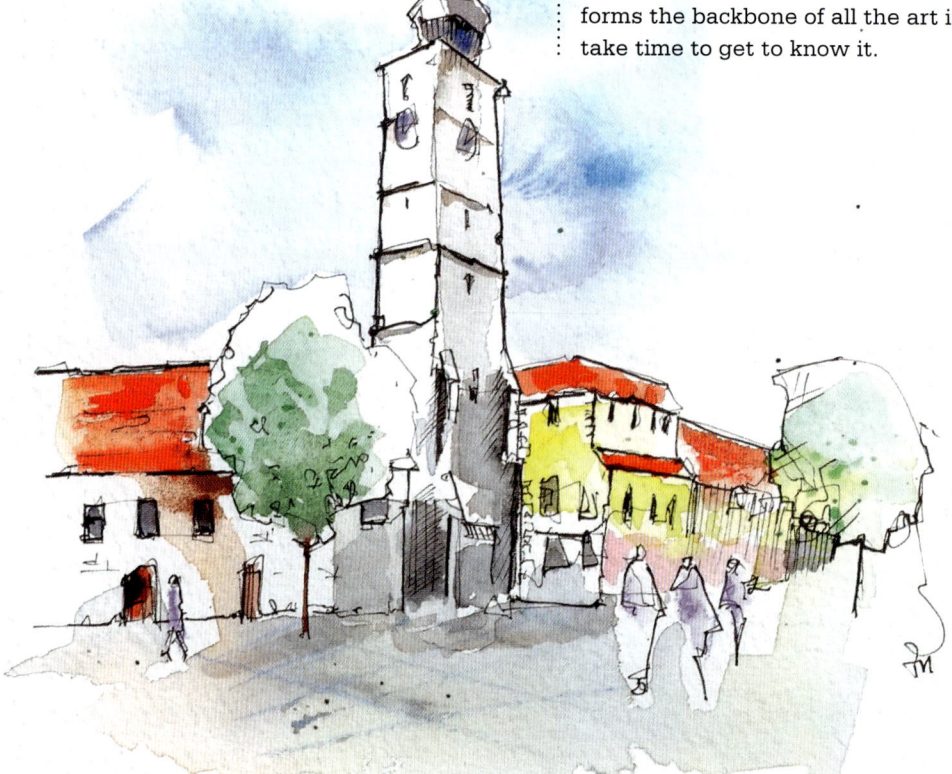

STEP ONE: SHAPES AND CONTOUR

1 Using light and loose lines, build up the contour of the scene. Focus on the biggest shapes and don't get stuck into details yet. For this stage, use a fineliner (around 0.2mm) or the reverse of your fountain pen nib.

2 With the initial structure on the page, now focus on restating key lines by gently retracing them. Using a bolder fineliner (0.5mm), or the fountain pen the normal way around, will naturally broaden the line. Be careful to keep the lines loose, and add variety with hatching for textures and shadow.

1

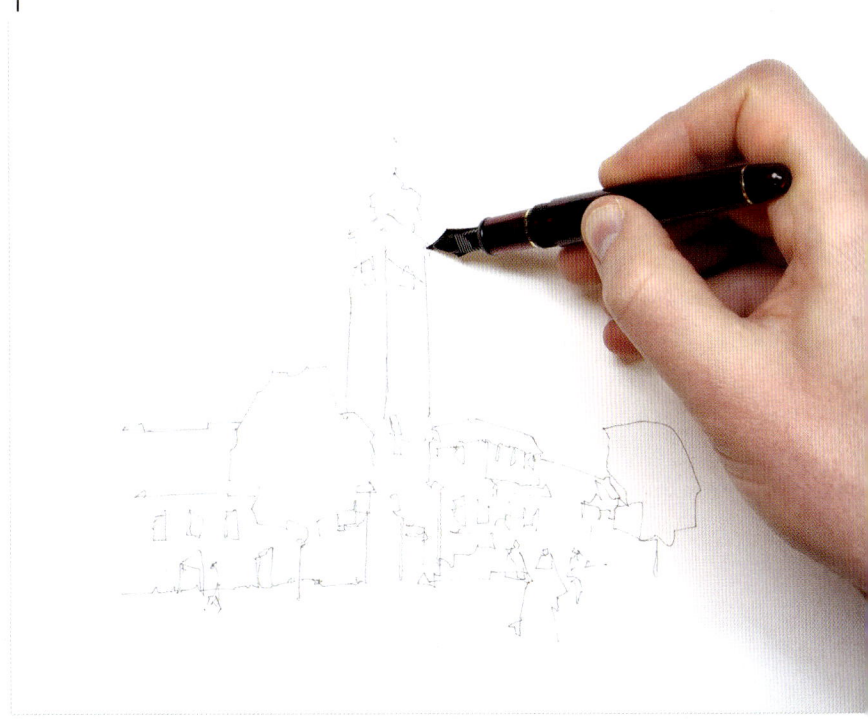

2

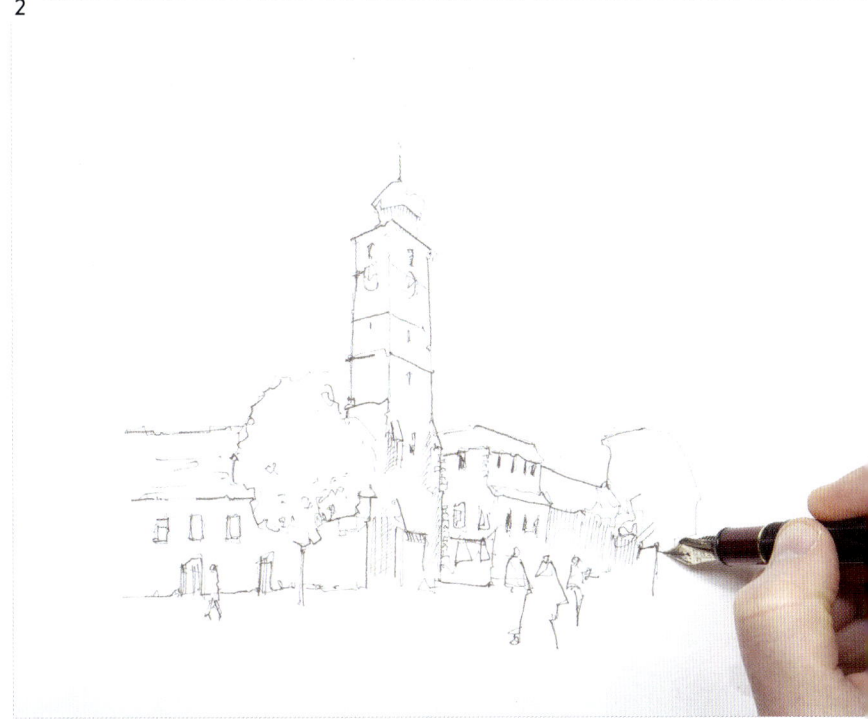

STEP TWO: LOOSE WATERCOLOUR WASH

3 Using a large brush, such as a size 20, apply a loose and watery wash starting in the sky. The page should be damp, but not flooded or pooling with water.

4 Now use the same loose wash throughout the rest of the scene, but be sure to leave some areas of white paper untouched. Leaving white space adds an airy, open feel to your sketch, enhances the contrast of your colours, and simplifies the overall process.

STEP THREE: WATERCOLOUR LAYERING

5 In watercolour painting, depth of shadow and richness of colour is achieved by layering the paint and using progressively smaller brushes. Look at your sketch and decide where to apply more paint. Between each layer, it's important to wait for the page to dry.

6 A small brush (such as a size 6) allows you to focus on more specific details, such as windows and doorways.

STEP FOUR: RESTATE THE INK

7 After waiting again for the colours to dry, you can restate your ink lines for a final time. Adding a little boldness and certainty to the key shapes and contours gives the image a little more impact.

STEP FIVE: ADD FINAL DETAILS

8 Finally, you might enhance the sketch with finer ink details, bold watercolour marks, or splatters. Using mixed media can add texture or highlights. Be careful not to overwork the sketch, but think outside the box and be creative to complete the five-step process.

3   4

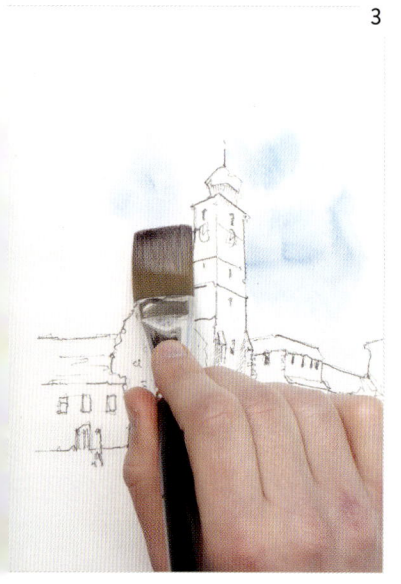
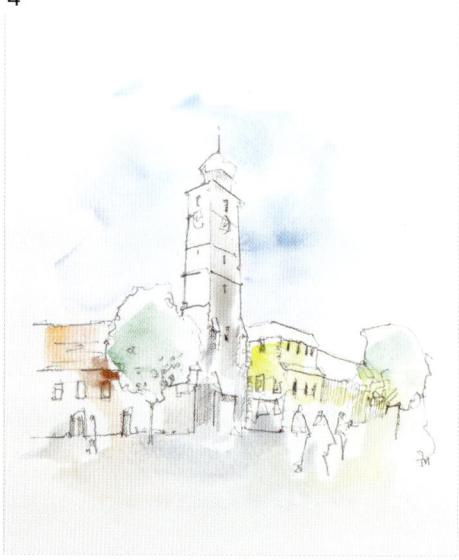

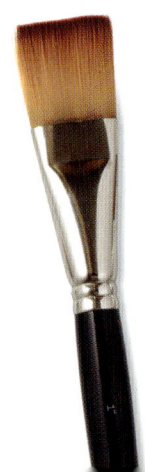

5

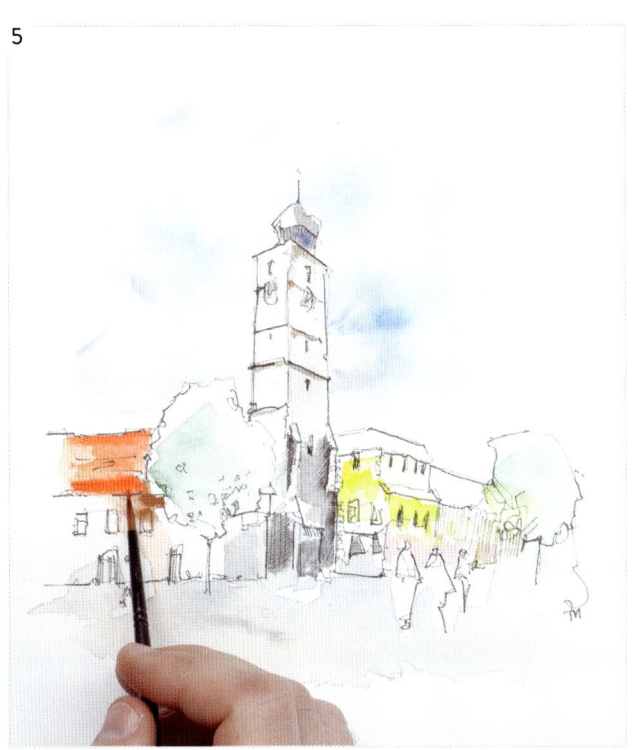

6

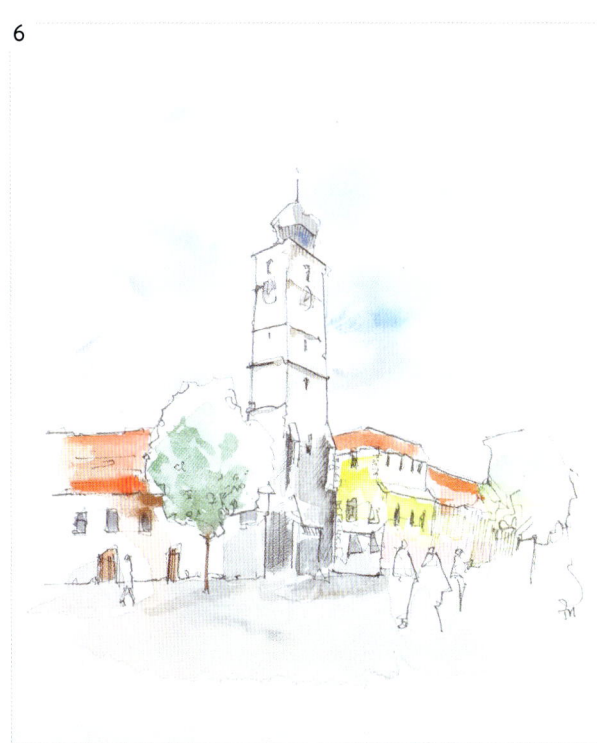

7

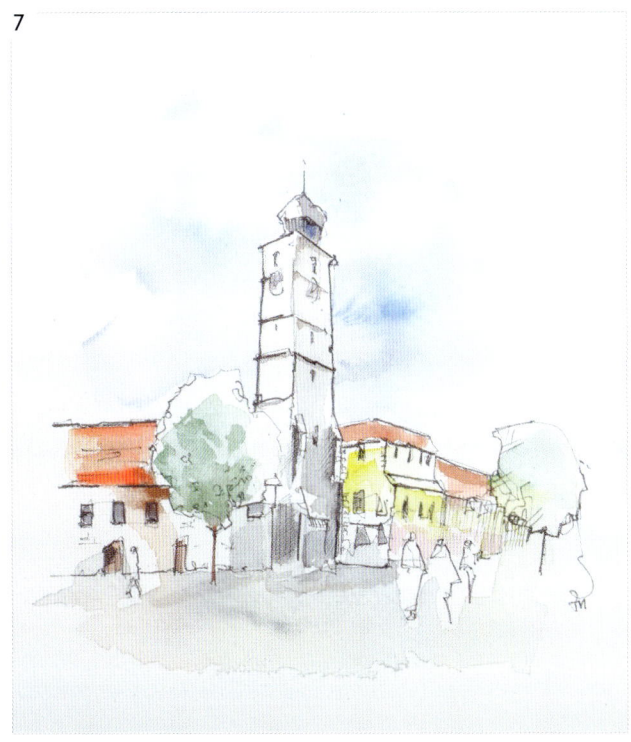

8

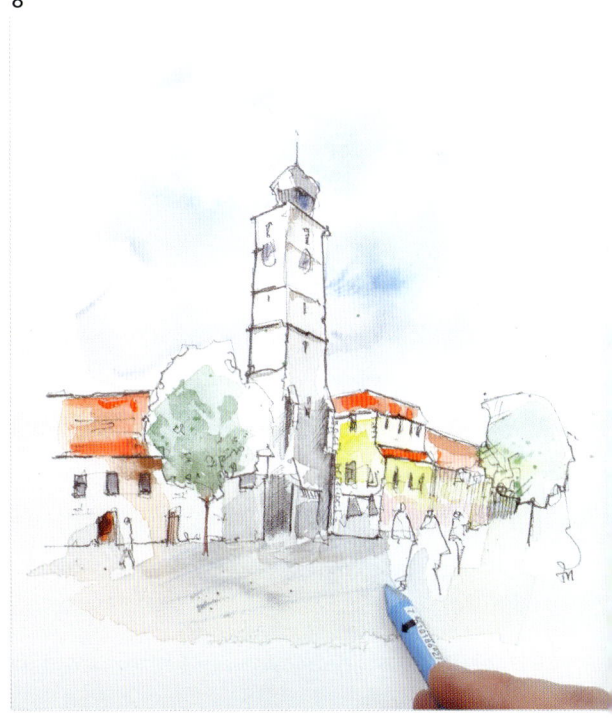

ADDITIONAL WATERCOLOUR TECHNIQUES

Watercolour is a wonderfully versatile medium, and its unique properties allow for techniques that are both expressive and freeing. These additional methods introduce an abstract touch to your work while retaining the loose, organic quality that makes watercolours so captivating.

NEGATIVE SPACE

Painting around a subject, while keeping the subject blank, is the purposeful act of leaving 'negative space'. The blank paper provides light to your painting, increasing the contrast in your image and creating more visual impact. It also simplifies a sketch, making it quicker to create and less likely to be overworked (B).

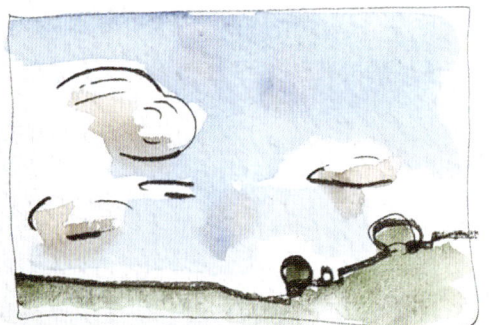

A

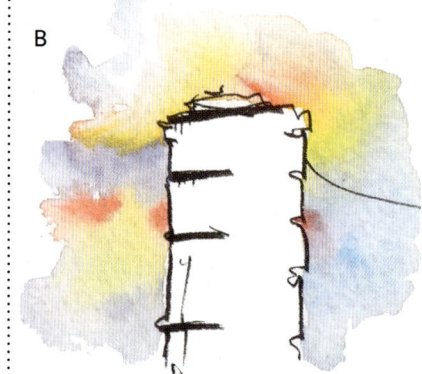

B

WET-ON-WET PAINTING

In this technique, the page is made wet before applying watercolour. The page can be pre-wet with pure water, or with a soft watercolour wash. This is ideal for quickly capturing atmospheric effects like skies, reflections, or rainy weather. Wet-on-wet painting also allows your colours to move in fascinating and unpredictable ways (A).

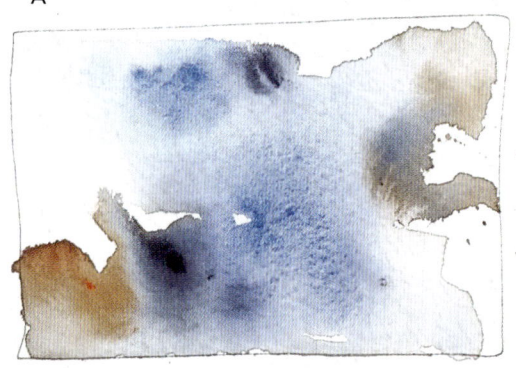

C

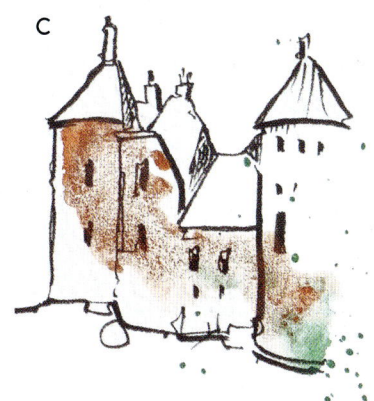

GRANULATION

Granulation is a property of certain watercolour pigments. It gives a sandy or grainy texture to the colours on the page. The effect is best brought out when there is plenty of water mixed with your pigment, or a wet-on-wet approach is used (C).

BLOOMS AND CAULIFLOWERS

Blooms occur when watercolour pigment diffuses outwards on your page – for example where the sky appears to glow in this street scene (D).

Cauliflowers occur when water is dropped into an area of watercolour and pushes outwards, creating irregular, feathery edges, which can be seen in the blues of the sky, and also in the road of the same street.

These effects can be purposefully created by introducing clean water or a watery pigment into a partially drying wash. The unpredictable results can add life and intrigue to your work.

SPLATTERS

Splatters are an energetic way to introduce texture and dynamic movement to your painting (E). Simply load your brush with wet paint and flick it onto the paper. Use splatters to suggest foliage, stars, or rain, break up large areas of flat colour with visual texture, or add an abstract, playful quality to your work. Control the effect by varying the amount of water or using tools like a toothbrush for finer splatters.

D

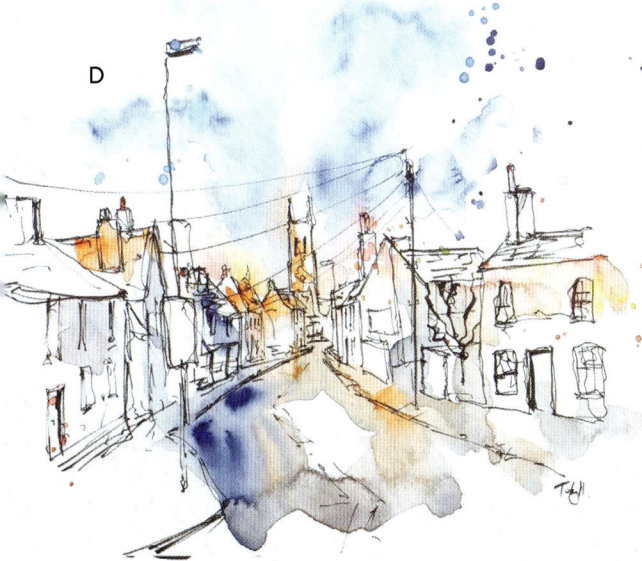

E

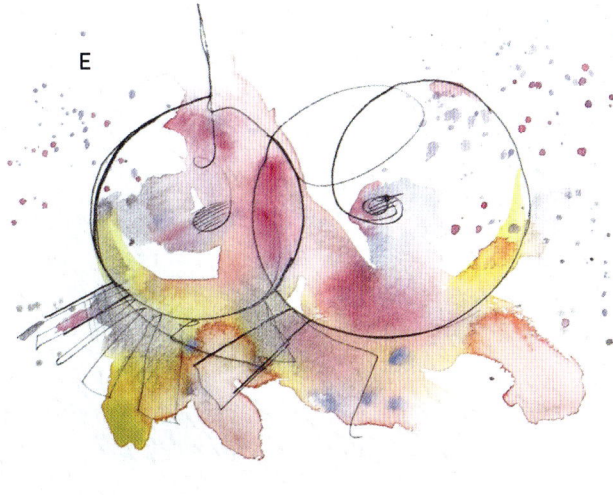

MIXED MEDIA

Mixed media opens up endless possibilities for creativity. Later in this book we will delve into projects focussed on mixing media, but here I will discuss my most frequently used mixed media that I blend into my normal processes.

A

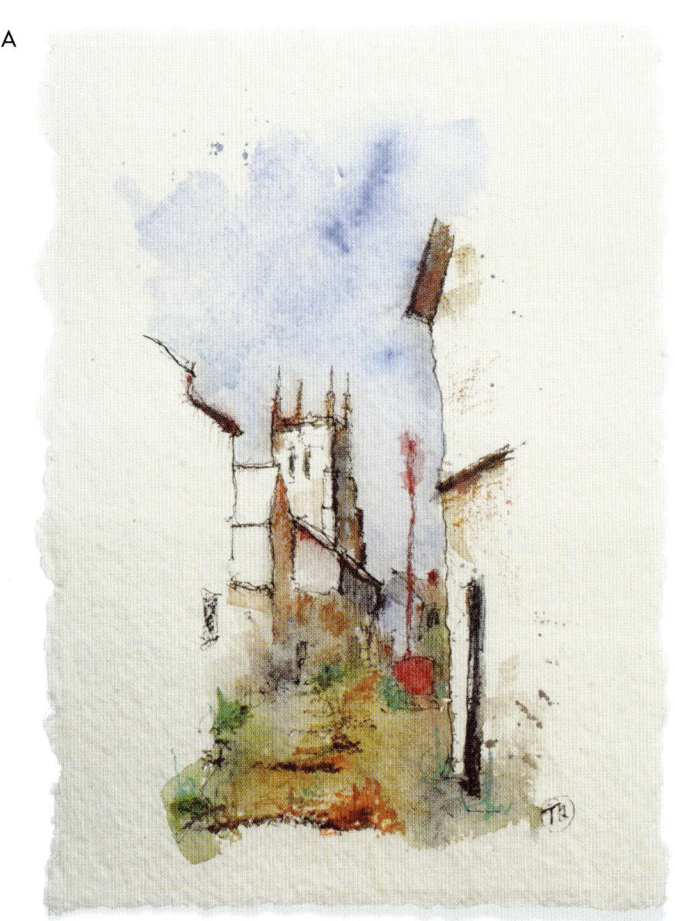

WATER-SOLUBLE PENCILS

Water-soluble pencils are one of the most commonly used mixed media tools in urban sketching – light, portable, affordable, and far more versatile than they might first appear. Try using them to:

- Provide added textures on top of your watercolours.

- Create finer and controlled details.

- Draw an initial outline before your first ink shapes.

- Create an ultra-portable palette by using them on their own.

In this grungy alley, I used water-soluble pencils to add distinctive textures in the road, as well as red and green highlights (A).

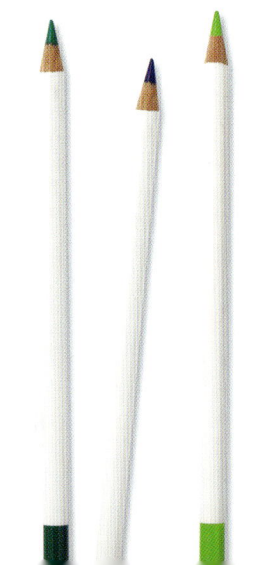

CRAYONS AND PASTELS

Artist-quality crayons and soft pastels bring bold colour and tactile texture to your work, as seen in this vibrant street (**B**). They are rich and opaque, which contrasts beautifully with the transparency of watercolour. Try using them to:

- Highlight key areas with vibrant pops of colour.

- Add texture to skies, foliage, or backgrounds.

- Create dynamic marks that evoke energy and movement.

BRUSH PENS AND MARKERS

Brush pens come in many forms and can be water-soluble or permanent, which are often alcohol based. They are usually transparent and can be layered like watercolours (**C**). Try using them to:

- Provide rich and controlled shadows with grey-scale markers.

- Add pops of colour to your watercolour painting while maintaining transparency.

- Provide a vivid and modern feel to your work.

ACRYLIC MARKERS

Acrylic markers come in various sizes, from finelines through to broad chisel nibs. They are opaque, meaning they sit on top of your watercolours, and provide a very different texture as seen in the splatters in this sky (D). Try using them to:

- Add bold, opaque highlights that stand out against any darker tones.

- Create crisp, graphic lines and details over ink or watercolour.

- Layer vibrant colours without worrying about transparency or paper texture.

B

C

D

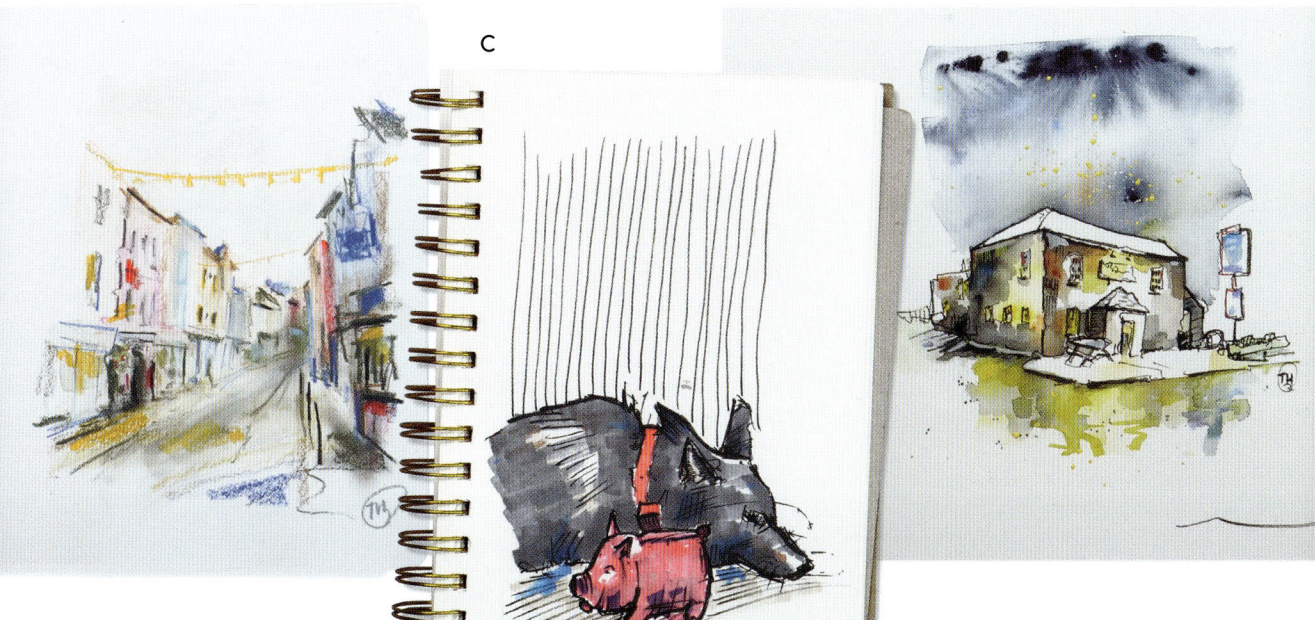

FIRST PROJECTS

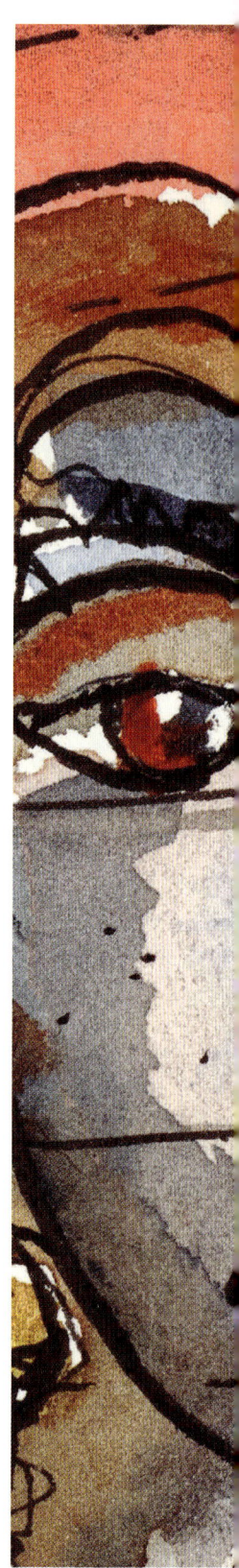

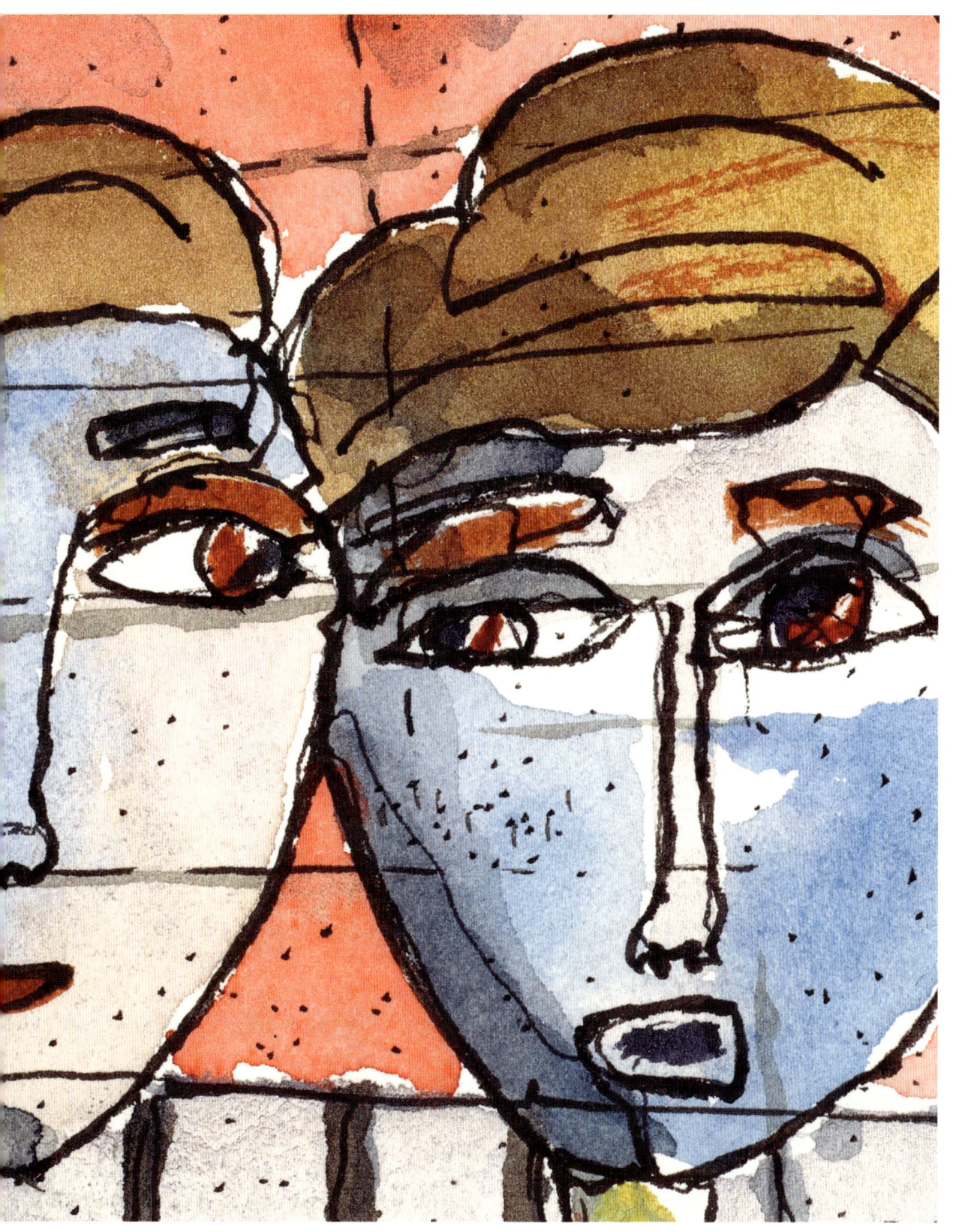

SUPPLIES

Cold pressed
watercolour paper
23 x 30.5cm (9 x 12in)
....
Fountain pen
....
Permanent and
waterproof ink
....
Round synthetic
brushes (size 12)
....
Flat synthetic
brushes (size ½in)
....
Watercolours –
lavender, ultramarine,
indigo, graphite grey,
organic vermilion
....

ONE–LINE SKYLINE

One-line sketching is exactly that: the process of creating a sketch with a single line and without lifting your pen off the page. This technique is a great place to start your sketching journey, as it will teach you to simplify your scene, get you to work quickly, and make decisions. It also requires concentration, so enhancing your observation skills. Here, we'll also add colour and texture to a New York skyline.

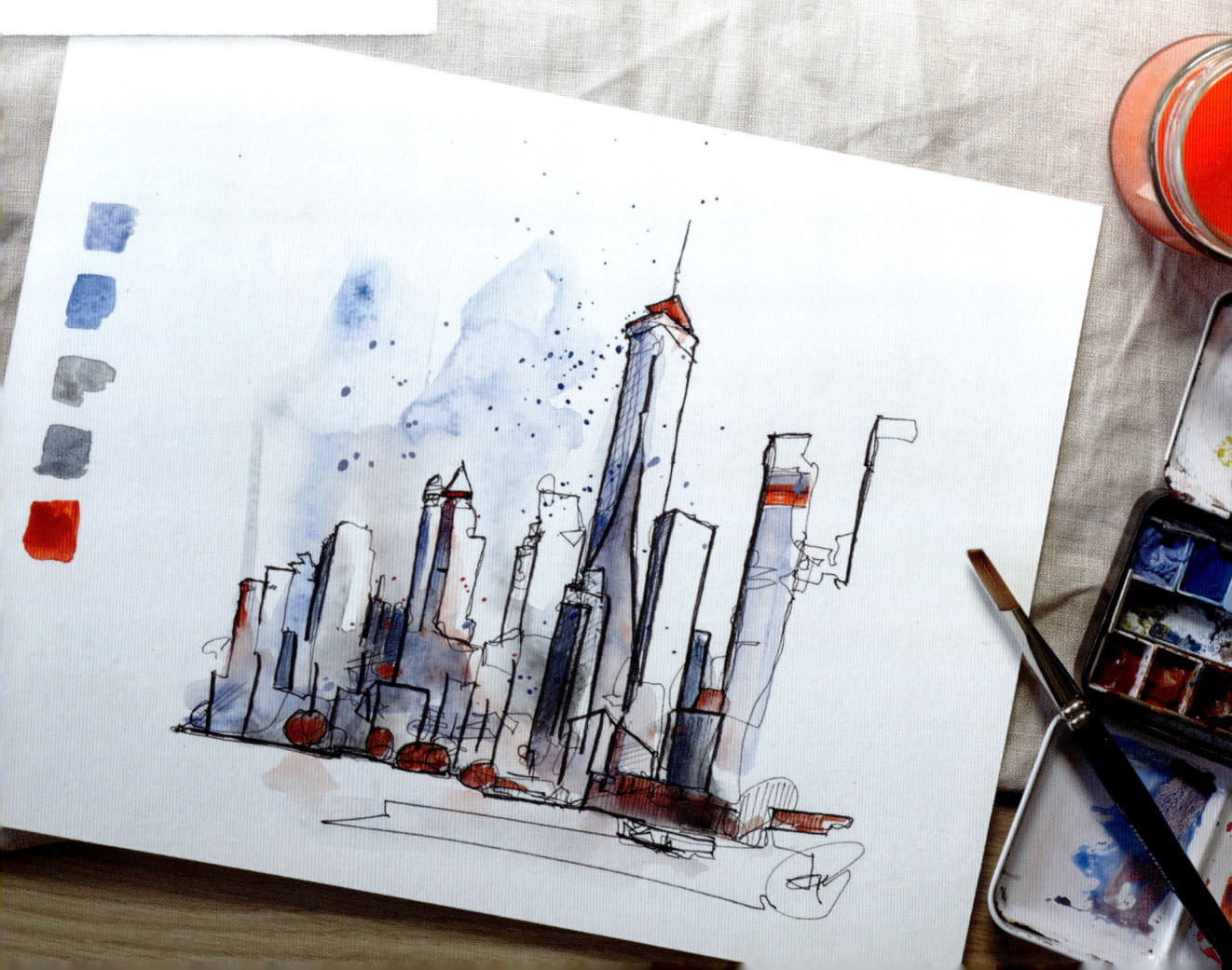

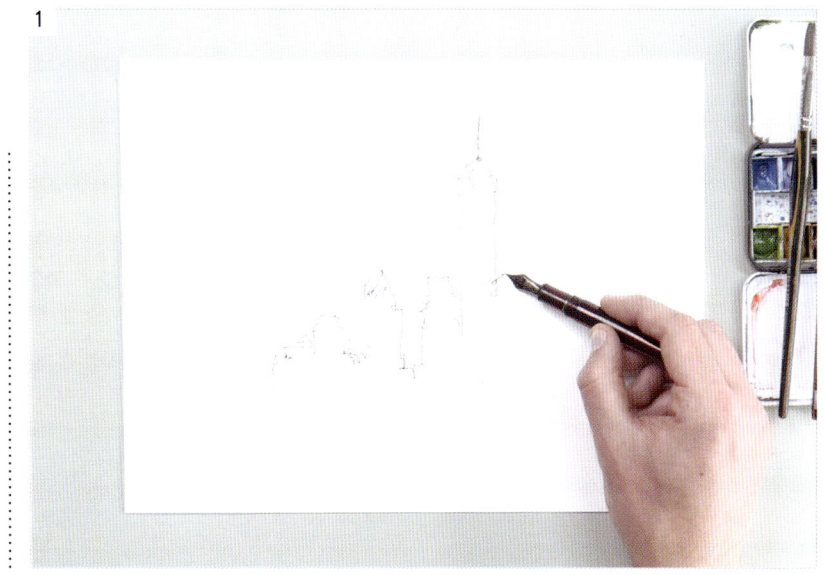

1 For capturing a skyline with one line, start with the 'top-line' of the silhouette. Use this to establish key landmarks and keep you on track. Allowing the line to be loose and gentle is key here, as it means the sketch will be more adaptable later.

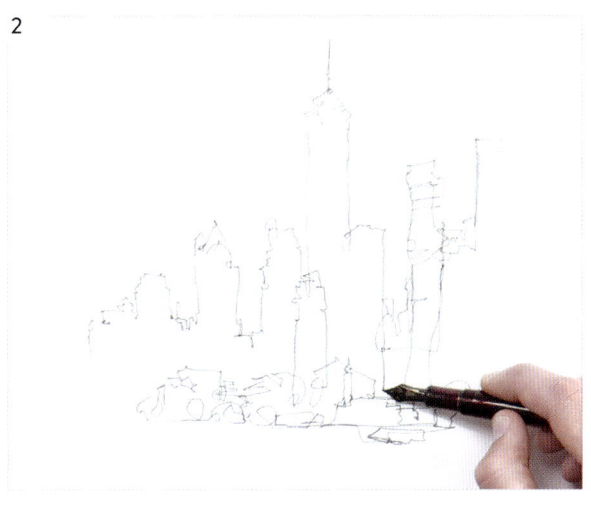

2 When the silhouette is complete, and keeping your pen on the page, come back across the bottom of the scene. This will allow you to fill in the foreground and start to introduce suggestions of textures and details. Use those key established landmarks to keep the scene approximately accurate.

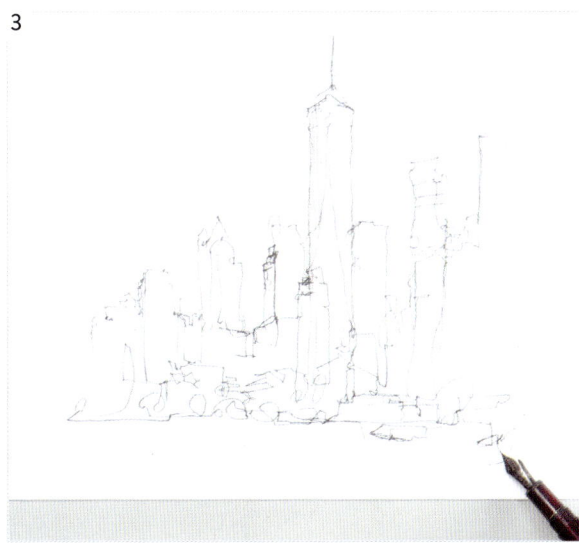

3 The line can continue as long as you want. It will be chaotic in places, but focus on building the idea of shapes in your scene. It's important to establish the vertical lines, especially when the scene features such tall and prominent buildings. Strong verticals add certainty and context to a wavy and connected line.

4 Once the line drawing is complete, use the pen to add hatching (see Line Work and Mark-Making in the previous chapter) to provide a sense of shadow and depth. Restate key lines to add structure and focus.

5 Now to paint the drawing. Use a simple palette to avoid adding too much complexity to an already complex set of lines. Pre-wetting your page with water and working wet-on-wet also reduces the complexity of your colours. Lift the page after you've wet it to encourage the flow of the water.

6 Start with the sky as in the Five-Step Process in the Tools and Techniques chapter. Next, work with a small flat brush and use more controlled touches to introduce shadows and highlights, starting with the shadowed edges of the buildings. Combining specific brushstrokes with touching pigment into the pre-wet areas gives a light, loose and varied wash across the page. Leave to dry.

7 Add another layer of colour, this time being more specific about where it is placed. Working on a now dry sheet of paper can enhance the shadows and bring out warmer touches to provide points of interest.

8 To complete the painting process, add splatters in the background and soft, gentle brush marks in the foreground. These prevent the paper from feeling too stark around the scene where there's large areas of negative space.

9 At this stage, with the paper dry, we have a loose and semi-abstract version of our scene. And there is a strong argument to say that it's complete at this stage.

10 For a stylised final step, restate key lines, focussing on the vertical lines that anchor the scene, as well as introducing a few new lines to add more suggestions of detail and to fill out the scene. This lends the painting more of a 'sketched' feel.

4
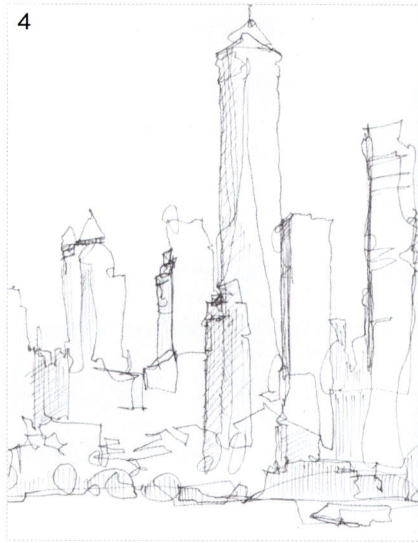

5
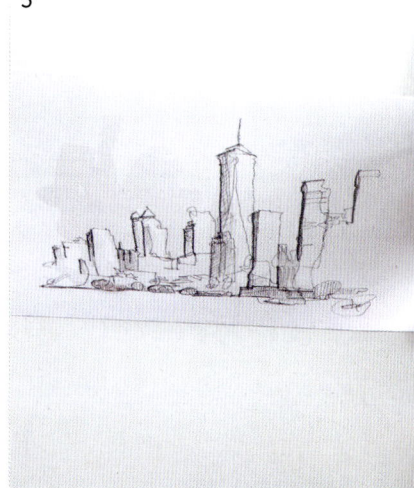

6
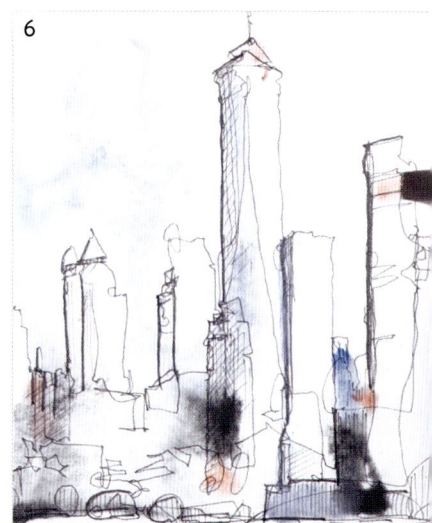

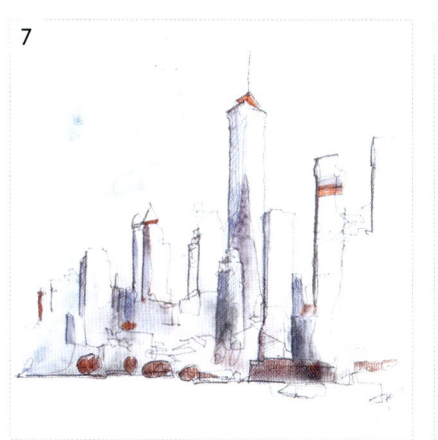

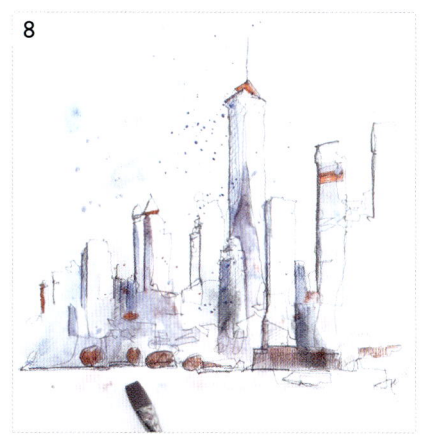

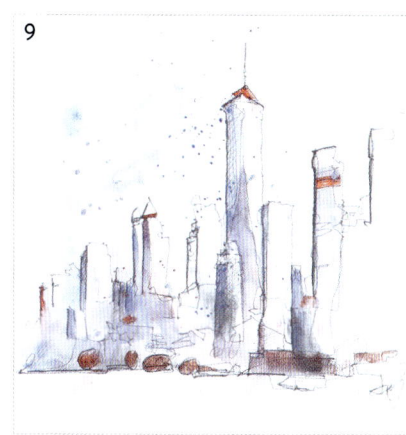

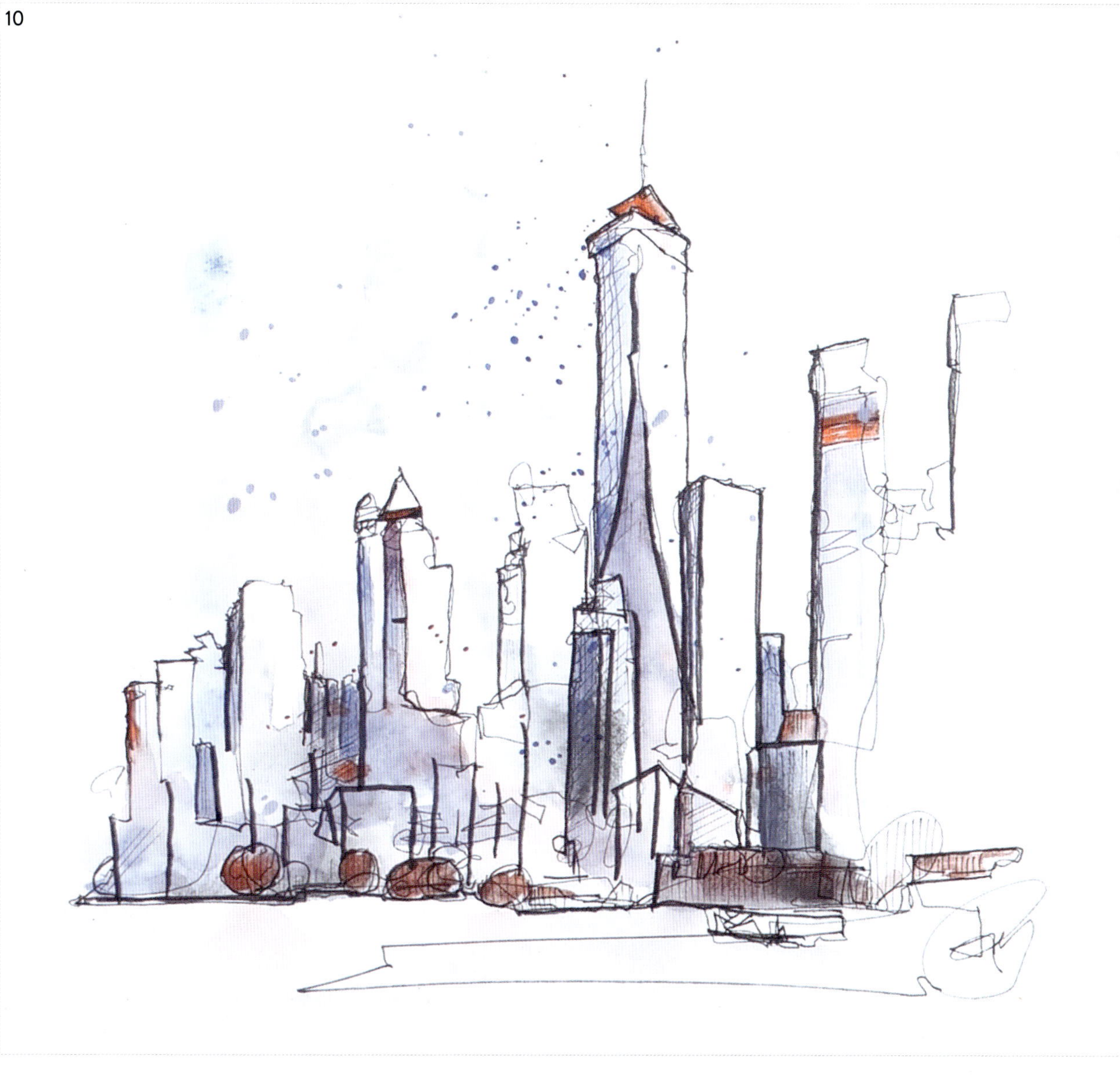

SUPPLIES

Cold pressed
watercolour paper
23 x 30.5cm (9 x 12in)
....
Fountain pen
....
Permanent and
waterproof ink
....
Round synthetic brushes
(sizes 6 and 10)
....
Flat synthetic brushes
(sizes ½in and 1in)
....
Watercolour – indigo
....
Watercolour
pencil – indigo
....

SKETCHING VALUES

Often a scene is interesting not because of its colours, but because of its shadows. In watercolour, the white page is our lightest value, and we achieve darker and darker values through progressive layering of our colours. This is what is meant by the phrase 'painting from light to dark'. Monochromatic paintings and value studies are not only an excellent way to practise watercolour control, they are also rather a lovely art form in their own right.

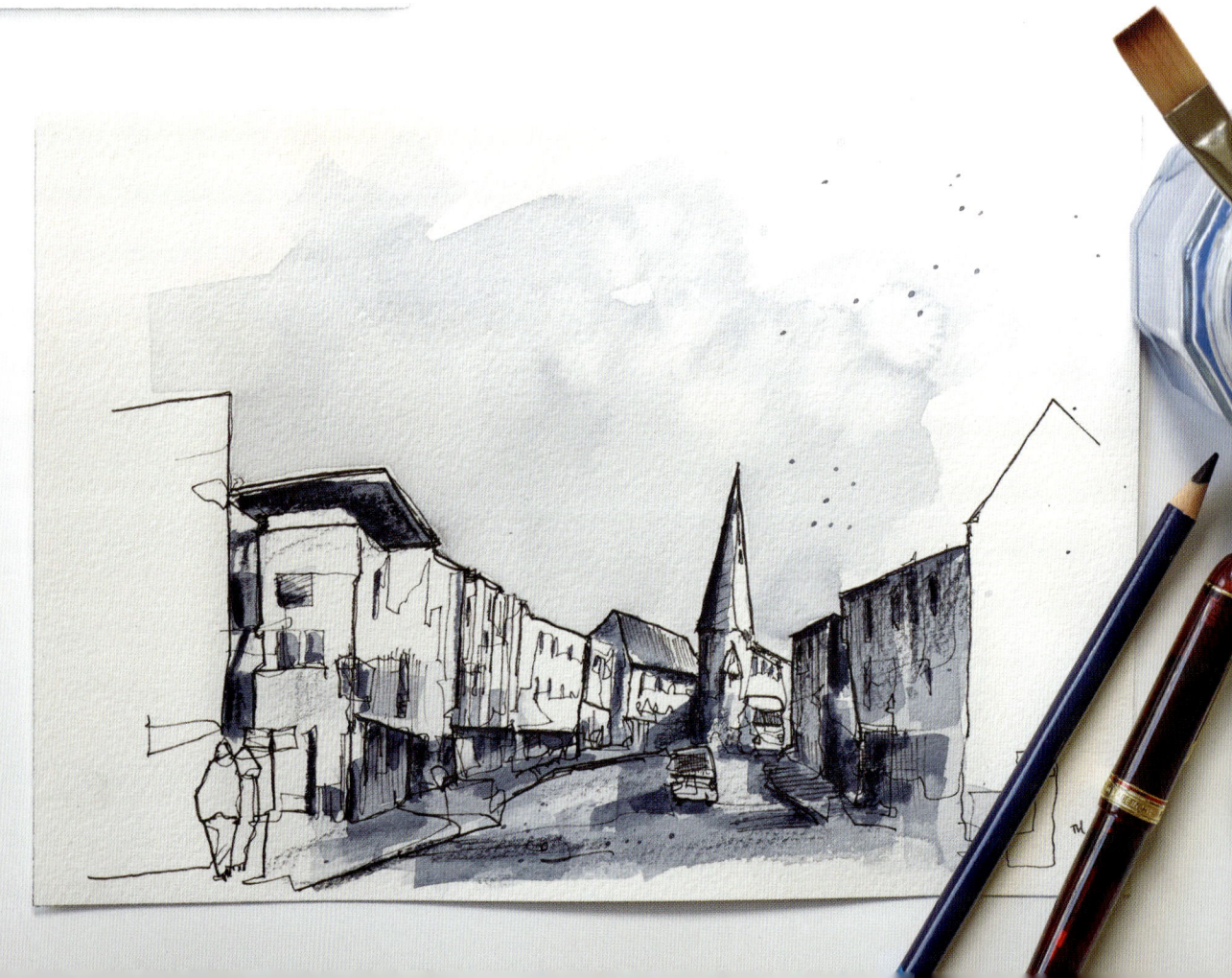

1 Start with a simple silhouette. Already this silhouette can make the scene feel recognisable. Next, fill out the middle of the scene, focussing on the large and medium shapes underneath the silhouette. Not every detail needs capturing – the essence of the scene is what we are seeking.

1

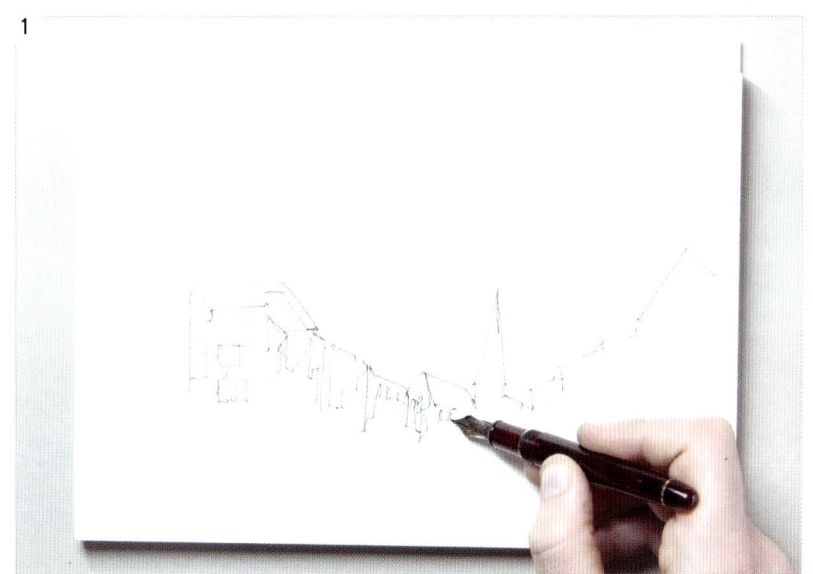

2 Add in more complex elements to the bottom section of the sketch, including details such as cars and people along the street. Try not to be too certain about where the buildings meet the street – notice how I have very few lines in my scene strictly defining the lower edges of the buildings.

2

3

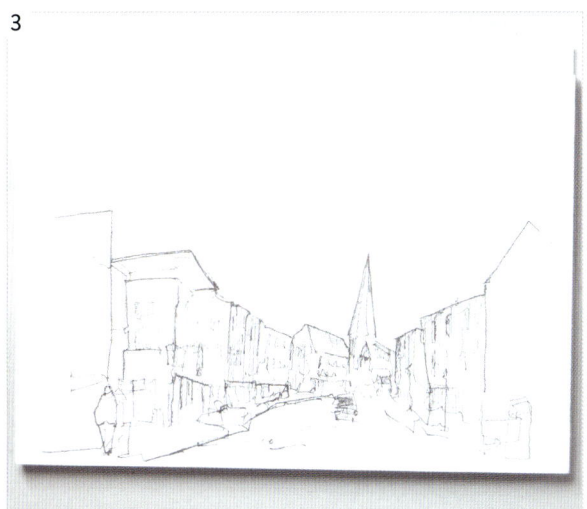

3 The last stage of inking is to add in the values in the scene. Bold lines accentuate the shapes, but also suggest the darkest shadows. Lighter hatching introduces a medium value.

4

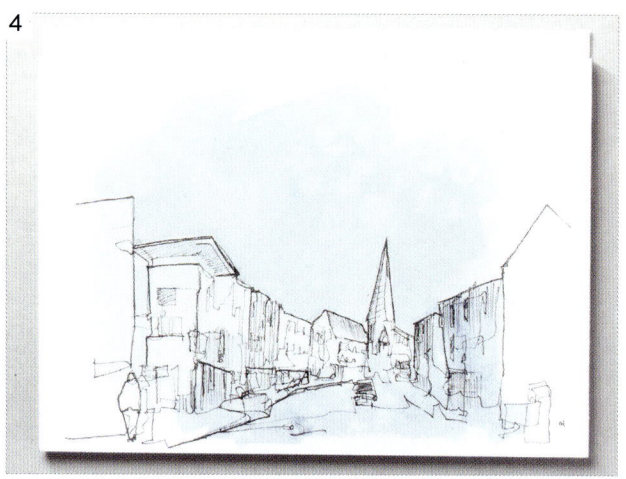

5

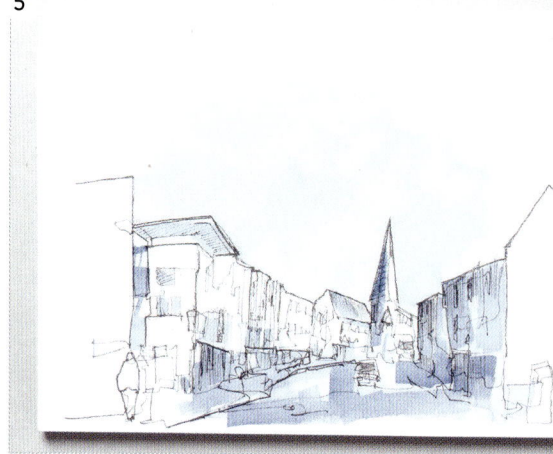

6

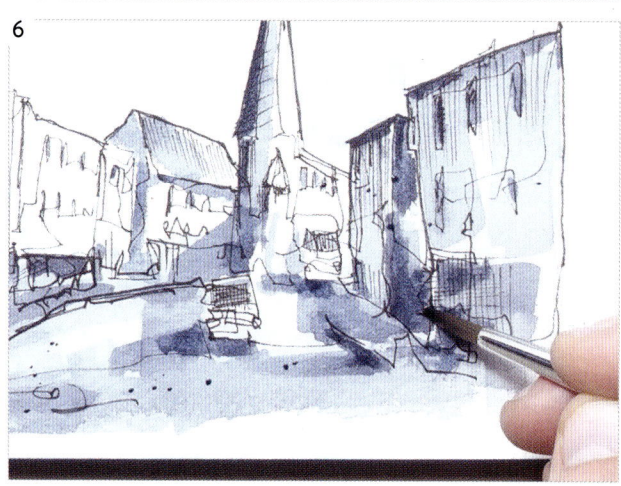

7

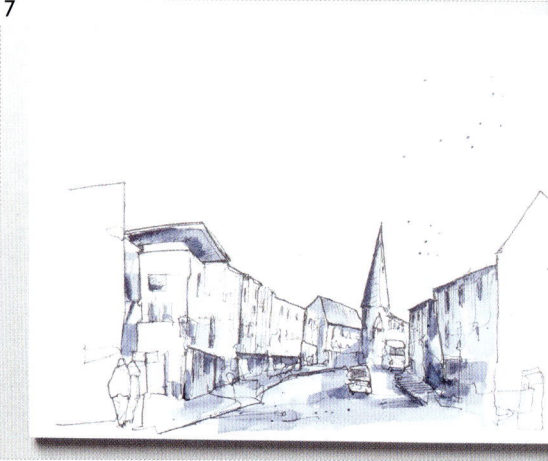

4 With a large brush, apply your lightest wash to the page, using indigo as your single colour. The white paper itself is the brightest value so leave plenty visible on the page, but apply a loose and continuous wash wherever you identify shadows.

5 Now gradually layer the watercolour. Each time, wait for the previous layer to dry, and add progressively more concentrated washes of colour to build up the values on the page.

6 As you build up the shadows, you will be working with smaller and smaller areas of shadow. Move gradually from a larger brush towards smaller and more pointed brushes to get more specific touches.

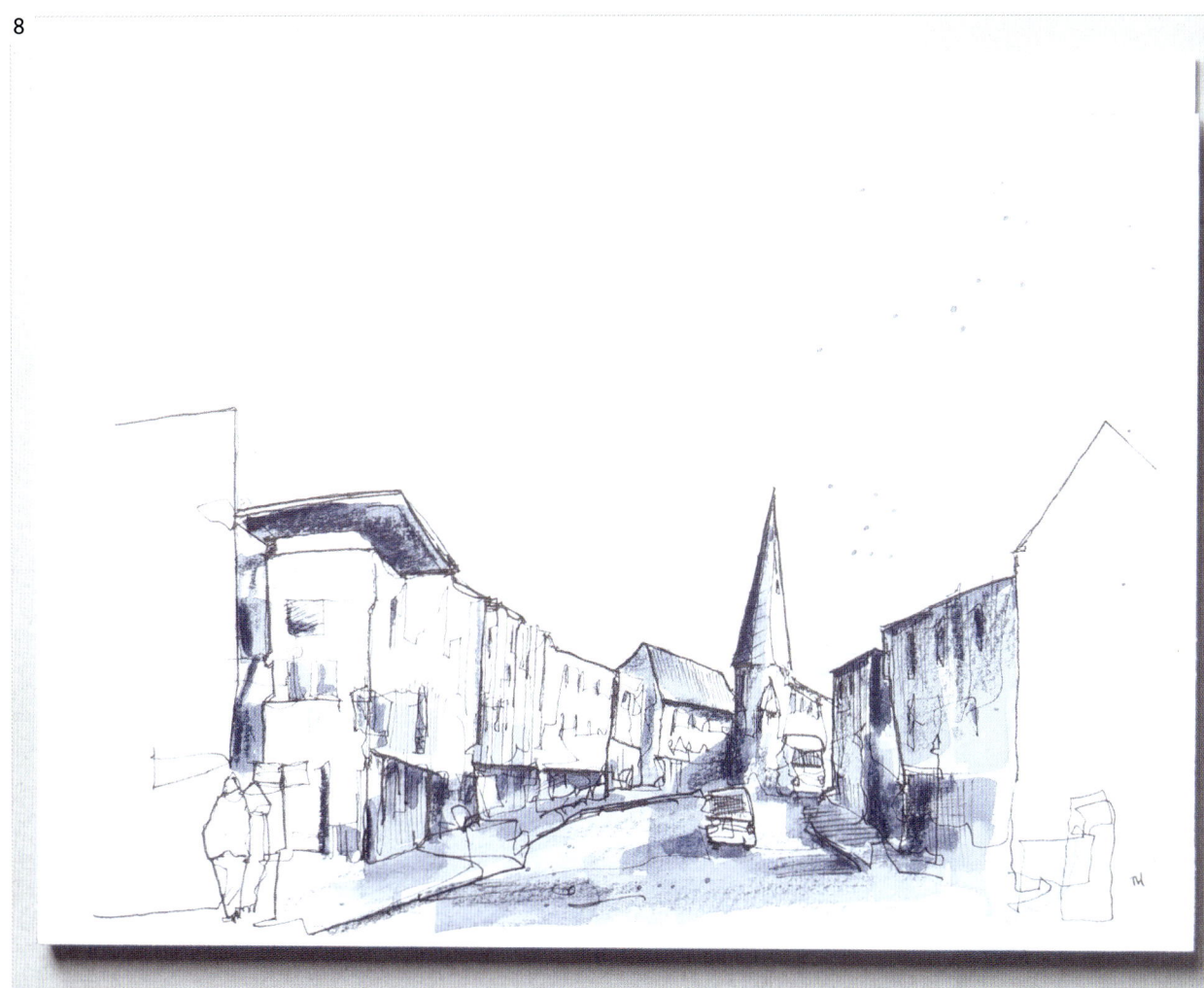

7 As you layer your paint, you will likely find your original line work becomes less distinct. After applying three or four layers of colour, go back in with ink to restate the key lines and bring some clarity back.

8 Watercolour pencils are fantastic for introducing texture to your painting process, as well as more controlled and specific touches of colour or value. Use the indigo watercolour pencil to help to create the deepest shadows, as well as some interesting textures on the tarmac of the road.

MICRO SKETCHING

Creating micro sketches is a fun way to
tackle complex subjects, focusing on limited
space, simplification, and artistic license.
When combined, these small sketches
have more impact than their simplicity
suggests. This approach is perfect for
outdoor sketching, allowing you to capture
interesting details around town and build
a captivating scene. Baroque architecture
works well for micro sketching, as there are
so many intricate elements to focus on.

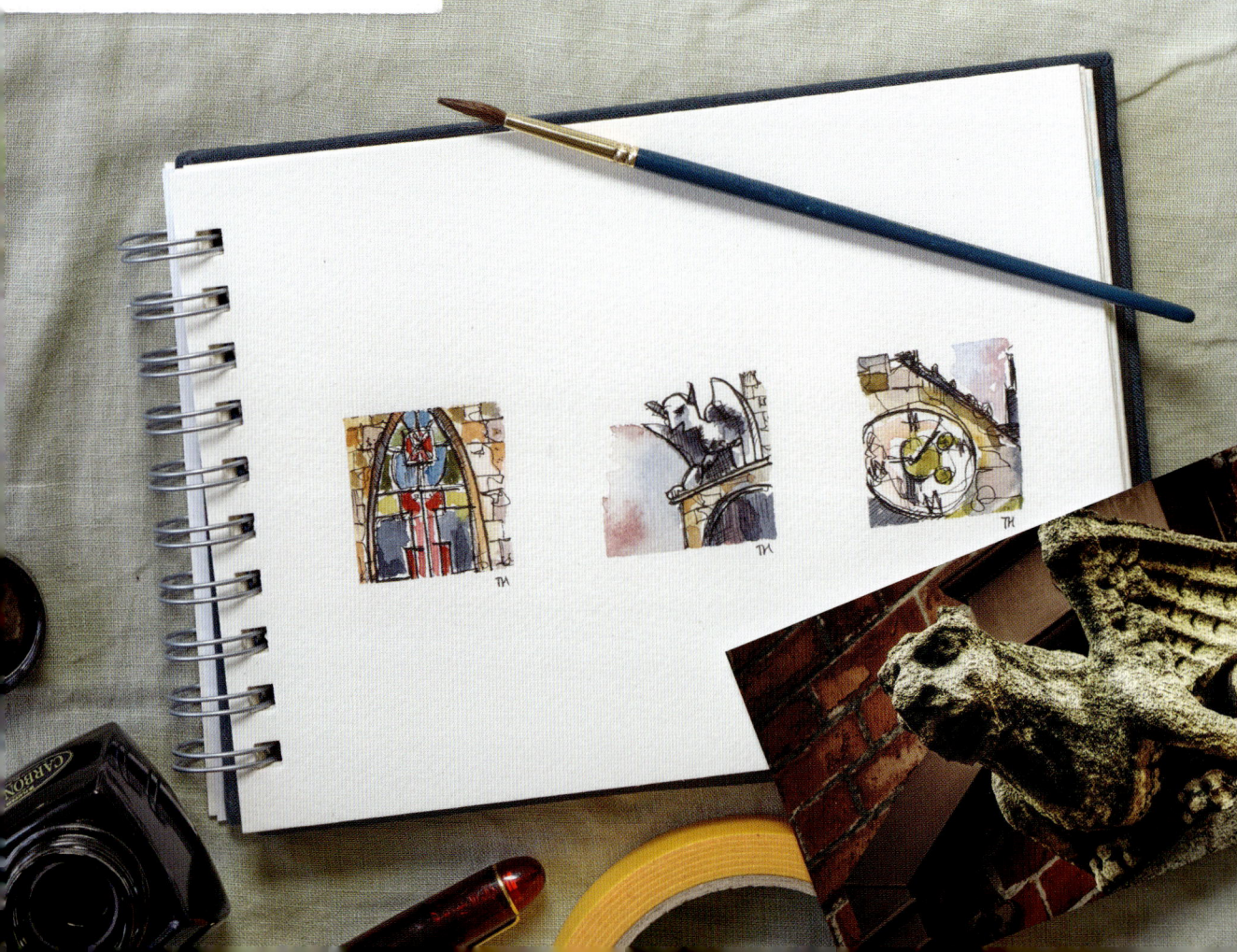

1 Firstly, lay out your page with tape, creating three equal squares around 5 x 5cm (2 x 2in) on your page. Burnish your tape by lightly rubbing it on a clean surface or your clothing before applying it to your page. This makes the tape even more low tack and can prevent damage when you remove it later.

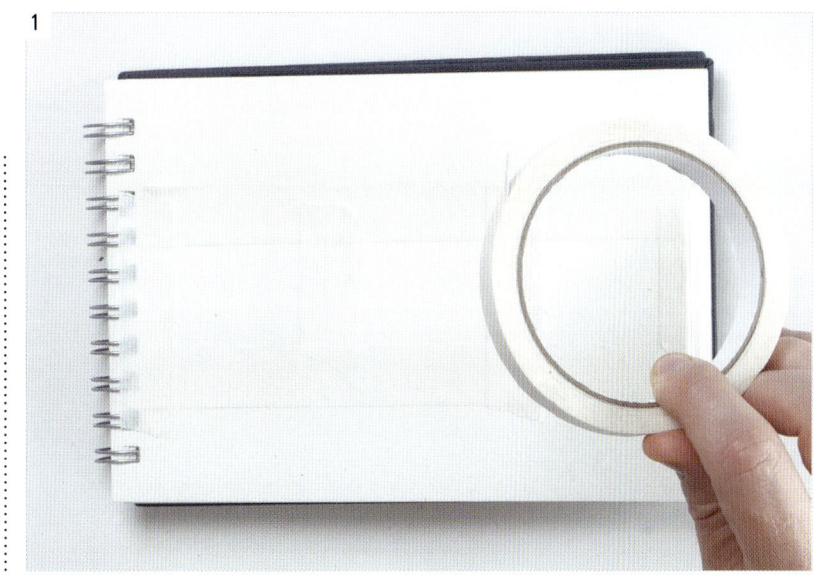

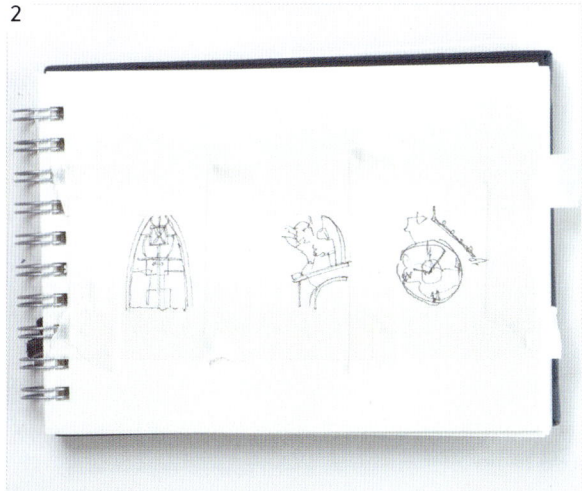

2 Each of these squares will now house a different but connected object. Sketch out the key shapes of a gargoyle, simplifying and altering as you wish. Next, add other features of Baroque architecture, inspired by churches and cathedrals near by – an intricate window on the left, and a large clock face on the right.

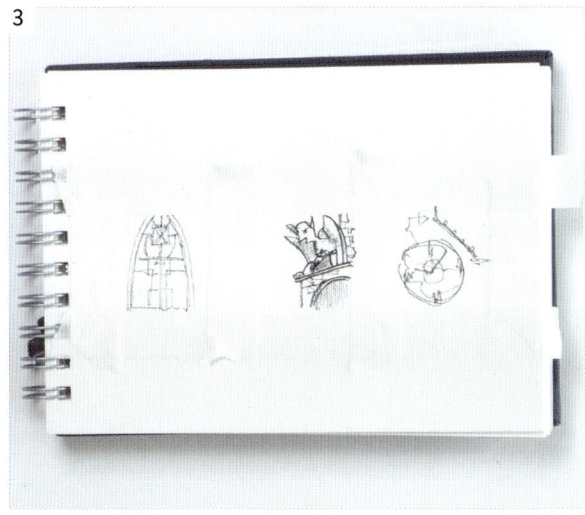

3 Pressing a little harder with your pen (or using a bolder fineliner), restate the main structural lines of the gargoyle, and add small textures. Consider the background a little more, allowing the gargoyle to sit proud on its ledge without competing textures behind it

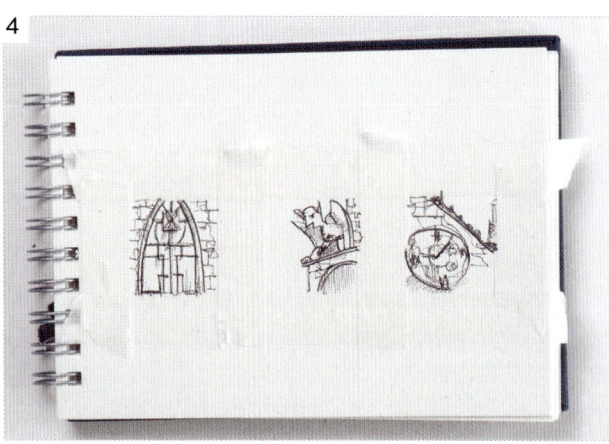

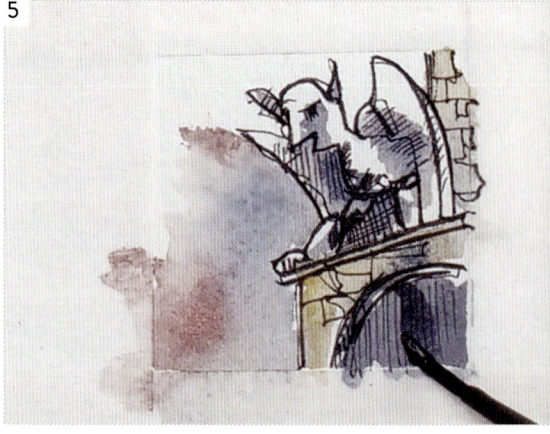

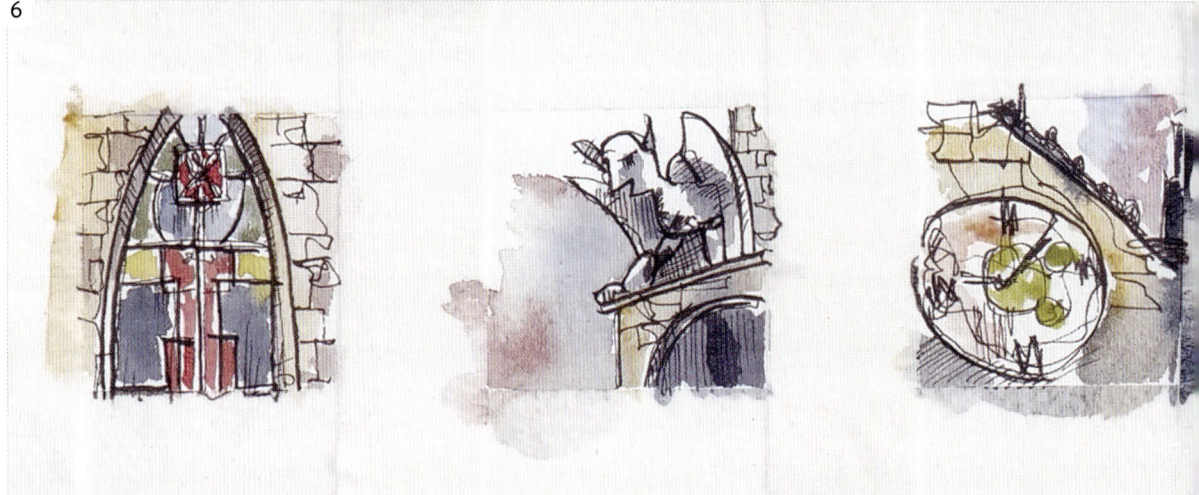

4 Consistency in approach is important, repeating the process in Step 3 on the other squares. This ensures your mini triptych works together as a finished page.

5 Next, add a loose wash of key colours. Given the scene, some imagination is needed in which colours to choose. Scale down your brush size to suit the size of the image. This helps as you gradually deepen some of the colours and shadows.

6 Repeat Step 5 in the adjacent squares, keeping the colours and quality of the wash consistent to match the main subject. Be sure to use enough water and start with a soft wash of colours. Allow to dry.

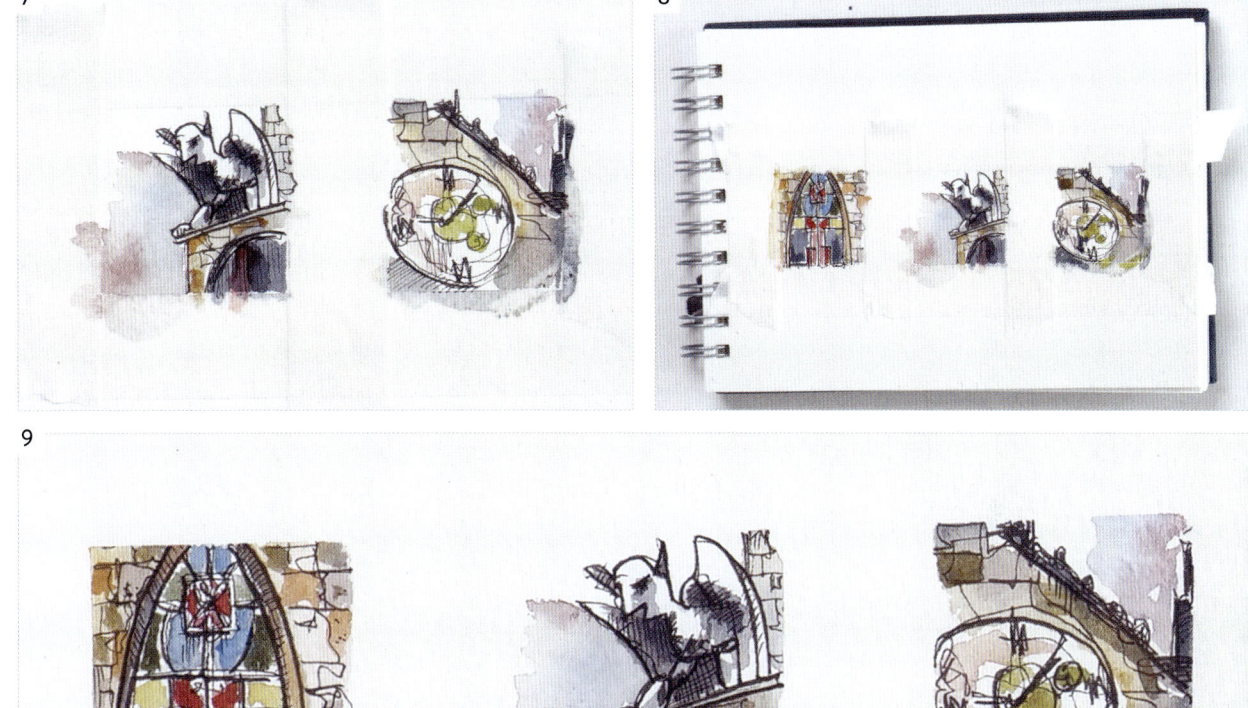

7 Approach each of the paintings in turn again. First, focus on adding shadows to improve the sense of the gargoyle being three-dimensional and imposing.

8 Next, enrich the colours of the window. Work to achieve a higher saturation, but allowing plenty of the underlying colours to shine through. Take the same approach to the clock. Each frame now has a similar value range and style, but with a slightly different focus in terms of composition and use of colour.

9 Remove the tape to leave a remarkably crisp and vibrant page. The consistent approach between each image means the triptych works well as a whole.

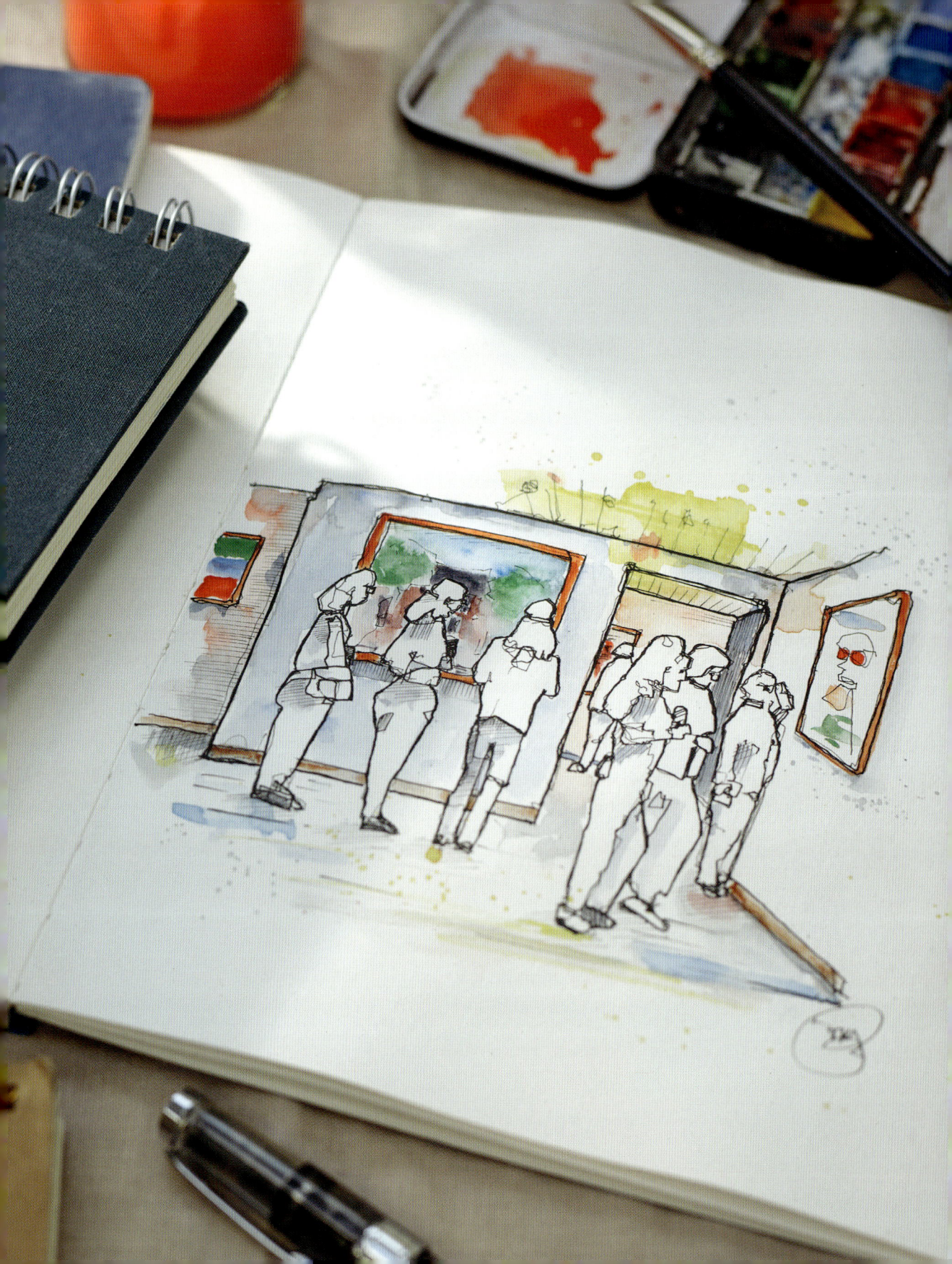

SKETCHING PEOPLE

Sketching people in a gallery offers a unique take on a potentially challenging subject. Unlike bustling streets or cafés, gallery visitors tend to move slowly or stand still, giving you a bit more time to observe and capture them. Even so, there's still movement to contend with, making this exercise about capturing the essence of a figure rather than striving for perfect accuracy. This approach allows you to focus on posture, gesture, and atmosphere, bringing life and character to the scene.

SUPPLIES

Mixed media sketchbook 20 x 25cm (8 x 10in)

Fountain pen

Permanent and waterproof ink

Round synthetic brushes (size 6)

Flat synthetic brushes (size ½in)

Watercolours – lavender, cobalt blue, organic vermilion, cobalt green, hansa yellow medium, quinacridone sienna, indigo

1

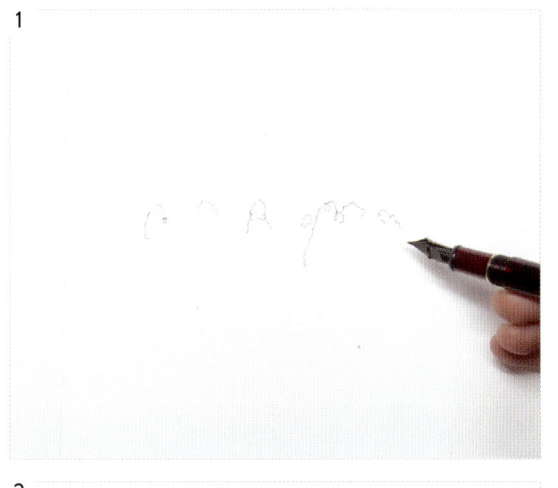

2

1 Using your pen, start with a very gentle line and a few simple marks to suggest the position of individual heads in the scene.

2 Build a few of the key lines and shapes in the scene, and then start to add the figures. Remember, people may move quickly, so capturing a snapshot is what we are aiming for.

3

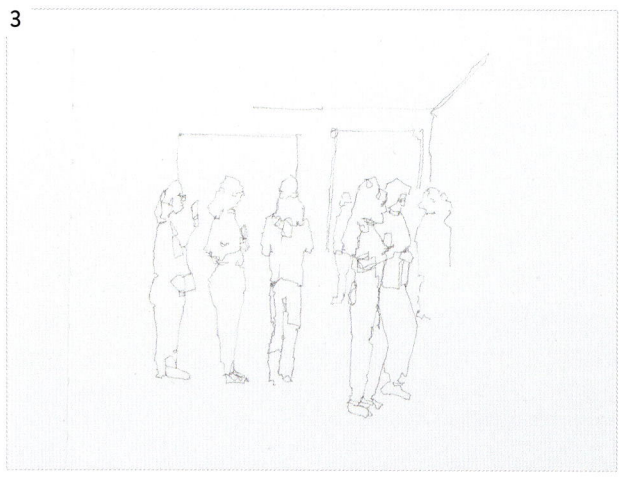

4

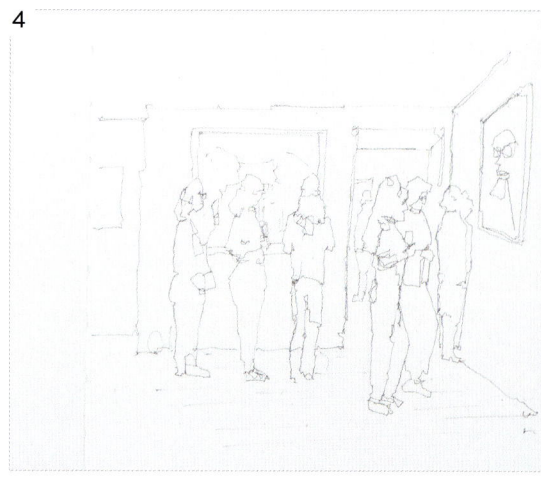

5

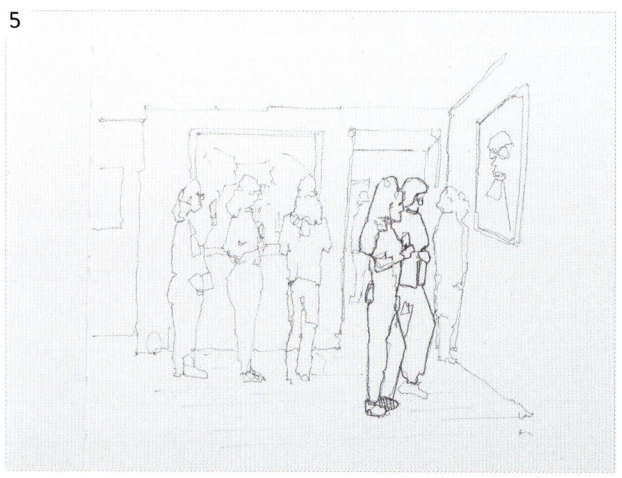

6

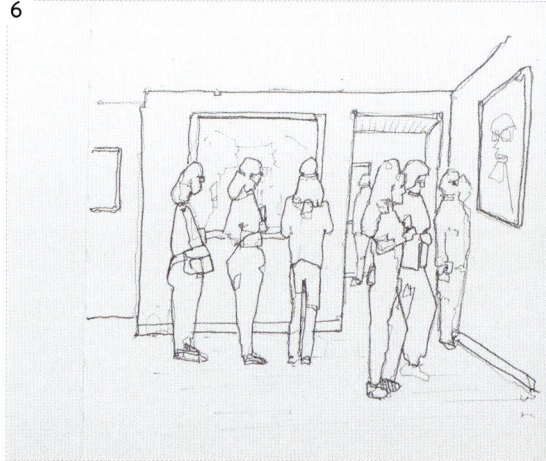

3 Continue through your sketch completing the figures. If you leave space in your scene, you could continue to add more people to the frame as they move through your view.

4 With your scene bustling with life, build the rest of the background around the figures. In a gallery, it can be fun to add details of the exhibits – for example a suggestion of a portrait hanging on the wall.

5 Next, work gradually through your lines to restate the figures. Focus first on the figures that have worked the best in your initial loose sketch.

6 And with the confidence gained from this, move through the rest of your scene repeating the process from Step 5.

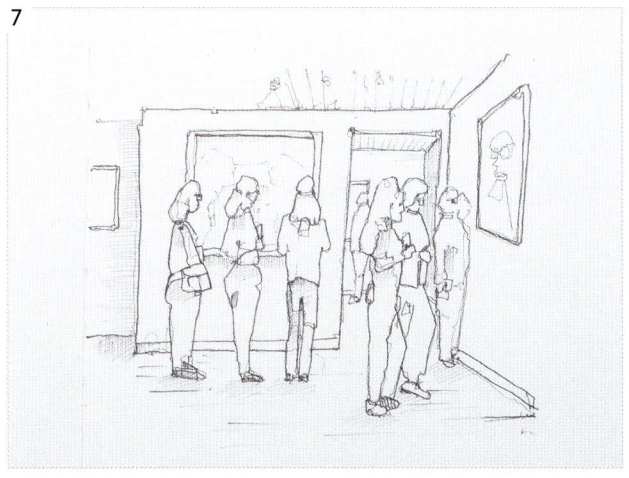

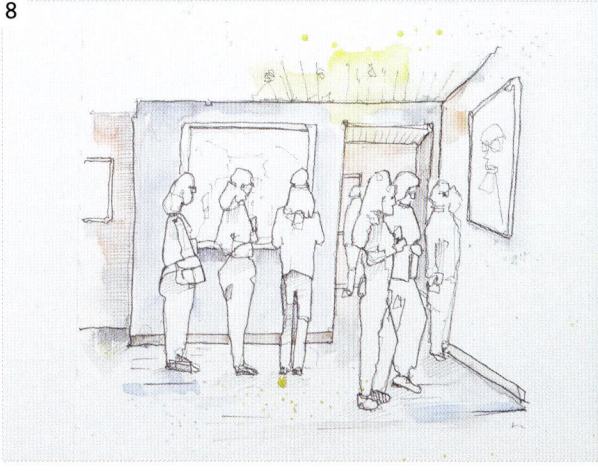

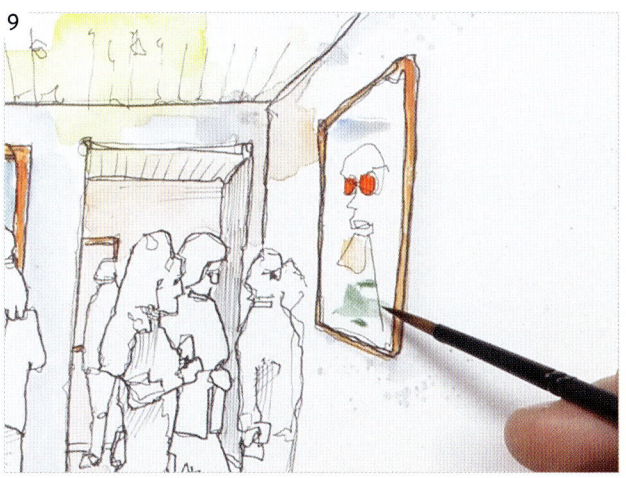

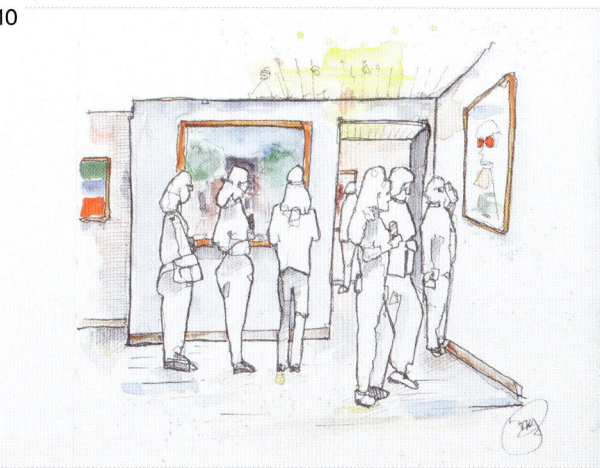

7 Add hatching and textures to both your figures and the background to start to introduce volume and form to your contours and shapes.

8 Once your ink is dry, add a light wash of colour with a larger brush.

9 Gradually layer the colours to build up the values of the shadows and the saturation of the your brightest colours.

10 Leave the people as negative space – it simplifies the painting process, making capturing a busy crowd quicker and easier. By adding a little hatching and shadow, the people feel three-dimensional and alive, but they also feel transitory, as if they are passing through the scene.

SUPPLIES

Cold pressed
watercolour paper
18 x 25cm (7 x 10in)
....
Fountain pen
....
Permanent and
waterproof ink
....
Soluble ink for
thumbnails only
....
Round synthetic brushes
(sizes 6 and 12)
....
Watercolours –
lavender, ultramarine,
indigo, pyrrol scarlet,
quinacridone sienna,
green apatite genuine,
hansa yellow medium
....

THUMBNAILS AND ARCHITECTURE

A great way to build confidence with a complex scene is to start with simple thumbnails. These small sketches help you explore compositions freely, without getting caught up in details. By sketching thumbnails first – like in this example of St Stephen's Basilica in Budapest – you can break down an overwhelming subject into manageable shapes, refining your approach before committing to a full sketch.

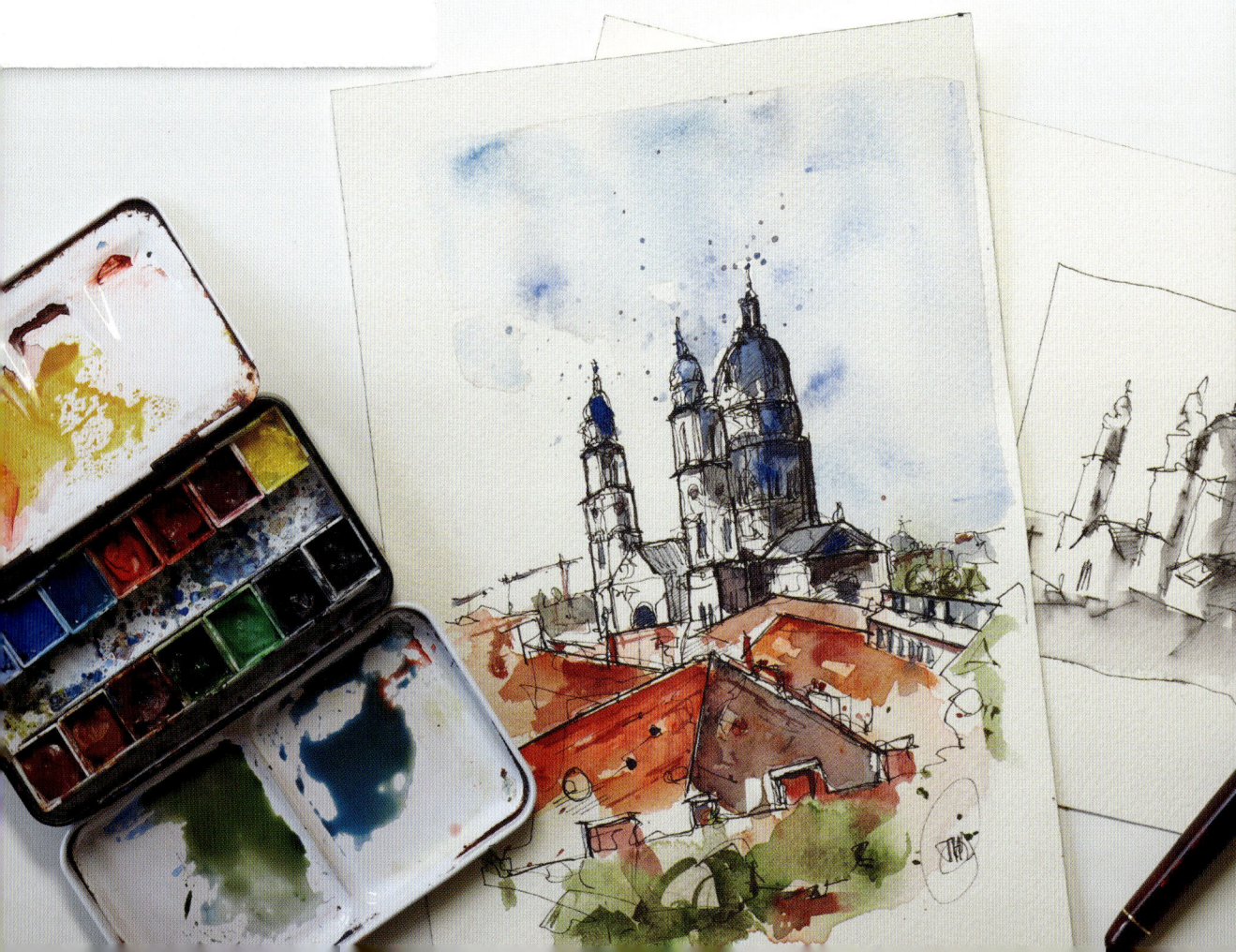

1

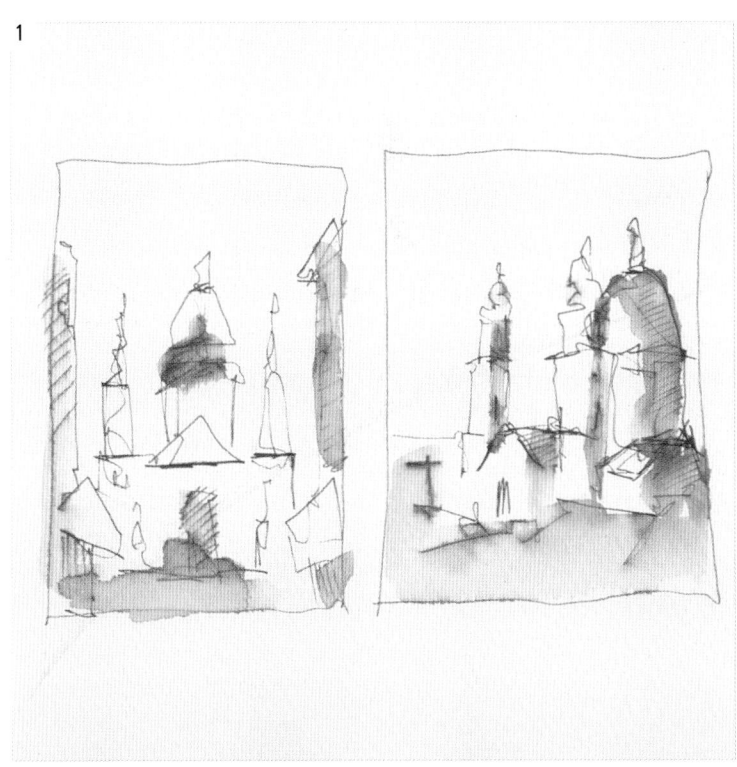

1 Before diving into a full sketch, explore the architecture from different viewpoints and quickly capture the main shapes in simple thumbnails. Keep your approach fast and loose, spending no more than five minutes on each. Use soluble ink to easily add contrast with a quick wash of water, or achieve a similar effect with hatching and shading. These quick studies will help you refine your composition and gain confidence.

2

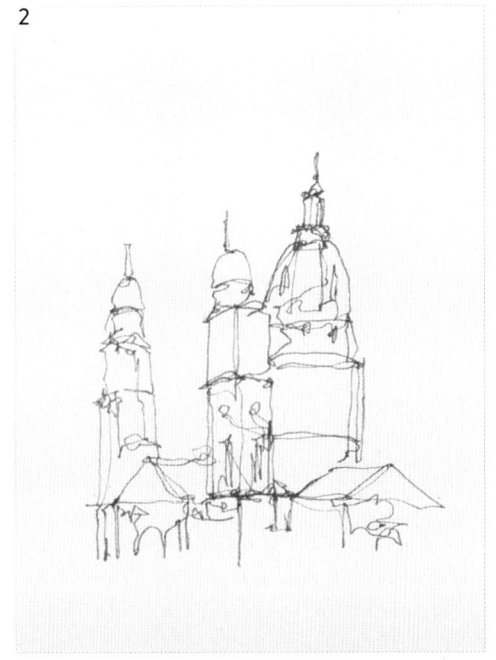

2 Now choose one of the thumbnails to guide your larger sketch. Thumbnails help simplify decision-making by giving you a clear starting point, allowing you to focus on refining shapes rather than figuring out composition as you go. Use your chosen thumbnail as a reference, capturing the key shapes with a bit more accuracy and detail, while still keeping your lines fluid and expressive.

3 Build the rest of the scene around that starting point, taking care to consider the perspective of the roof tops.

4 Add bolder structural lines, along with hatching, to bring out key values through the image. The most care and attention should be taken on the focal point – a higher density of ink will naturally draw the eye.

5 Starting with the sky, apply a soft wet-on-wet wash of colours with a large brush. Use a mixture of warm colours from the palette and a wet-on-wet wash to provide variety to the texture and hues within the roofs, adding immediate interest.

6 When the first layer is dry, pick out more specific hues in the roofs with a second layer of colour, as well as shapes and textures in the foreground.

7 Allow the page to dry again before working on the basilica itself. Focus just on the values of the building using a neutral wash (mine is a mix of indigo and quinacridone sienna). In deep shadows like this, adding a touch of ultramarine blue gives the shadows another dimension.

8 Focus on what your page needs at this point, not just what is accurate to the scene. We typically want the biggest contrasts around the focal point. By leaving plenty of negative space in the towers and enhancing the shadows in this area, the focal point grabs the eye because of the bold contrast. Also explore other elements of your scene that may benefit from a few extra touches. At this point, I enjoy adding splashes and splatters in the sky using the same neutral and blue colours as used on the tower.

9 The final step is to bring back the pen to restate key lines, particularly around the towers and main shapes of the focal point. Be careful not to overdo this stage, but also don't overlook the power of a subtle increase in line weight to make the whole image pop a little more.

3
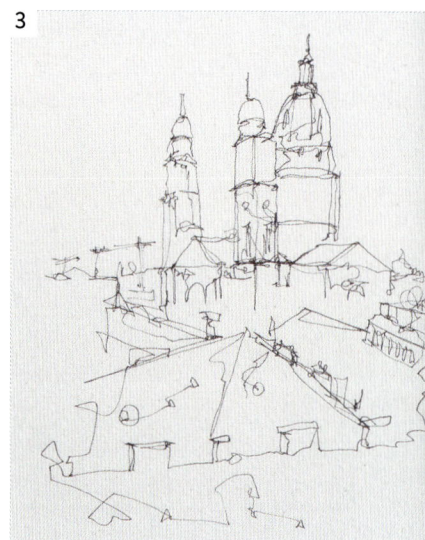

4
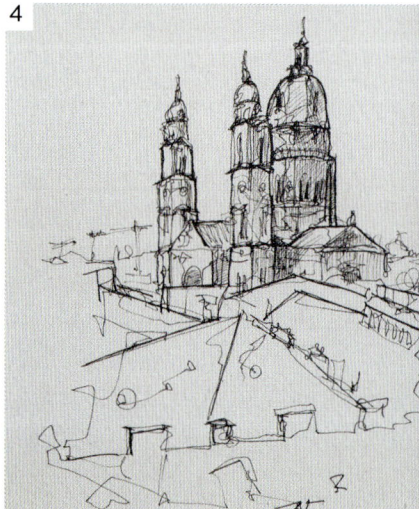

5
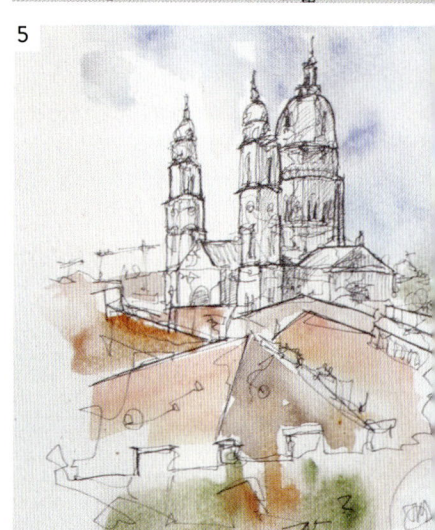

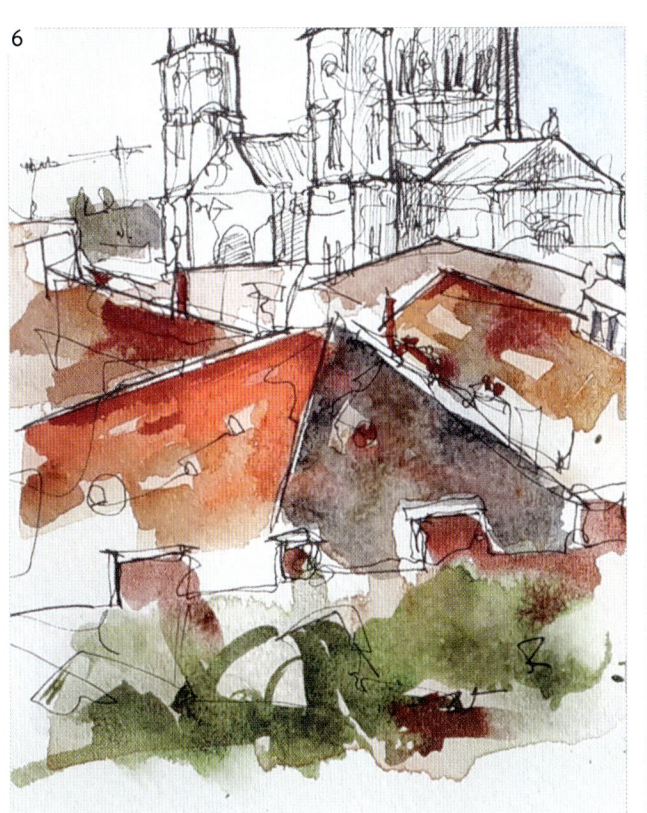

6

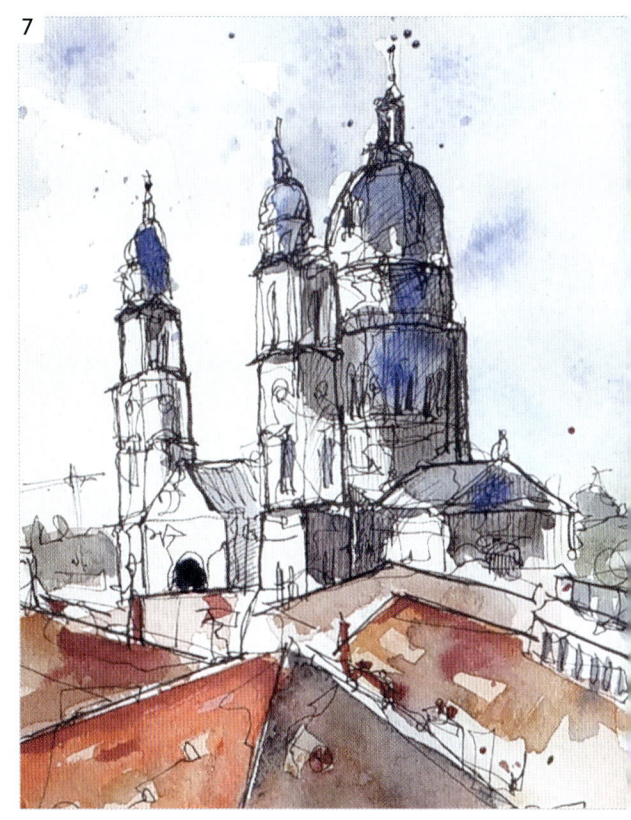

7

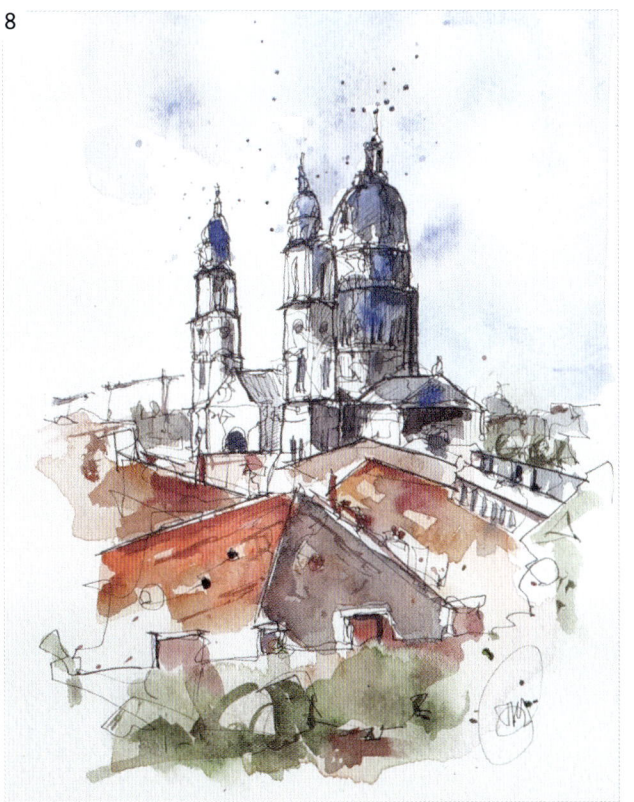

8

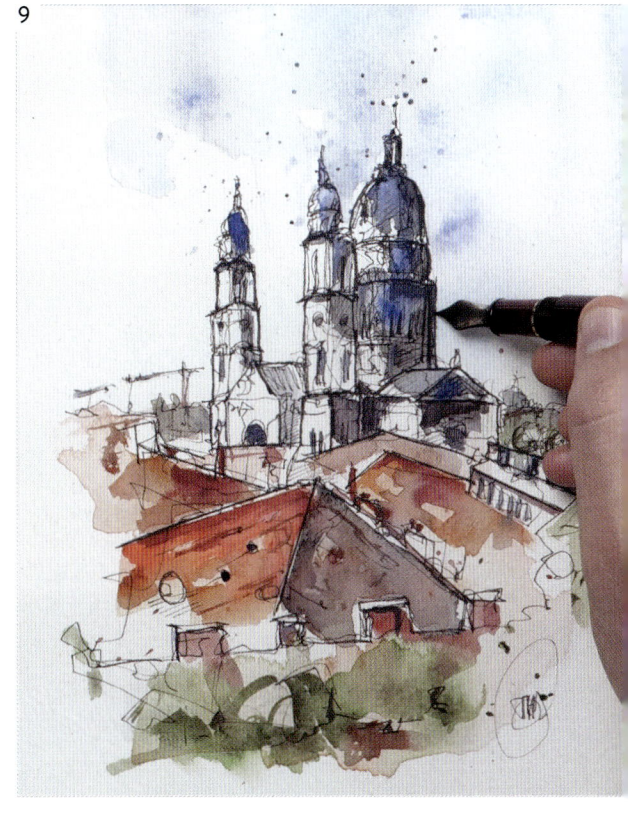

9

GRAFFITI AS ART

The masters of old learned and honed their skills by studying and emulating the work of other great artists. Likewise, we can learn and explore our craft in a more modern and unconventional setting by sketching the work of city artists and recreating it on our page – whether that is sketching a monument, a statue, or in this example, bringing to life some graffiti from the streets of Valparaiso, in Chile.

SUPPLIES

Cold pressed watercolour paper 18 x 25cm (7 x 10in)

Fountain pen

Permanent and waterproof ink

Round synthetic brushes (sizes 6 and 12)

Watercolours – lavender, ultramarine, indigo, pyrrol scarlet, quinacridone sienna, green apatite genuine, green gold, hansa yellow medium

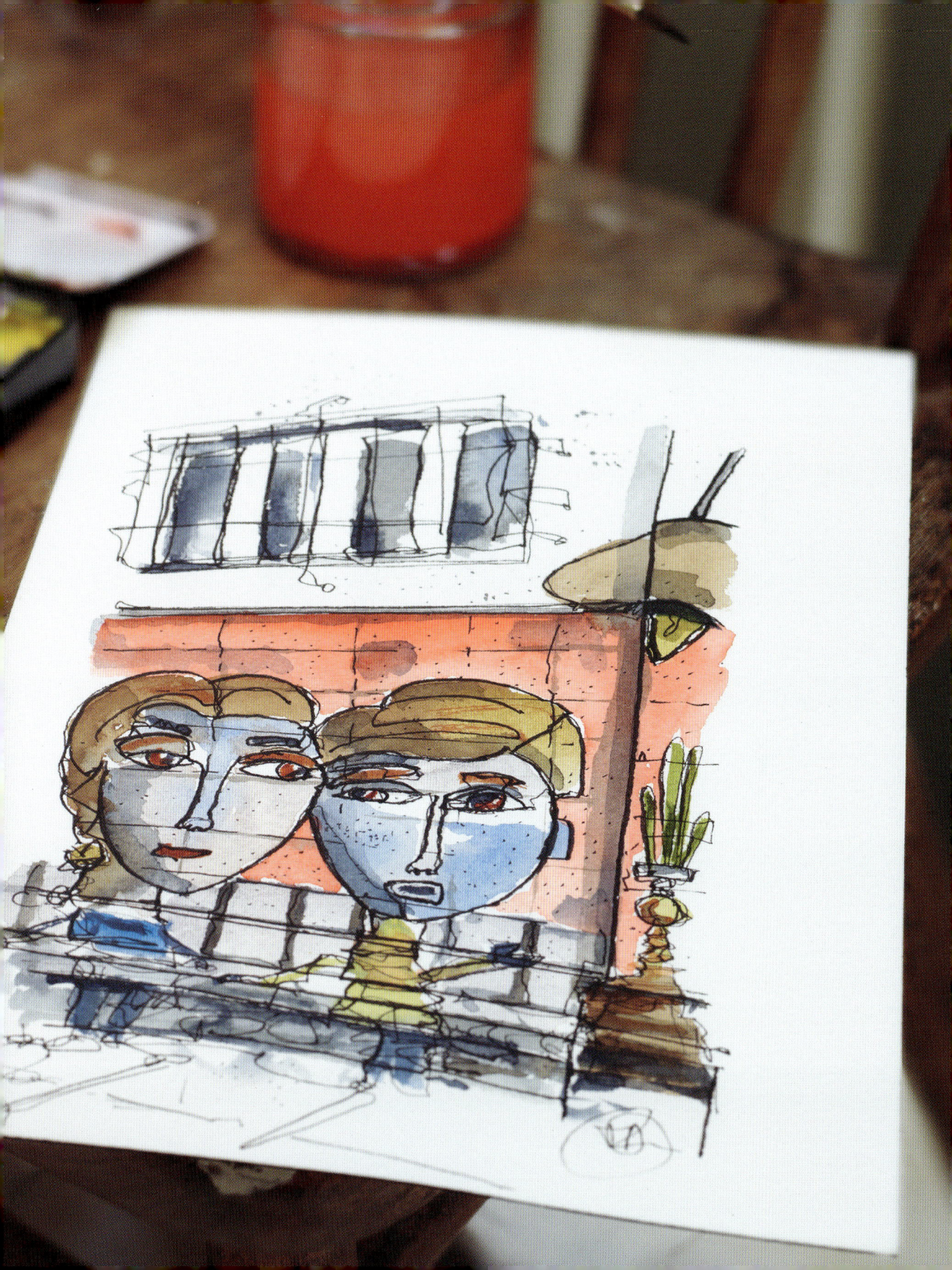

1 This scene has some simple but strong perspective, so a good starting point is to mark in these lines before adding on the contour of the main subjects of the scene. Careful observation is needed, because the flat graffiti on a three-dimensional wall curves and bends in unexpected ways.

2 Next, start to build up the first layer of the lightest colours. The graffiti is bold and bright, but don't rush ahead. Keep your colours light at this stage.

3 Next, begin to find the darker areas. This includes darker paints used to imply shadows in the graffiti, but also literal shadows formed by the wall, and the small gaps between bricks. Use a smaller brush to bring out specific details.

4 Create a light and loose background above the wall to complete the composition. Remember, the further from the focal point, the less detail and accuracy is required. Use the same colours from the background to enhance the darkest areas of the characters.

5 With the colours dry, the image may now appear a little flat or lacklustre.

Use bold ink marks to outline the blocks of colour to quickly change that.

6 Work through the scene with your pen. Be careful not to make your lines too strict. Keep the initial looseness. If we allow the lines to wobble a little, it gives the image a sketchy feeling.

7 Now add more details and textures. The scene itself is literally flat so there is a lack of depth and shadows. Focussing on the smallest shadows that define the textures throughout the scene is another way to bring a sense of dynamism to the sketch. You might also invent or enhance textures here – adding a sense of paving slabs in the foreground, for example.

8 Loosely imply the ironmongery on the window, and add ink marks to give the shadows in the gaps between bricks more definition.

9 For some final touches, closely observe the textures through the image. Your pen can be used to add dots, scratches, and scribbles to simulate these and add an extra layer of interest. This can really help the sketch feel more dynamic.

1
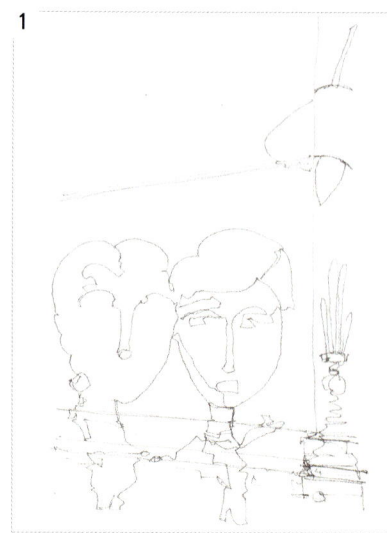

2
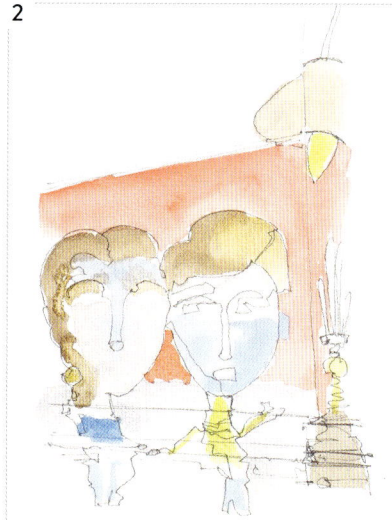

3
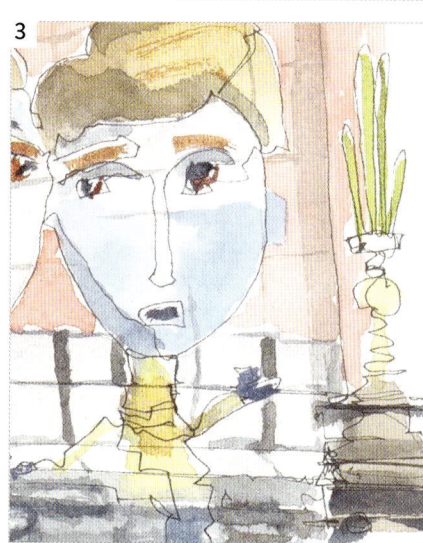

4

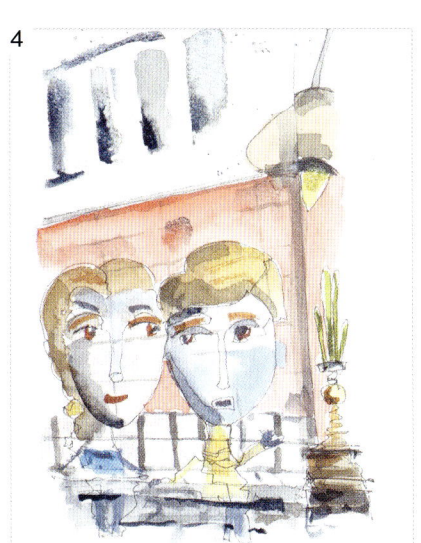

5

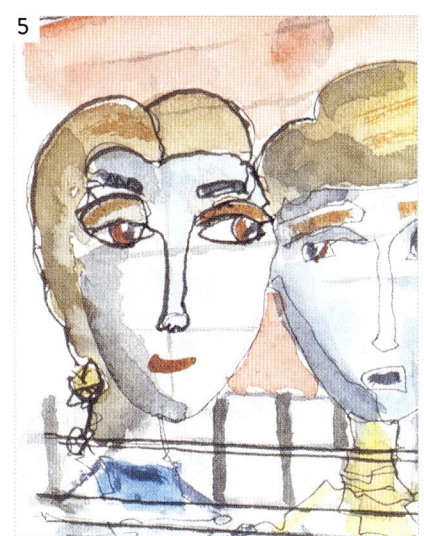

6

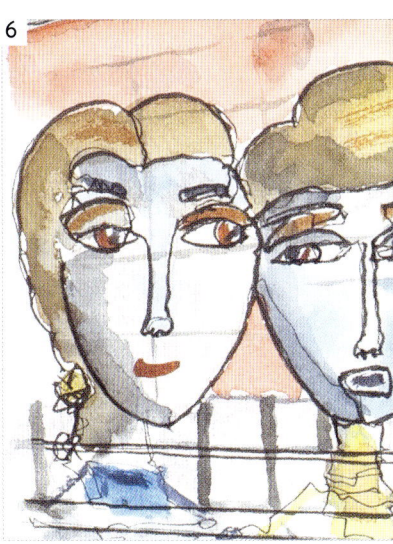

7

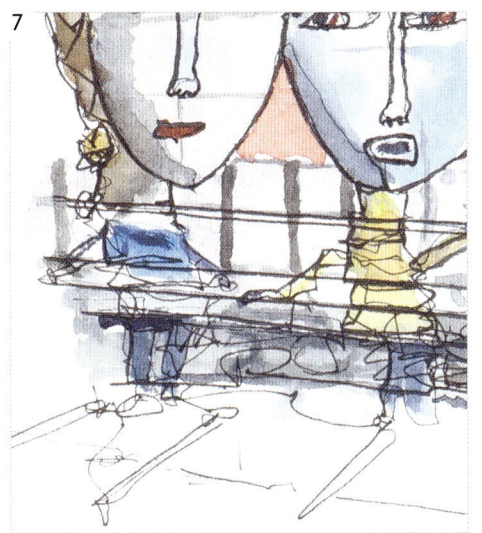

8

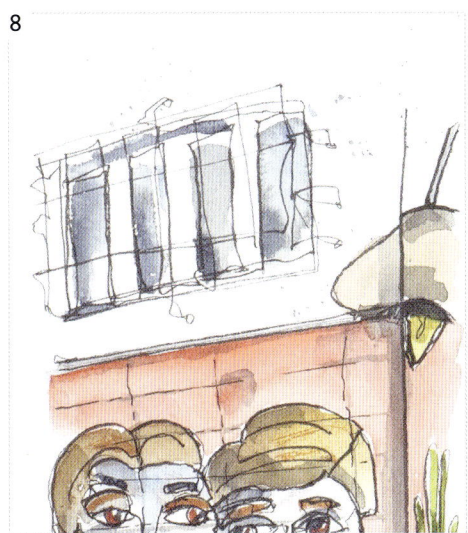

9

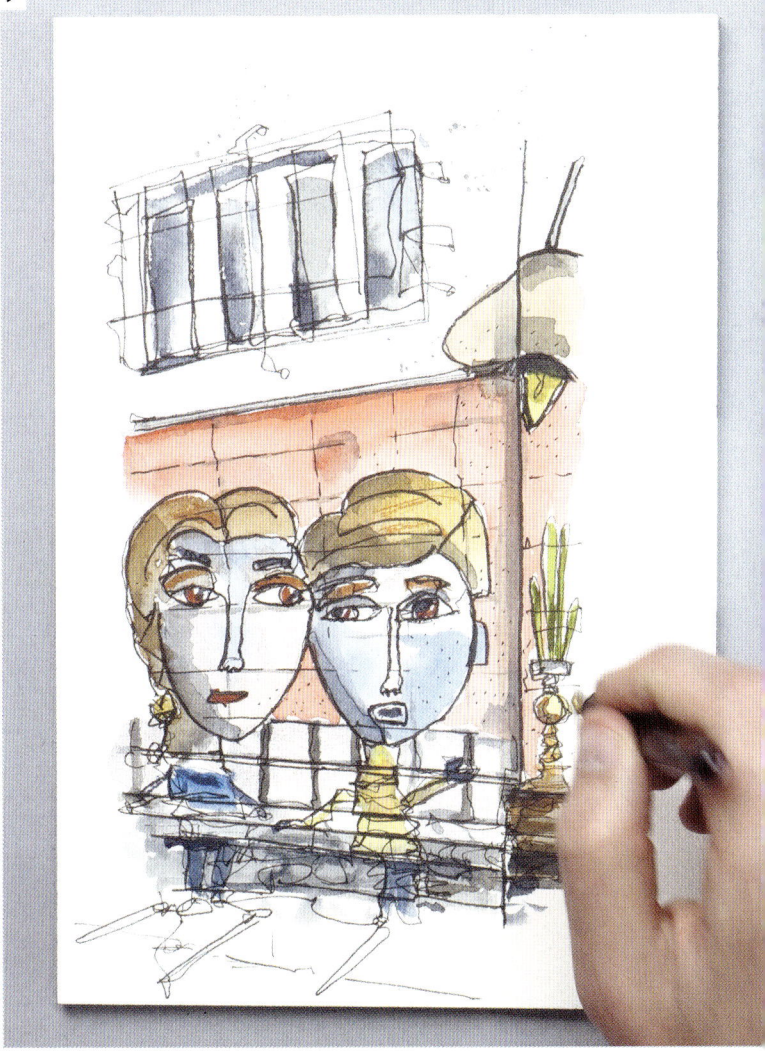

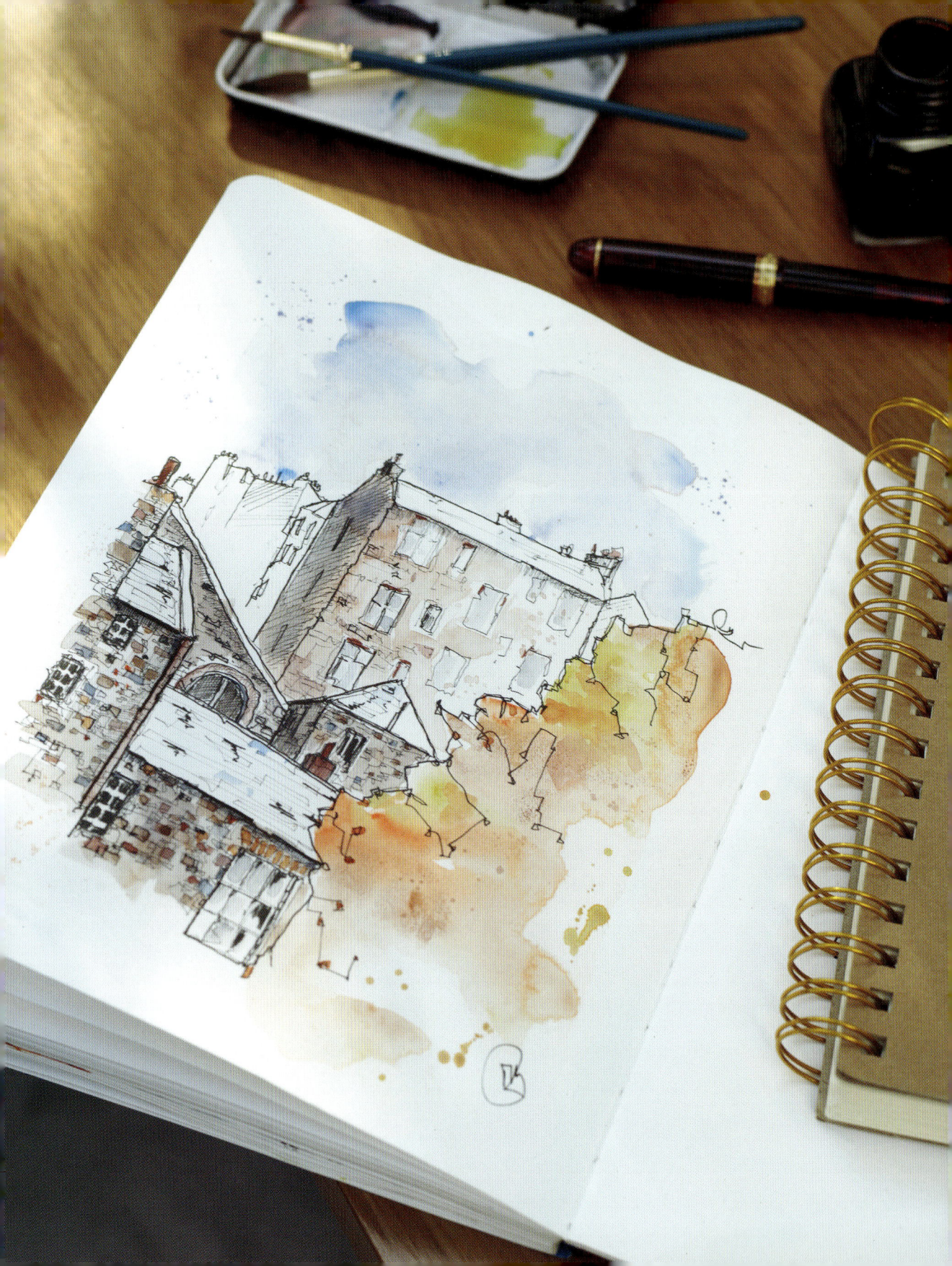

DETAIL AND TEXTURE

Cities are teeming with intricate textures, from sleek modern façades to the weathered stonework of older streets. Stonework, in particular, offers a wealth of detail, but trying to capture every texture can quickly become overwhelming. In this project, we'll look at how to use detailed textures strategically. By balancing these intricate sections with simpler, looser elements, you can achieve a light, lively composition that conveys the essence of the scene without becoming overly laborious.

SUPPLIES

Mixed media sketchbook 20 x 25cm (8 x 10in)

Fountain pen

Permanent and waterproof ink

Round synthetic brushes (sizes 3 and 6)

Flat synthetic brushes (size 1in)

Watercolours – lavender, cerulean blue chromium, cobalt blue, indigo, organic vermilion, Indian red, pyrrol scarlet, quinacridone sienna, green apatite genuine, cobalt green, hansa yellow medium

1 Start with finding and gently marking in the key shapes of the scene. Focus on introducing texture into the contours that suggest the interesting brickwork in the scene already.

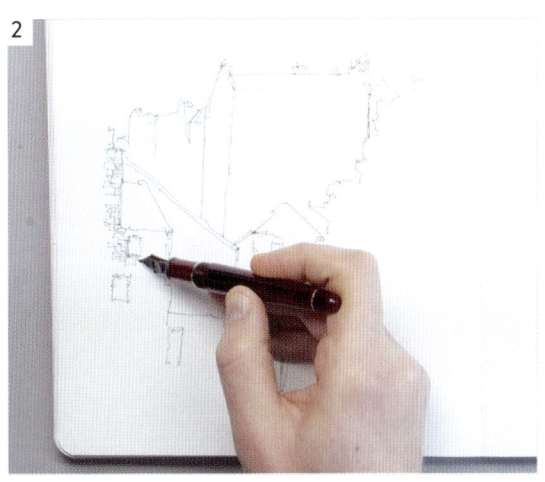

2 Creating texture in ink is often about choosing repetitive marks that best represent the textures in your scene. Use your pen to slowly and carefully draw these marks on your page. Keep your marks simple and light. Adding texture can be a painstaking process. Be prepared to take a little longer than usual to complete this texture-heavy sketch.

3 Move gradually around the scene, working in sections. This will help keep you focussed on the correct textures for each area.

4 As you work into the distance, reduce the density of the ink lines and lighten up the amount of texture on the page. This helps create the sense of 'atmospheric perspective', where details and contrast are decreased in the distance.

5 Work through the scene again from front to back. Restate the most important shapes, and add contrast with hatching and blots of ink. Again, be sure to consider atmospheric perspective.

6 Add the first layer of watercolour. With so much ink on the page, excessive colours will quickly feel murky or overworked. Instead, work with a light and varied wash in ink-heavy areas with room for bold bright colours where the ink detail is less.

7 Use a small brush to pull out the different colours and tones of the varied stones in the walls. Allow a little artistic licence in the interpretation – you may find reds, blues, yellows, greys, and more that can be accentuated.

8 As with the ink, take your time and be careful not to overwork your initial marks. Aim to have your boldest colours at the front of the image, and lightest and most limited suggestions in the back. With the stonework complete, consider the other elements. Adding a little tone into the windows can make them feel more part of the scene, and textures in the golden trees add a sense of fun.

9 Finally, a little extra ink neatens up the edges of the shapes after all the delicate watercolour painting, and the scene is complete. It can be tempting, when you start adding detail, to keep going until things become a little too much. Aim to use the detail to help guide the eye to the most interesting part of the image, while elsewhere is left blank or greatly simplified to balance out the image.

3

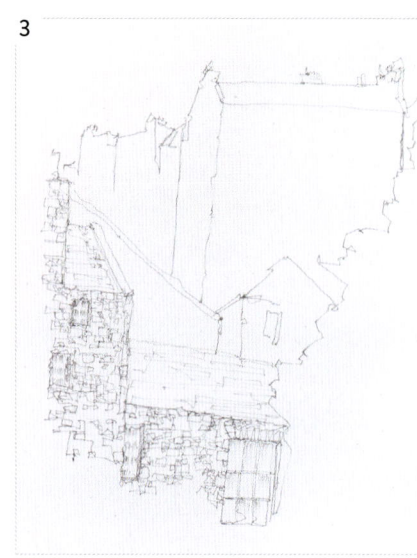

4

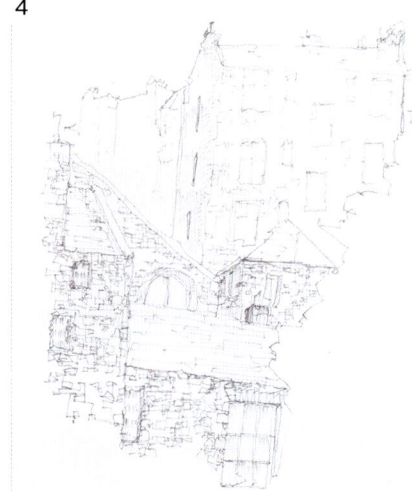

5

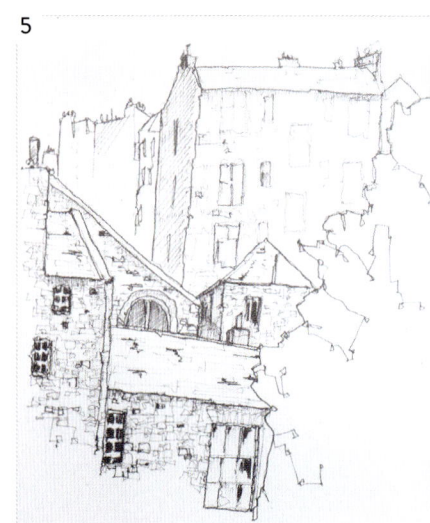

6

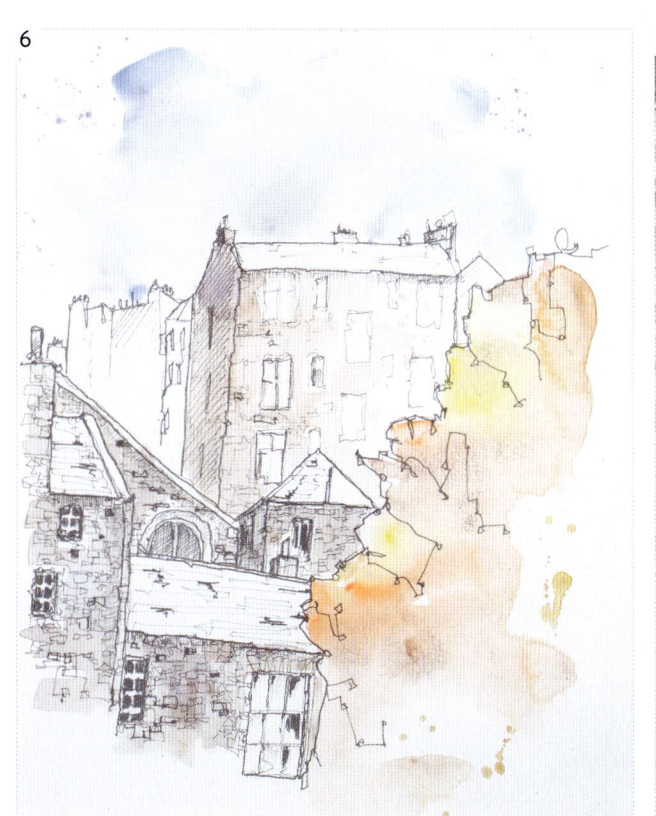

7

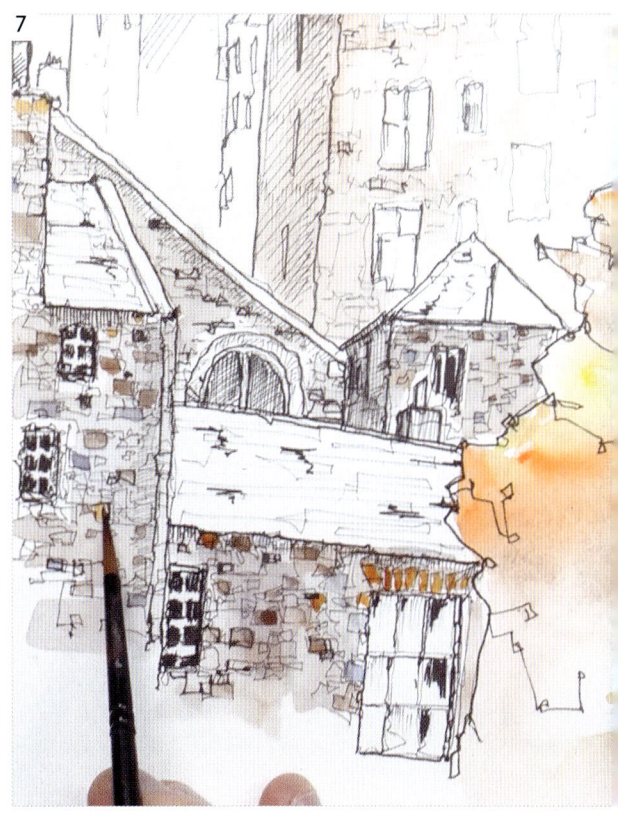

8

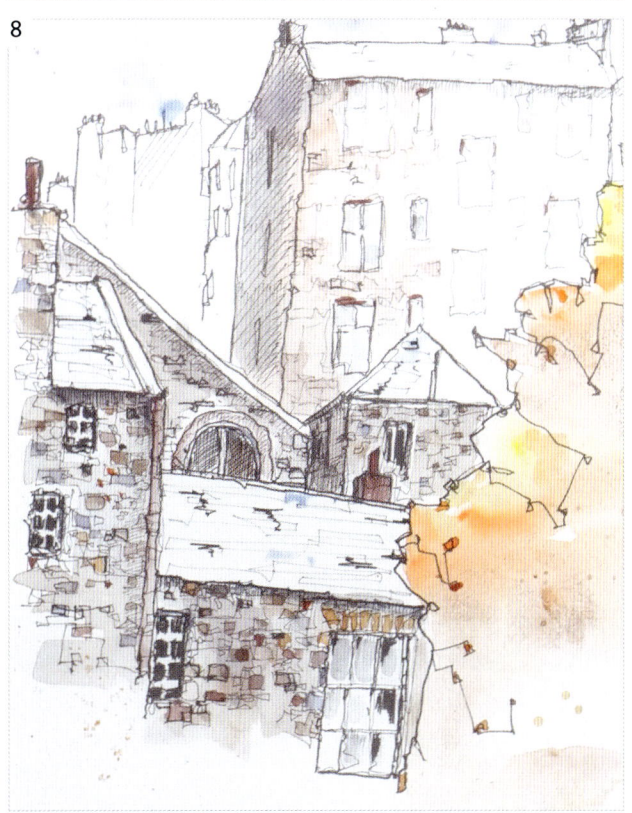

9

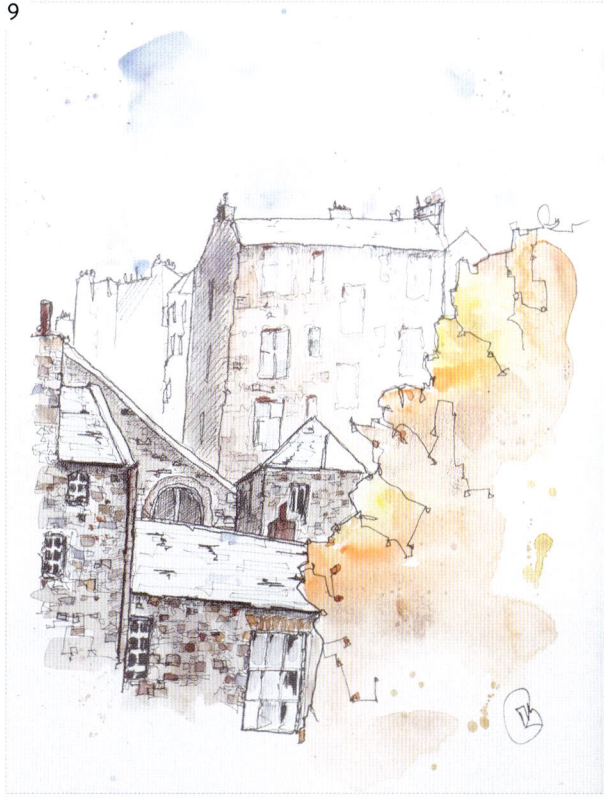

RIVERS AND BOATS

This river scene seem challenging, but it offers many delightful features to capture – textures of the water, the shapes of the boats, reflections, and more. When sketching water, focus on its movement and how it interacts with the surrounding elements. Reflections are key; they often stretch vertically, while subtle horizontal strokes can suggest ripples and disturbance on the surface. With a thoughtful approach, the complexity of water can be simplified into an expressive and dynamic element of your scene.

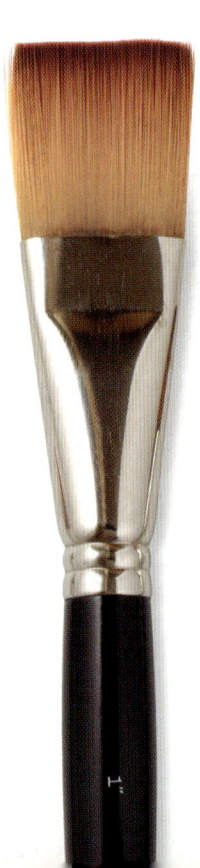

SUPPLIES

A5 mixed media sketchbook
....
Fountain pen
....
Permanent and waterproof ink
....
Round synthetic brushes (size 6)
....
Flat synthetic brushes (size 1in)
....
Watercolours – ultramarine, indigo, organic vermilion, mars yellow, pyrrol scarlet, quinacridone sienna, green apatite genuine, azo yellow
....
Posca pens – white, yellow, red, blue (0.7mm)
....

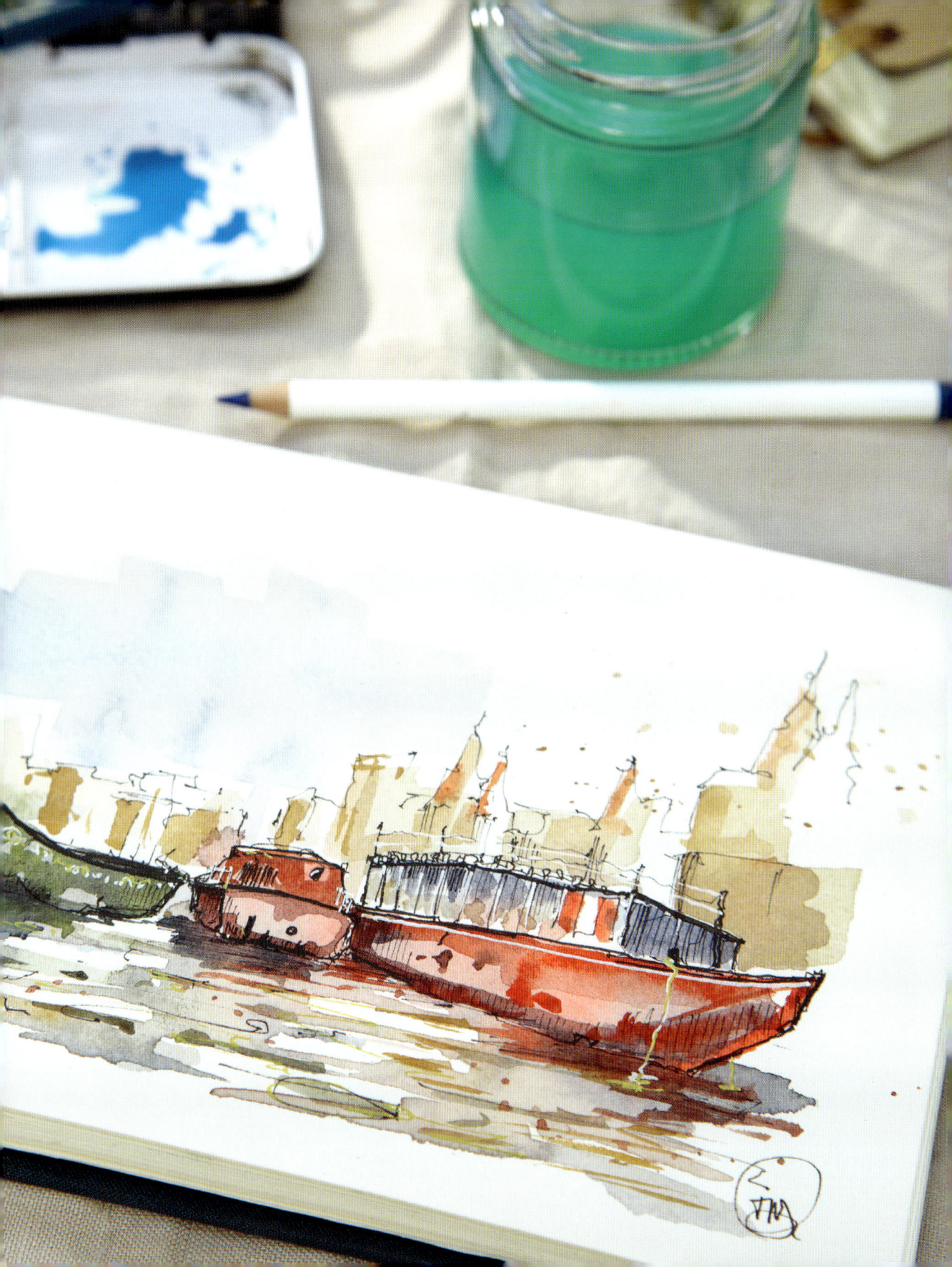

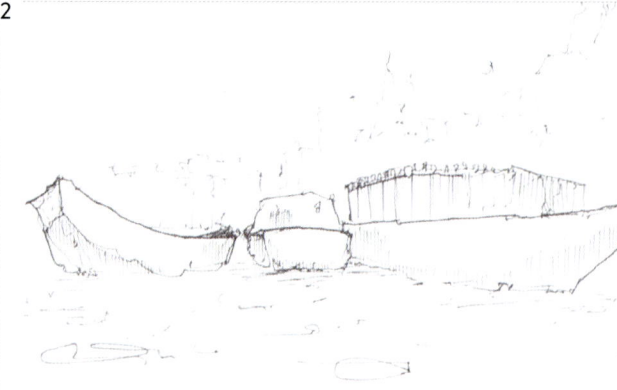

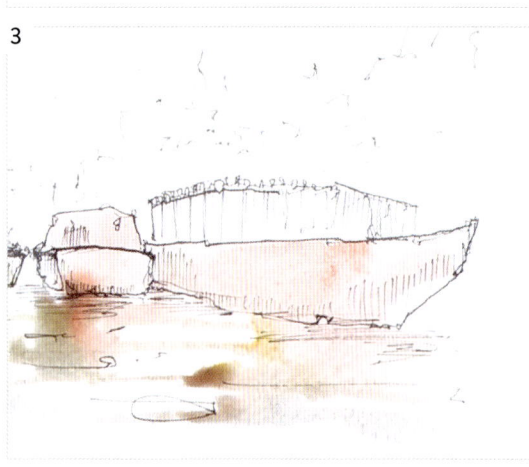

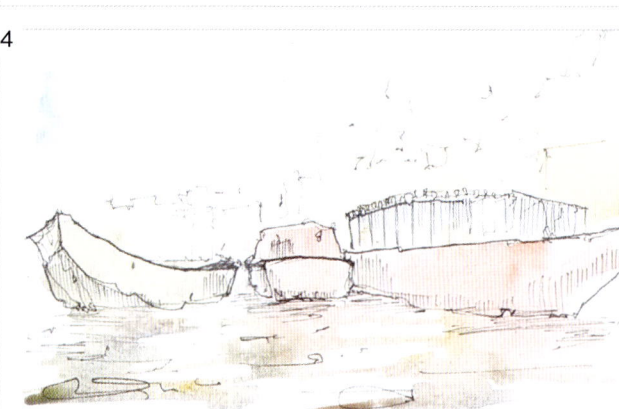

1 Start with the main focal point – the three boats – focusing on contours and key shapes. Keep the background minimal to avoid clutter. Use light hatching to define the boats and their connection to the water.

2 Strengthen contours and add details to bring the boats forward. Take time to observe water textures – ripples often appear as parallel lines that widen as they approach, but also include looping and elliptical patterns. Adding a few of these will enhance the scene's character.

3 Due to the complexity of water textures, working wet-on-wet is ideal, requiring some speed before the page dries. Take a moment to observe the water – it's rarely just blue but a mix of murky greens, whites, blacks, and scene reflections. Apply a light wash to the boats, then create reflections by dragging their reds and greens downward. Soften these vertical marks with gentle horizontal strokes using a neutral mix like indigo and quinacridone sienna.

4 Paint the background in the simplest and lightest of washes. It's not the focus of the sketch, so don't try to make it detailed.

5

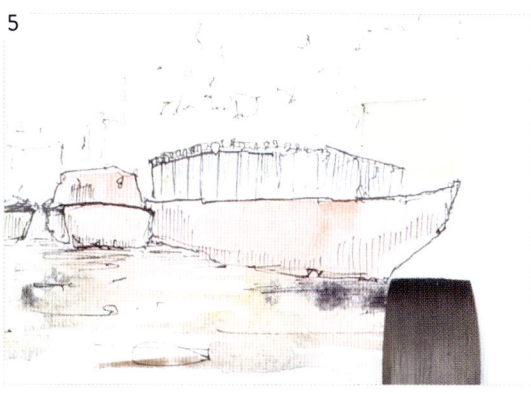

6

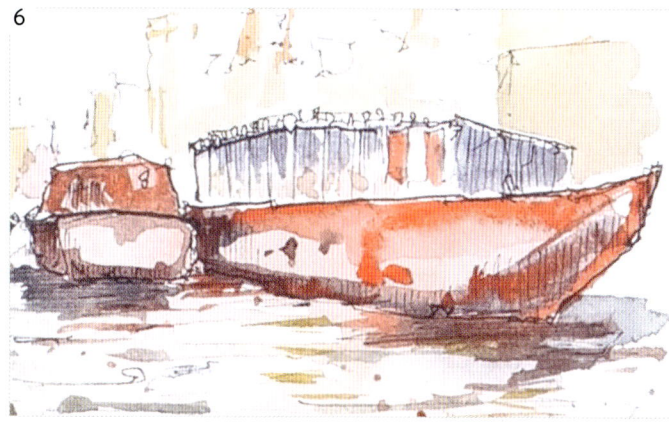

7

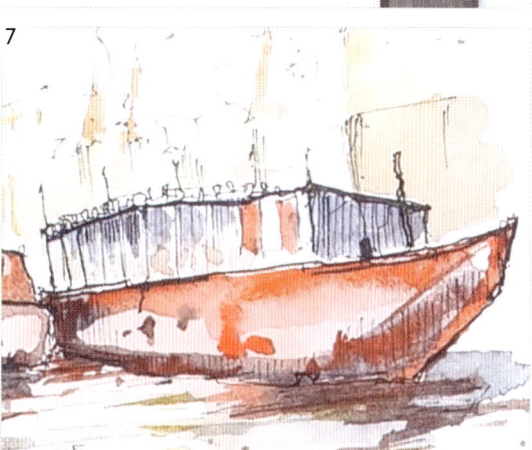

8

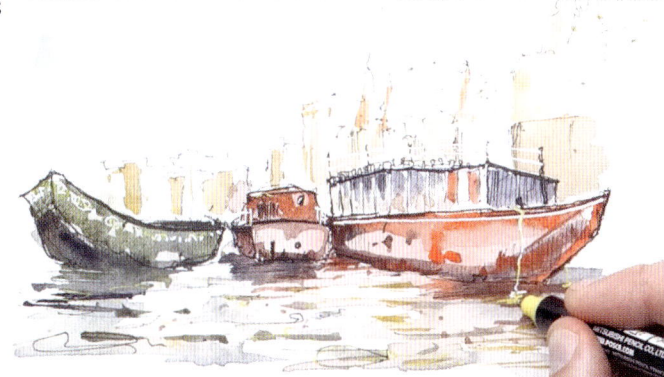

5 While the page is still wet, add darker values using the same neutral mix from Step 3, but more concentrated. Drop it into the deepest shadows and let it diffuse naturally. If the pigment spreads too fast, the page is too wet – wait a few minutes and try again. If it doesn't blend, re-wet the area lightly.

6 Once dry, use a smaller brush to refine the reds and greens, enhancing light and shadow on the boats and their reflections. Add subtle background details to suggest light and dark, and the 3D form of distant buildings.

7 Restate the lines of the boats to bring them back into the foreground, and respond to any shifts in the shapes that may have happened with the watercolours. Reapply hatching or add further details at this point.

8 Use light touches with Posca pens or acrylic markers to bring out the reflections in the water and highlights on the boats. Add in further details, such as the anchor lines reaching down below the waterline to complete the scene.

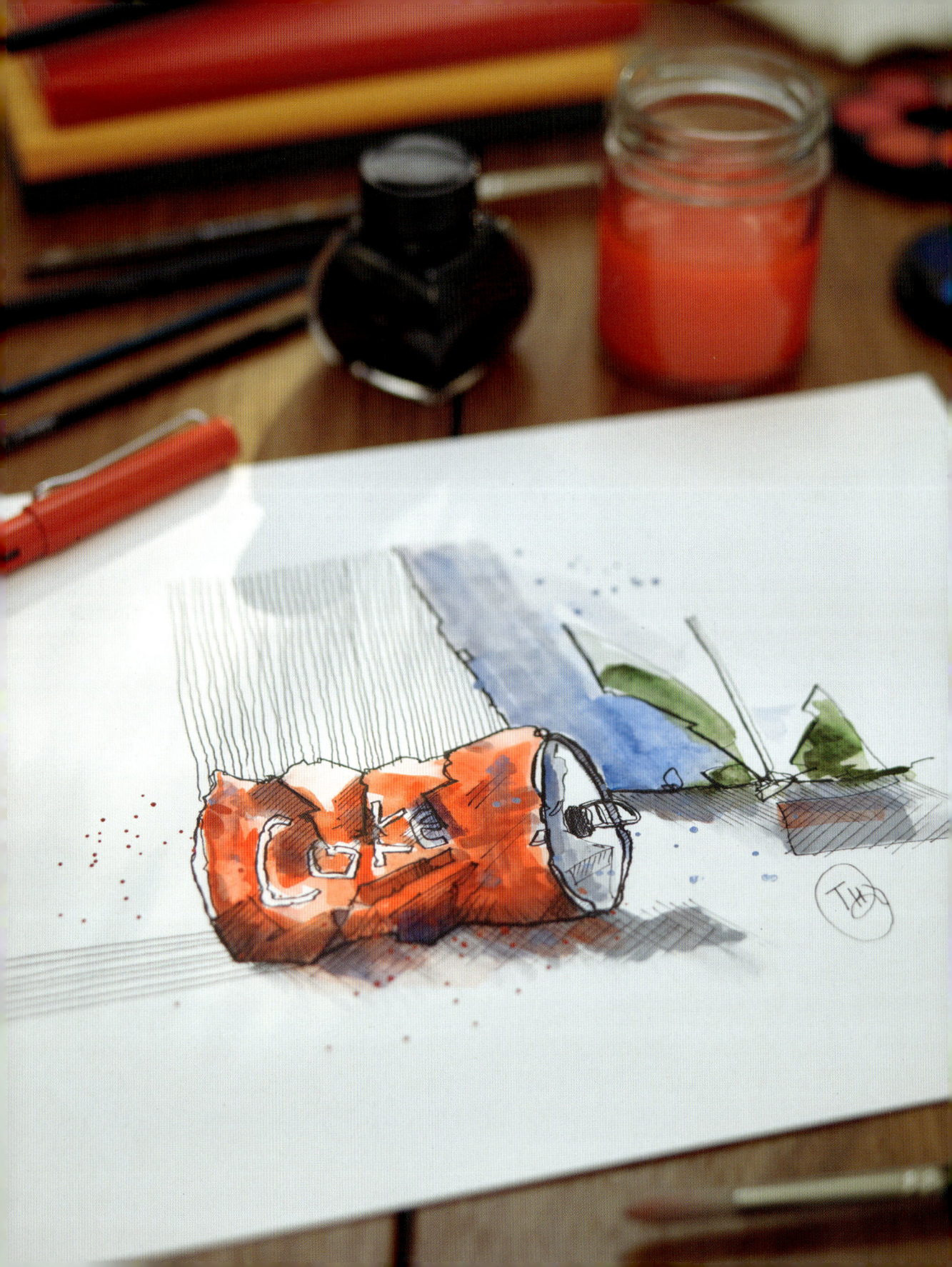

URBAN STILL LIFE

Sketching something as simple as a discarded drinks can offers a rich exploration of value, form, texture, and colour. Modern city living provides endless inspiration for contemporary still life art, with crumpled snack packets, squashed wrappers, or any other forgotten debris that you come across. Still life offers a chance to experiment with art materials, or to simply enjoy creating a playful composition – a sketching approach to still life can add a fun, quirky, and contemporary feel to your art.

SUPPLIES

Cold pressed watercolour paper 23 x 30.5cm (9 x 12in)

Fountain pen

Permanent and waterproof ink

Round synthetic brushes (size 12)

Flat synthetic brushes (size ½in)

Watercolours – lavender, ultramarine, organic vermilion, pyrrol scarlet, green apatite genuine

Alcohol ink markers – light grey, medium grey

Gouache or acrylic marker – white

1

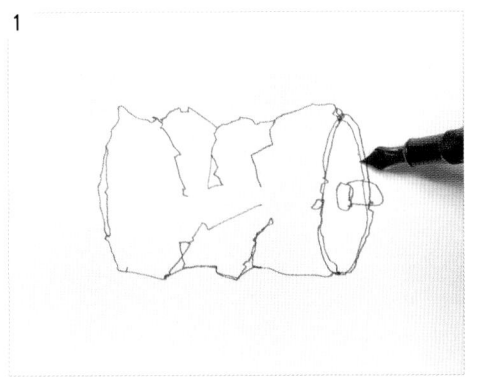

2

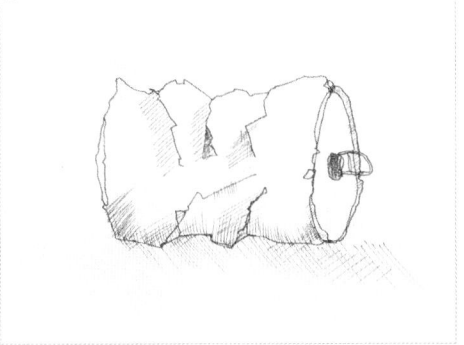

1 Start with a contour of the can, and mark in the key folds as well. There will be surprising angles and shapes, so focus on what you see, not what you think you see. A loose grip on your pen helps your line stay agile and characterful.

2 Now try squinting at your object. The darks and lights should become more obvious. This will help you find the folds that create the darkest areas and the reflections that give the brightest spots. Continue to build value. Simple linear hatching can be remarkably versatile. Try to vary the direction of the lines to stay consistent with the form of the object. Use crosshatching for darker values.

3 Add a few background marks to suggest a bin with a plant growing out from underneath, with hatching to keep the direction of light consistent.

4 In a scene that focuses on objects with complex or unexpected forms, tackling the shadows of the scene before adding colour can be helpful. First, add the lightest shadows with alcohol ink markers to the main subjects of the scene.

5 Just as with watercolours, these marker pens can be layered – use a darker pen to create the next highest value of shadow.

6 Now layer a light wash of watercolour on top of these values. To create a varied and interesting wash for the can, use organic vermilion and pyrrol scarlet, two different reds, to allow varied hues to develop. Keep the background scenery light and simple. Allow to dry.

7 Build saturation with a second wash, and use ultramarine blue to add richness to the shadows and depth to the reds. Don't neglect a little colour in the shadows, reflected from the objects casting them.

8 Allow the watercolours to fully dry, then restate key lines – adapt your lines to the object you're observing but also be guided to some extent by the watercolour's movements. Try simple linear hatching marks to flatten the background area and guide the eye to the can. Notice the vertical hatching in the background implies a vertical surface, while the horizontal hatching to the left of the can implies it's on the ground.

9 Tap your brush to create a light splatter of watercolours on your page. This takes a little practice to control, but the effect helps to fill up blank space on the page and enhance the sense of colour through the image.

10 The final step is to make sure the highlights and key details are evident by restating the writing on the can. You might add white gouache or acrylic marker here to enhance any highlights that have been lost in the painting process.

3
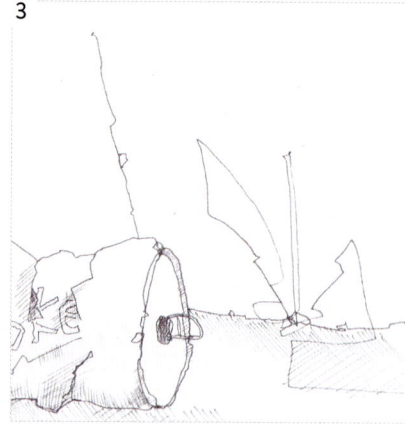

4
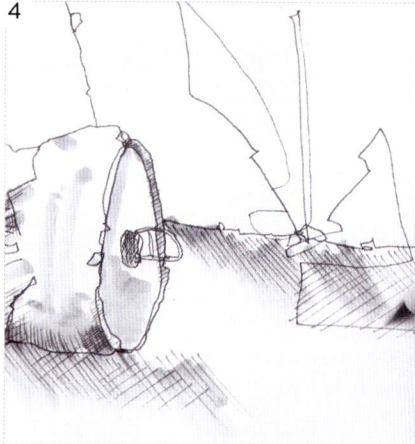

5
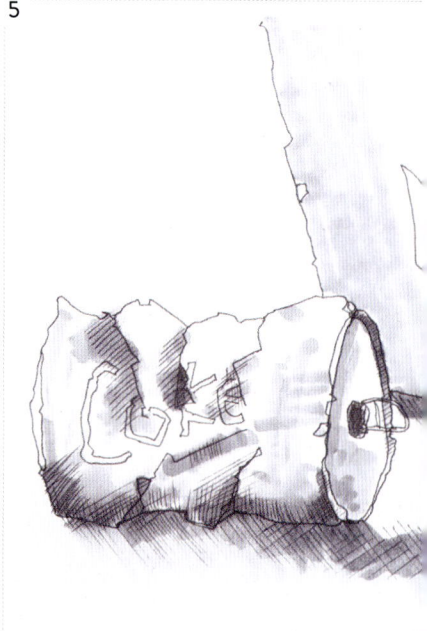

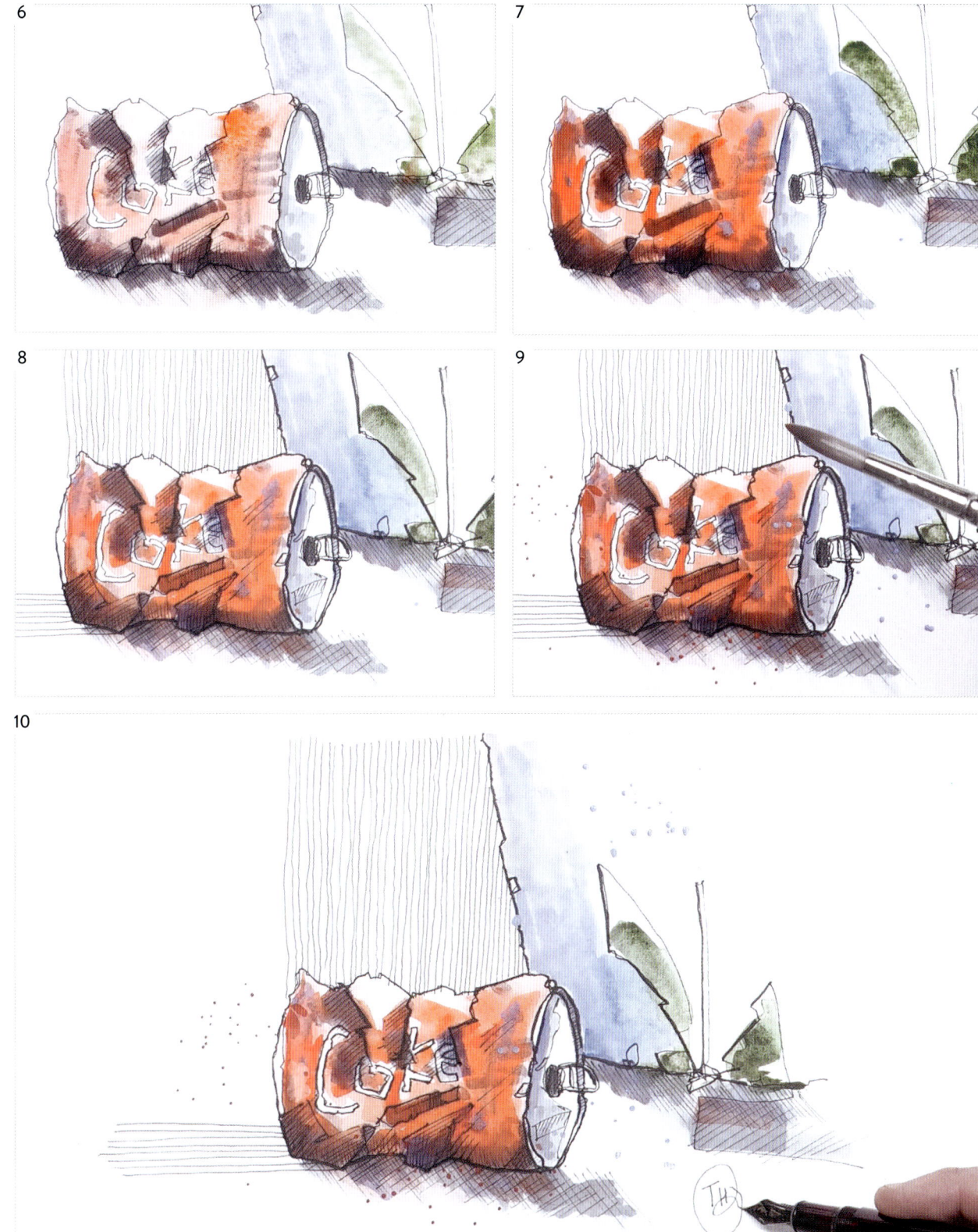

SUPPLIES

Mixed media sketchbook
20 x 25cm (8 x 10in)

Fude pen or brush pen

Round synthetic brushes
(sizes 6 and 10)

Flat synthetic
brushes (size 1in)

Watercolours – cobalt
blue, indigo, organic
vermilion, pyrrol scarlet,
quinacridone sienna,
hansa yellow medium,
cobalt green, lunar earth

VIBRANT MARKET SCENE

Sketching crowds, especially in a bustling market, can feel intimidating. However, by focusing on the scene's essence and simplifying elements to create depth, you can turn a challenging subject into a rewarding experience. Remember, mistakes and extra lines can enhance the sense of life and energy, so don't worry about perfection – let the chaos work for you.

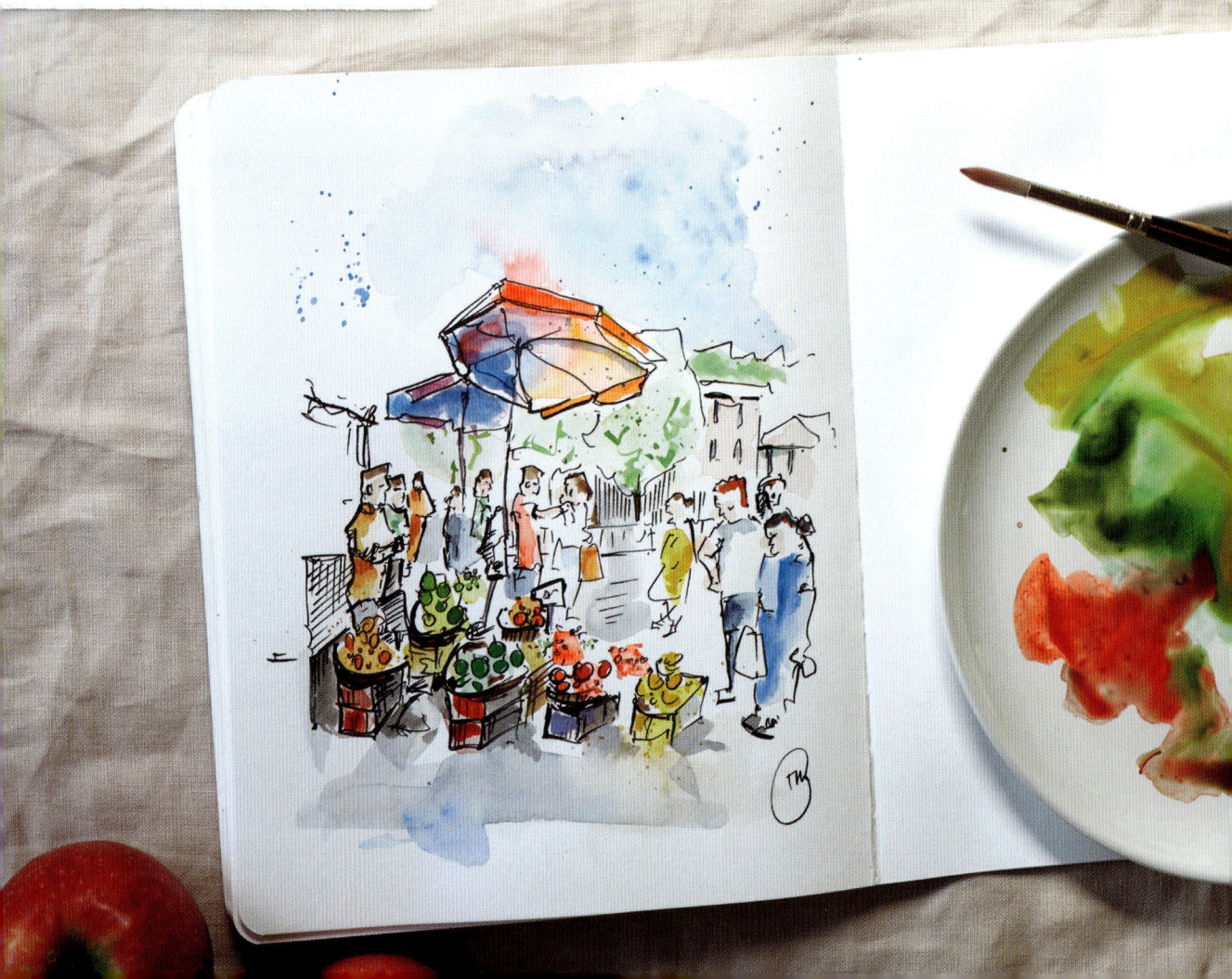

1 Start with light, loose lines to indicate the heads of the crowd. This is my usual approach to drawing people, and a busy crowd is no exception. With the heads in position, it ensures the perspective of the scene will feel good.

2 Continue to build the scene, adding shapes to create people's figures and add in foreground details of the market.

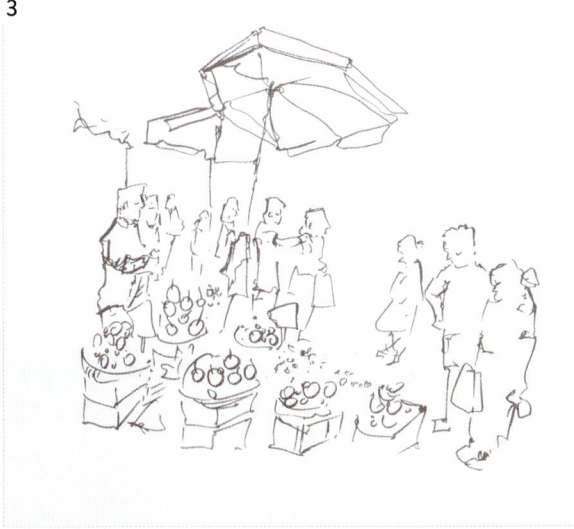

3 A market can feel like an overwhelmingly complex scene. Try to pick out key shapes and ideas, rather than creating a literal representation of every fruit, veg, and box in the scene.

4 With a busy foreground, add a simple background to complete the scene before restating elements of the foreground to enhance the depth of the image.

5 Now add your first, light wash of colour. Think about what attracted you to the scene in the first place, as this can become your focal area. I found the shapes and colours of the fruit fascinating, so I started my colouring there to highlight those features. Next, add colours around your focal area in a light and loose fashion.

6 Remember that in watercolour painting, vibrancy is achieved through layering. So the next step is to allow the page to dry, before using a small brush to apply a second bolder layer of colour to the fruit.

7 Use this layering technique on the people and on elements of the background to ensure the rest of the scene doesn't feel flat.

8 Vibrancy is often more keenly felt when contrasted against light and shadow. Plenty of white paper and light watercolours means the image has lovely light.

So now is the time to provide some depth of shadow, in particular to the foreground.

9 With the watercolours dry, restate a few key lines, suggest details, and provide some extra structure to the background. Flicks and splatters of the brightest colours in the foreground add to the suggestion of complexity on top of what is quite a simple sketch.

4
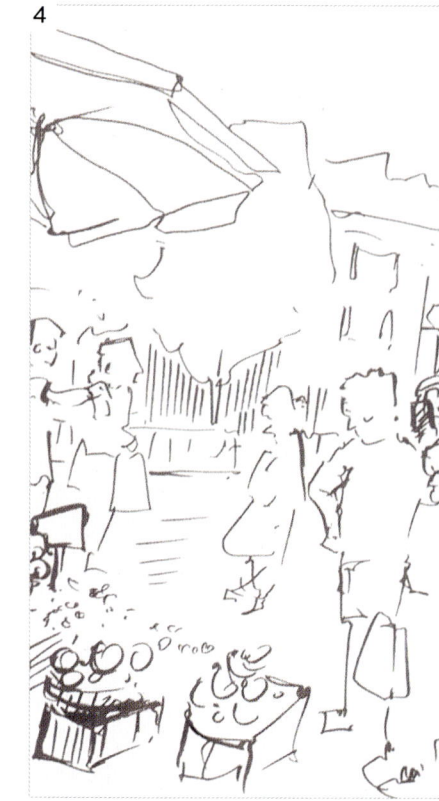

5
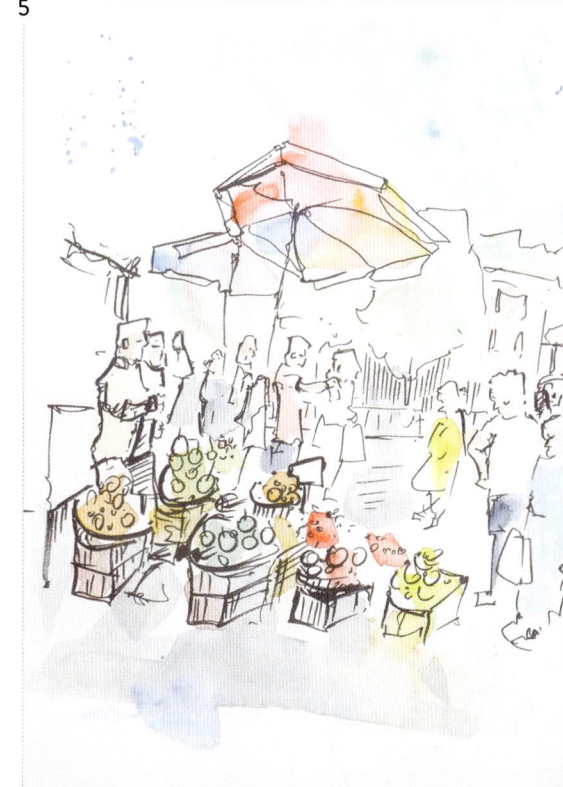

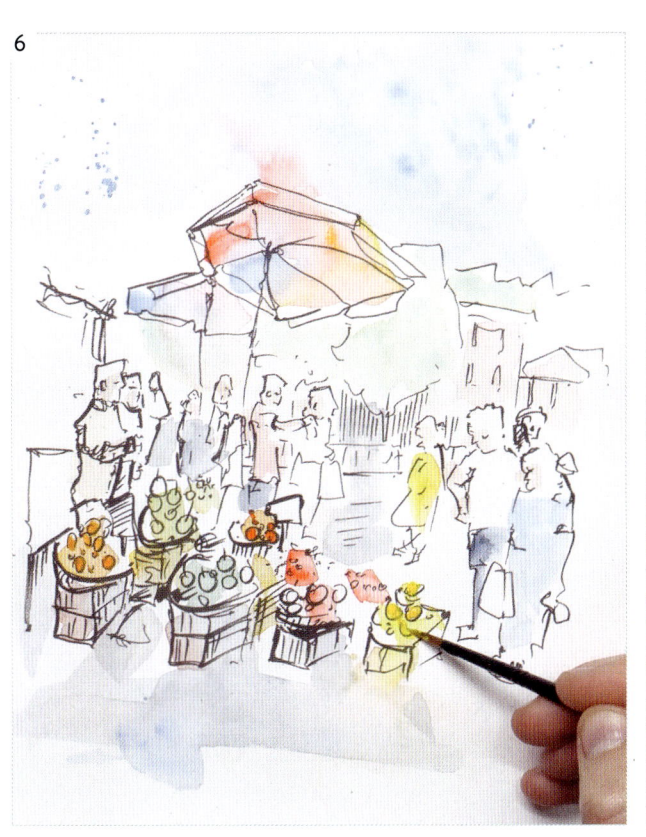

6

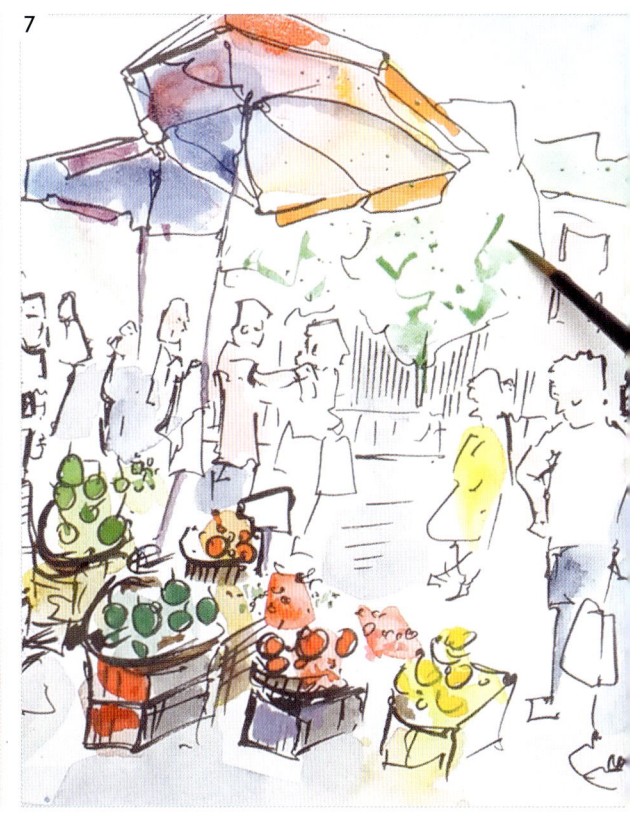

7

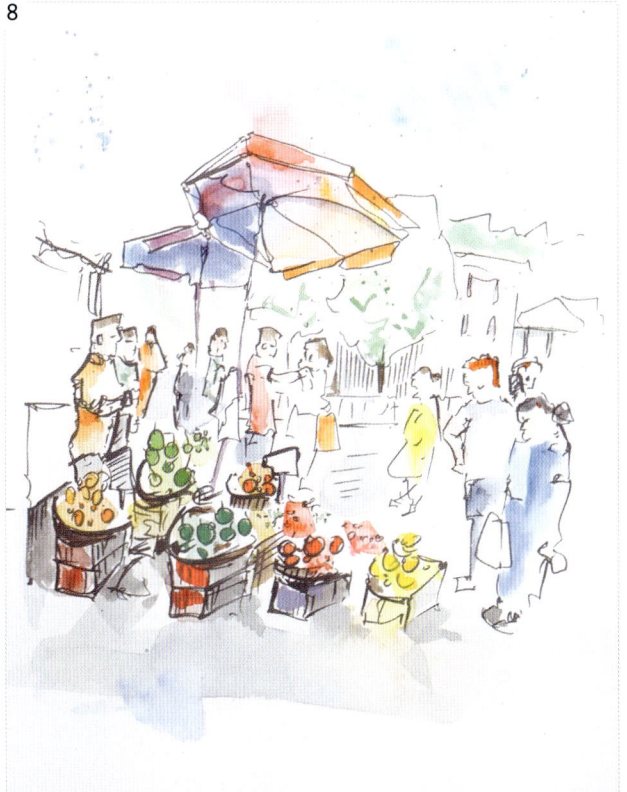

8

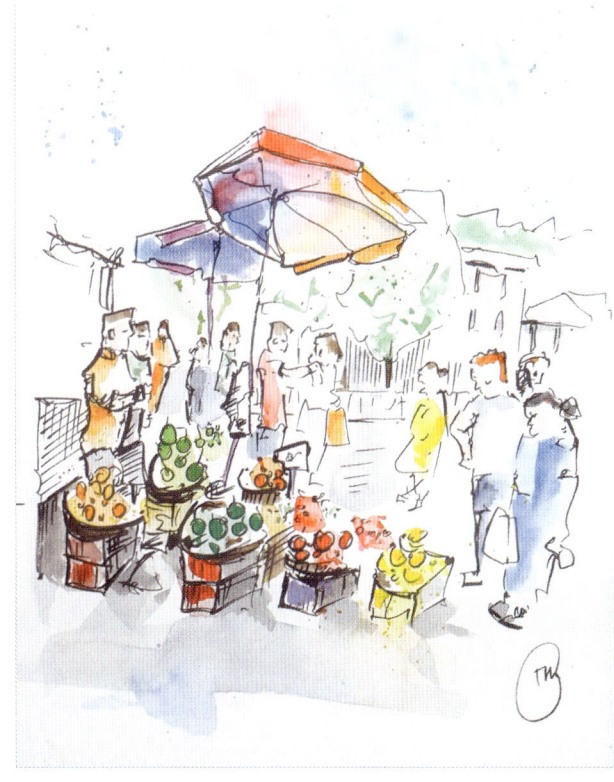

9

INSPIRATION FINDER

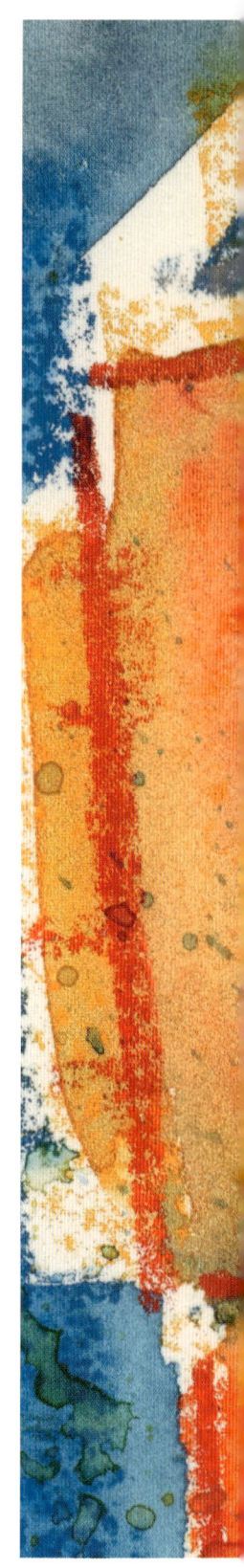

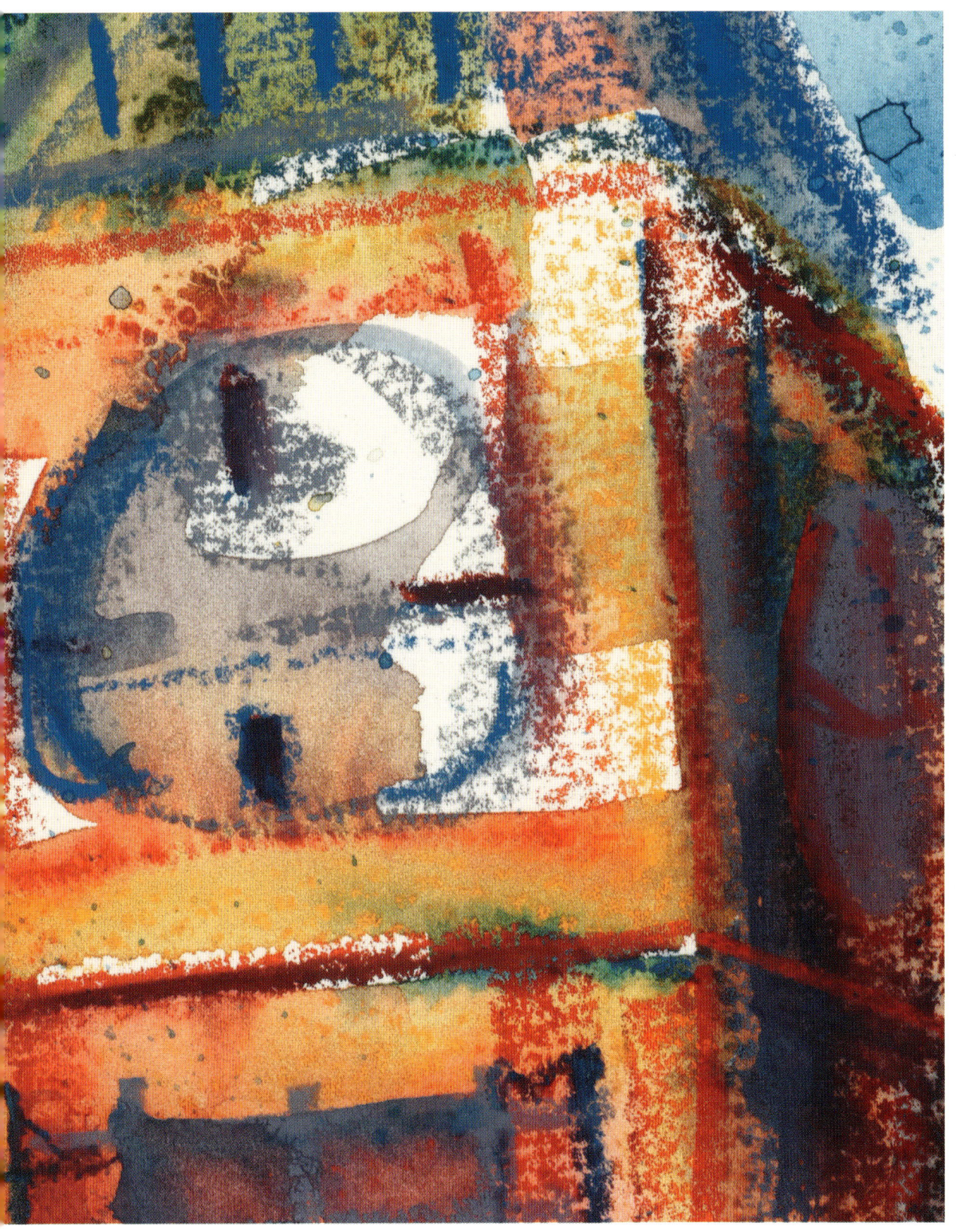

QUICK-FIRE SKETCHING

Capturing the essence of city life doesn't always require grandeur – sometimes, it's the small, overlooked details that tell the best stories. One of my favourite activities is to just get out, and sketch anything. Combining lots of small scenes on a page, fleeting images and small studies, can create something that is more than the sum of its parts. The small and simple approach to sketching is quicker, puts less pressure on you, and can be used to practise complex subjects or just to enjoy yourself and experiment.

A

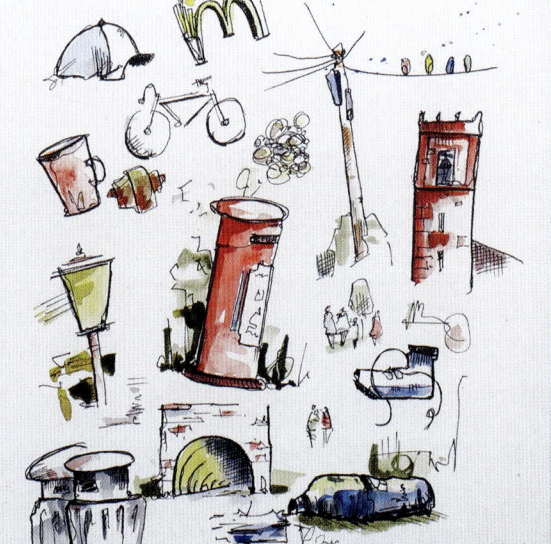

Pages like this (A) are a cornerstone of my sketchbooks. The ink work is what I call 'doodley', where observation and imagination come together to create something simple yet recognisable.

Instead of sitting down to capture a perfect, complete scene in one go, this page came together throughout a day in multiple locations. The starlings on a wire were sketched from my front door, while the tunnel and the McDonald's sign are familiar features of my town centre. Little doodles of people filled in the gaps, and I used this opportunity to tackle more intimidating subjects, like the bicycle, as practice.

I added the colour later at home with pencils and watercolours, bringing the page to life and making my sketchbook feel vibrant and dynamic.

This page of miniature sketches (B) came together during a walk through my hometown. I started in the town centre with a coffee, then made my way back along the river and through the parks. Along the way, I stopped to capture small glimpses of the scenery, adding bold, bright colours with water-soluble crayons. It was a relaxed way to sketch without putting pressure on any single image, and I really like how it all came together.

The approach of simple, doodle-like lines and quick splashes of colour can be a wonderful way to capture memories. For example, this page from my sketchbook (C) – featuring my wedding venue, family, and our house – is one I've cut out and kept safe. This technique can also be used for playful experimentation, creating small doodles on scraps of paper to practise techniques, explore ideas, or even turn into bookmarks (D).

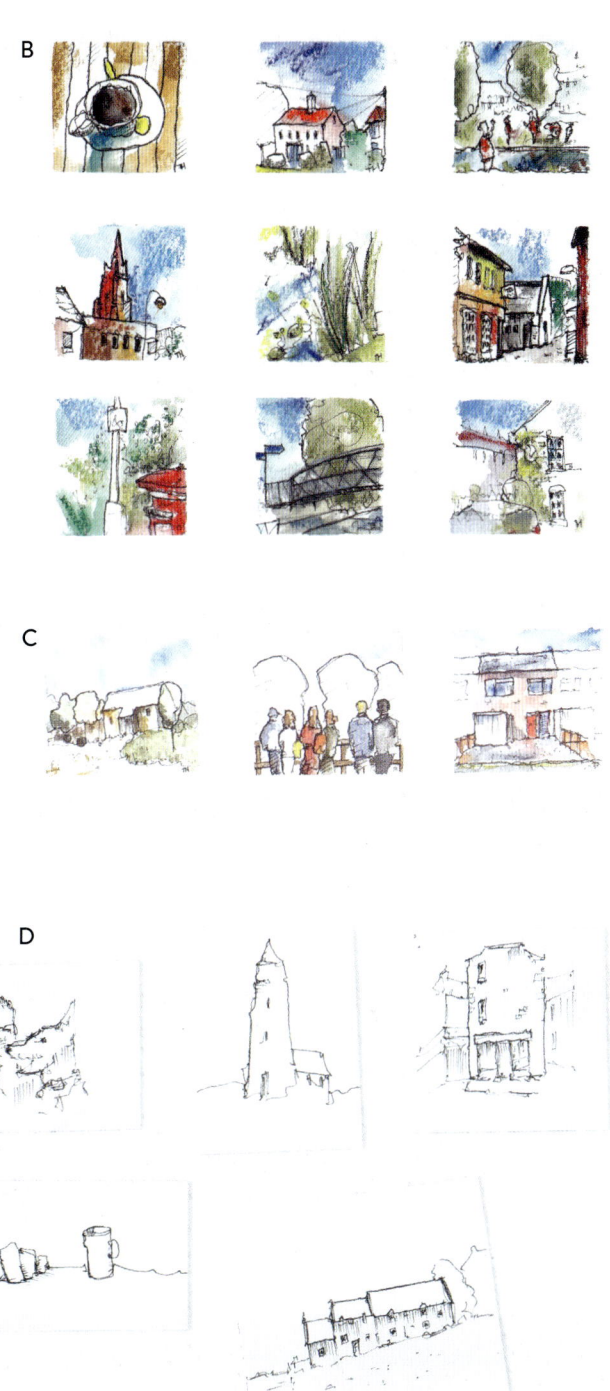

CHANGE YOUR VIEWPOINT

Cities offer endless variety, not just in scenery, but in the perspectives they offer. From a block of high-rise flats to rooftop cafés, urban life provides unique viewpoints that can transform how we approach a scene. Sometimes, a little creativity in interpretation achieves something far more exciting than strict accuracy ever could.

This painting (A) captures the essence of a wide, sweeping landscape in Durham, UK, through a playful fish-eye perspective. The scene features a street climbing up to the right and another descending steeply through the centre. Rather than adhering strictly to linear perspective – which would be both challenging and require a much larger canvas – I chose to warp elements of the scene to fit the page and convey the essence I wanted.

This approach isn't about achieving perfect accuracy but about embracing the freedom to interpret the scene. Letting go of the need to 'get it right' can feel daunting at first, but I find it liberating to play with perspective and create my own version of the view. The result is a unique and expressive take on a complex and dynamic landscape.

A

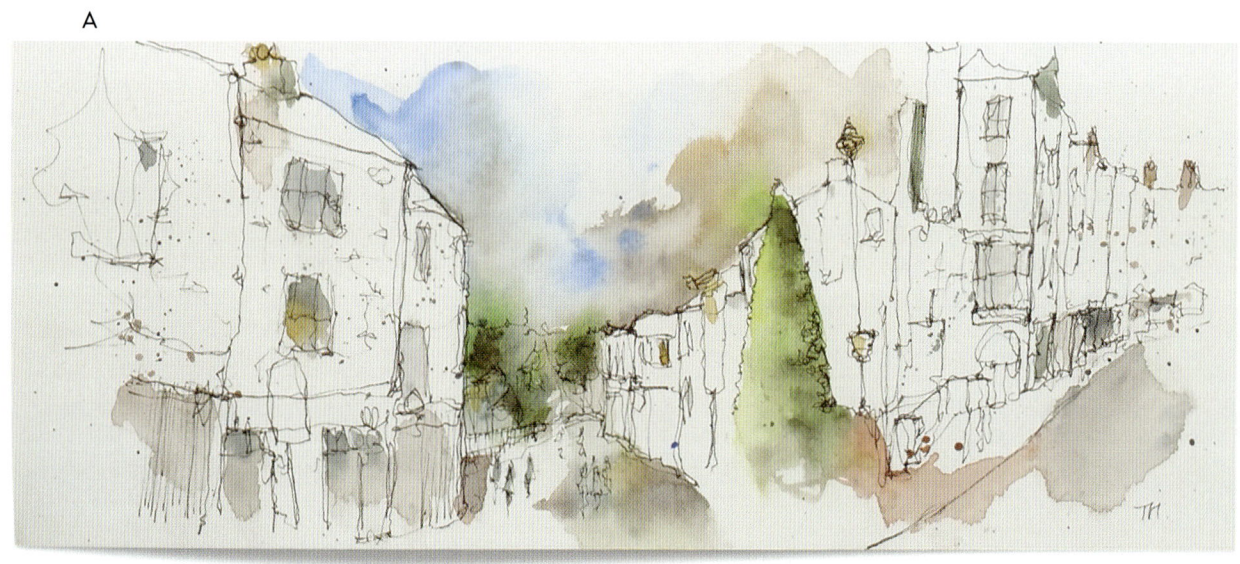

The next painting (**B**) captures a top-down view, offering an unusual perspective that required careful observation to draw what I saw rather than what I assumed. Instead of looking up at tall buildings, this scene demanded a focus on the shapes and structures below. I started lightly, sketching the key forms to ensure the composition felt balanced and accurate.

From there, I added textures to bring the rooftops to life. Rather than meticulously copying every detail, I used repetitive shapes and marks to suggest the variety of textures, simplifying the scene for clarity and working through the complex shapes in stages.

To contrast with the detailed ink work, I kept the colour application loose and fluid (**C**). This prevented the piece feeling overworked and allowed all that effort spent on sketching to shine through. These bold, expressive touches helped complete the piece, blending ink structure with fluidity of more moody colours.

B

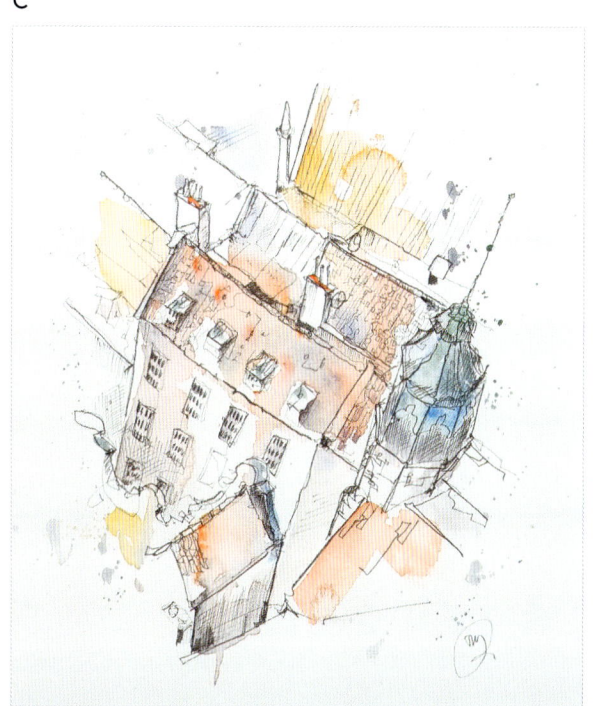

C

MUNDANE MADE INTERESTING

Transforming the mundane into something quirky and creative brings new life to often overlooked parts of city life, from pigeons and gritty alleys, to tangles of wires overhead. These urban details are full of potential for artistic inspiration. We just need to think a little more creatively about what's in front of us. We can use the observation skills we worked on in Urban Still Life in the First Projects chapter to consider what we might want to sketch.

The focus could be on a drainpipe and the gritty character of the scene (A). Layered watercolours allowed to literally drip down the page create a playful suggestion of grime and urban texture.

The bricks are brought to life with varied ink marks, adding depth and interest to the background. A subtle pink tinge enhances their texture, injecting an unexpected warmth into the scene. This unusual colour choice adds to the theme of making mundane more interesting. An abstract colour can turn an overlooked detail into something visually engaging. Meanwhile, the pigeon – a mere bystander – adds a touch of life and movement to the composition.

A

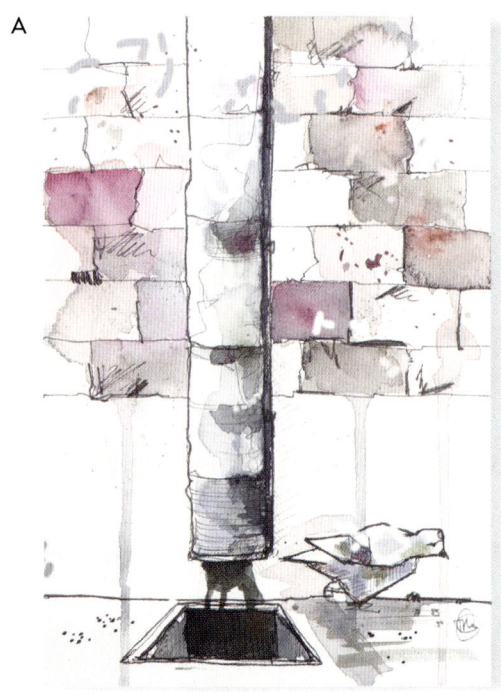

B

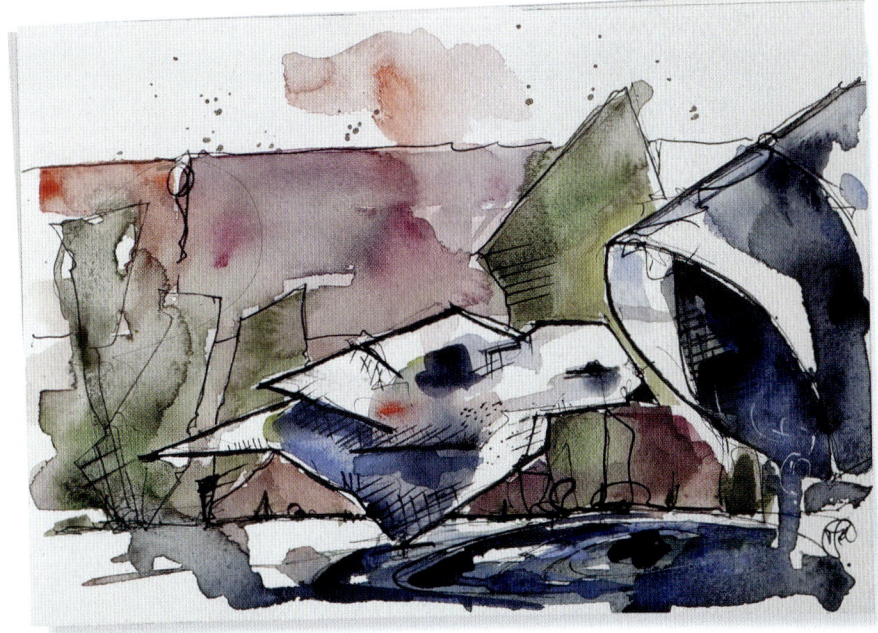

The exact background, foreground, subject, or animal may change, but the concept of transforming the mundane into something exciting remains constant. The pigeon now takes centre stage (B), boldly contrasted against the scene as it leans inquisitively over a drainpipe, perhaps investigating what lies within.

Now looking upwards, we can capture the tangled chaos of overhead wires and utility poles (C). These everyday structures form intricate patterns against the sky. Amongst the sometimes random-feeling wires, there is also a surprising amount of structure to be found. Bold ink links can follow this structure and anchor the art, while more fluid colours and watercolour splashes represent the chaos. A few birds sitting on the topmost wires add a little life.

C

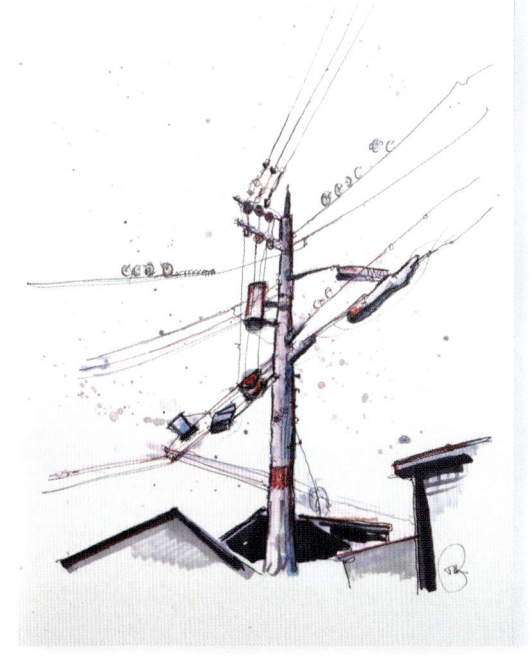

ICONIC VIEWS REIMAGINED

Not every scene needs to be rendered in full detail to make an impact. In fact, those idealized and overdone images often seen on postcards or souvenirs can feel intimidating. As artists, we have the freedom to reimagine these views with abstraction and simplicity. By reducing a scene to its essential shapes, we can be playful with colours, tones, and textures, creating something both unique and recognizable. This approach provides an exciting way to reinterpret iconic views with your own creative flair.

The Eiffel Tower, with its intricate web of ironwork, is both incredibly complex to draw and immediately recognizable (A). By using a sketcher's eye, we can break it down into simplified shapes. Here, I've taken a visual shortcut by repeating a basic square with an 'X' inside to suggest the intricate iron lattice-work and it gives a pleasing result.

To complement the sketch, I've added a light watercolour wash. First, a loose splash of lavender and ultramarine blue sets a subtle background. Then, I applied a more deliberate wash of hansa yellow medium and green apatite genuine, carefully bringing it right to the edges of the tower. Finally, the pyrrol scarlet within the tower itself serves as a nod to its iron construction, adding warmth and a touch of character.

A

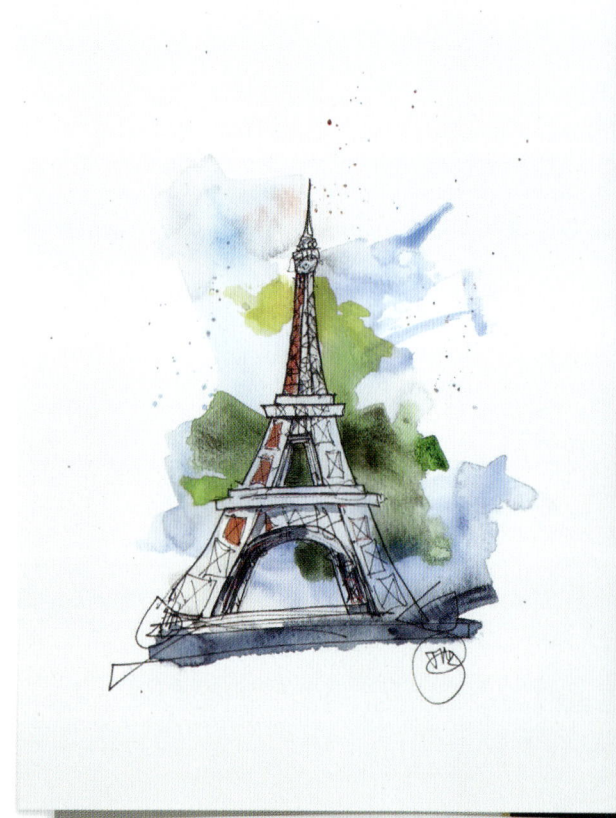

B

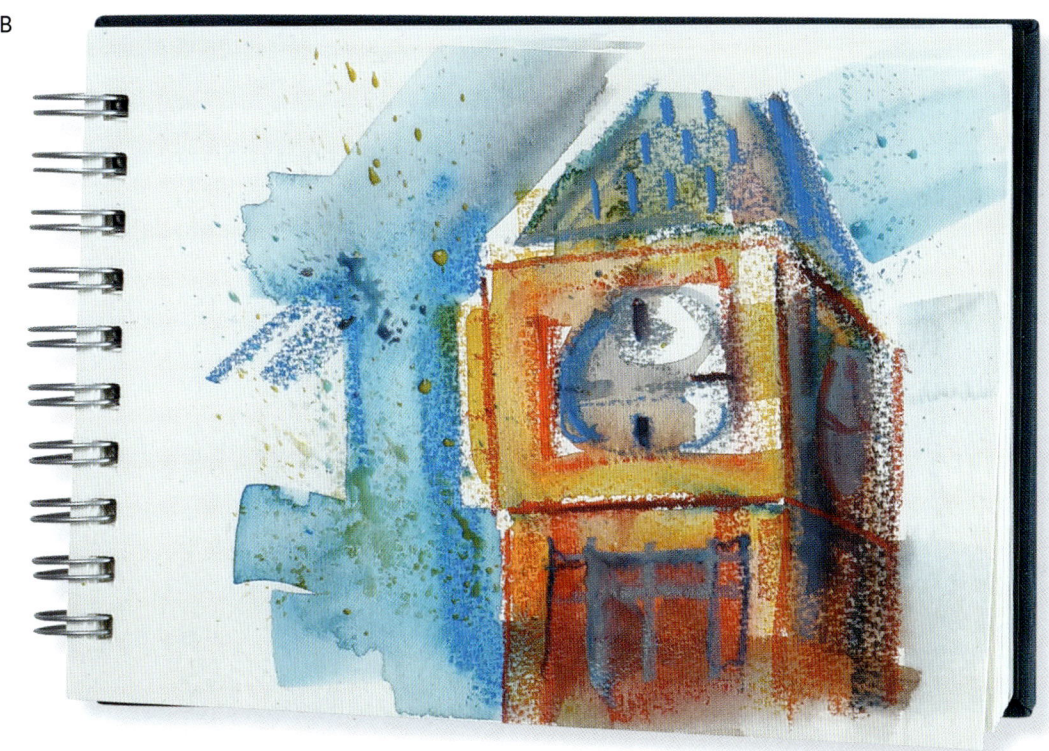

Sketches needn't seek to capture the entirety of a subject. Inspiration can be found by picking out a key element of a scene. Big Ben (B) sits surrounded by Westminster, but is recognisable for its clock face alone.

In this sketch, I opted to use water-soluble crayons to create the initial shapes instead of ink and watercolours. The bold blue background, indicative of sky, helps to understand the scene. Loosening them up with a wash of colour allows the water-soluble colours to mix and create the essence of shadows on the right side of the clock face. I added very minimal texture and a suggestion of detail to complete my simple scene.

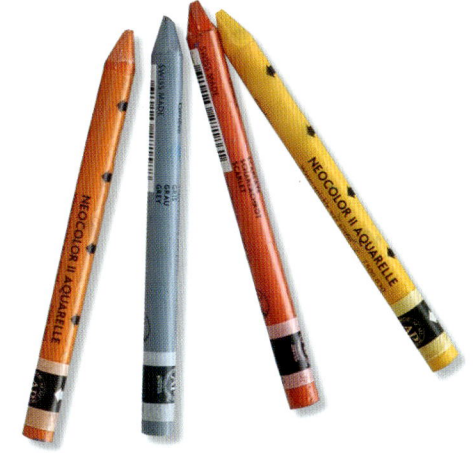

RAINY WEATHER

Rainy weather evokes a strong mood in a scene, but can also be quite a challenge to sketch. The rain itself will blur and obscure outlines, the clouds will be darker and more dramatic, and the water on the streets gives an ethereal glow. Capturing these elements requires a balance of loose, fluid washes and more controlled mark-making.

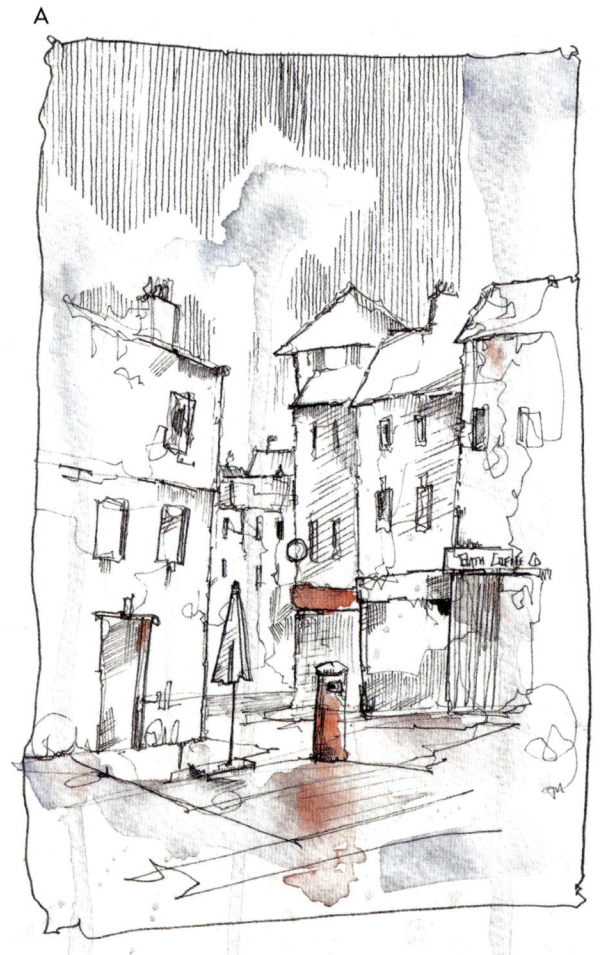

A

In the first scene (A), I used linear ink marks to suggest falling rain, creating movement and reinforcing the moody atmosphere. These fine lines break up the sky, toning it down and giving a sense of depth. To enhance this effect and experiment with simple hatching, I left purposeful gaps in the sky. Within these gaps, I added light and tonal watercolours, tilting the page to encourage drips that mirror the natural flow of the rain. This controlled movement helps unify the scene, making the rainfall feel more tangible.

In contrast, this second scene (B) takes a bolder, more illustrative approach. I used the wet-on-wet technique to blend blues, reds, and neutrals, letting the sky wash bleed into the foreground to unify the composition and emphasize the weight of the rain.

The glowing buildings, soft trees, and street reflections emerged through fluid washes, with water droplets creating organic cauliflower patterns that resemble puddles.

I added final rain effects with an acrylic marker. Vertical strokes and small dots mimicked raindrops, while hints of colour suggested reflections and city lights. This contrast between soft washes and crisp, opaque highlights demonstrates how different techniques can evoke a rainy atmosphere in distinct ways.

B

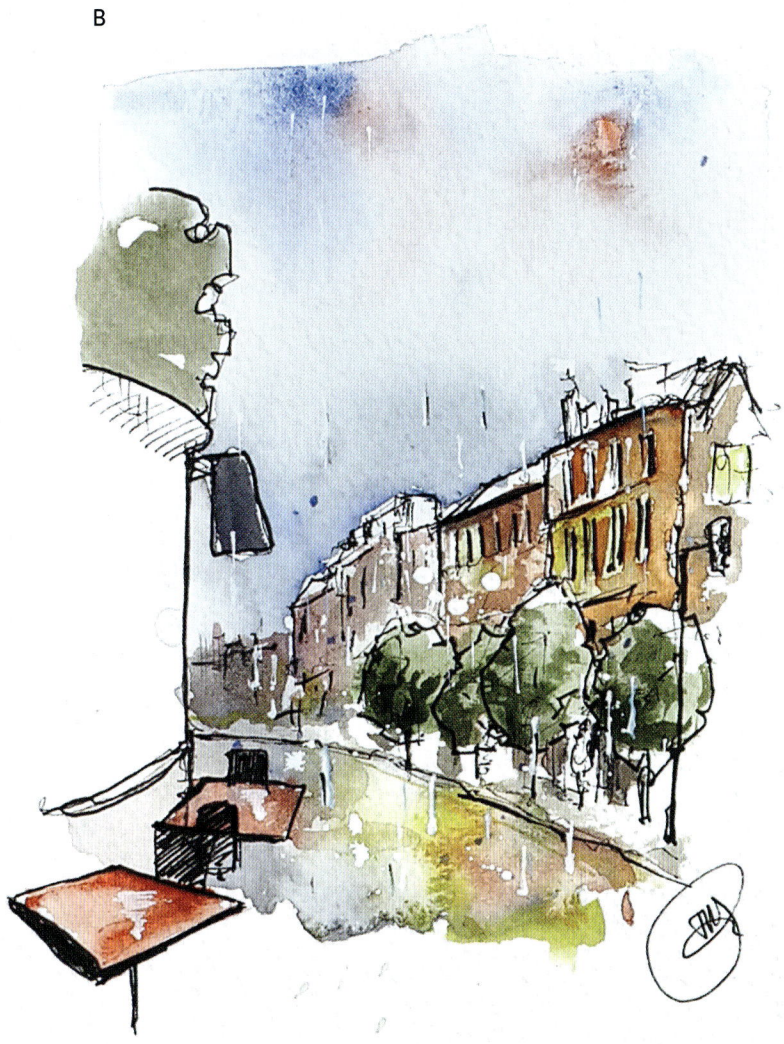

THE CITY GLOWS AT NIGHT

The light at night in the city offers a completely different atmosphere from the daytime. Bright, glowing lights from street lights and windows add warmth and drama, while the sky often features a mix of soft glows and deep, near-black shadows. Walls and surfaces vary greatly, from areas that are harshly lit to others that fade into near invisibility. Capturing these contrasts can be challenging but also rewarding.

In the day time, the sky is lighter than the walls of buildings, with the deepest shadows at the base of structures. However, in a city at night, these values can fluctuate dramatically, and often the sky becomes the dominant presence. In this scene (A), inspired by a kebab shop in Bath, UK, I used indigo to create a deep, rich sky, while layering watercolours below the buildings to form soft shadows. A wet-on-wet approach allowed the lights to glow naturally, capturing the warmth of the window and street lights. Notice how I've left areas of white paper, focusing on key contrasts of shadow and light to keep the sketch dynamic and simplified. Subtle touches of opaque mixed media – fine white and yellow acrylic lines – enhance the glowing effect. While there is plenty more that could be developed in the scene, this approach remains freeing and effective for sketching a street at night.

A

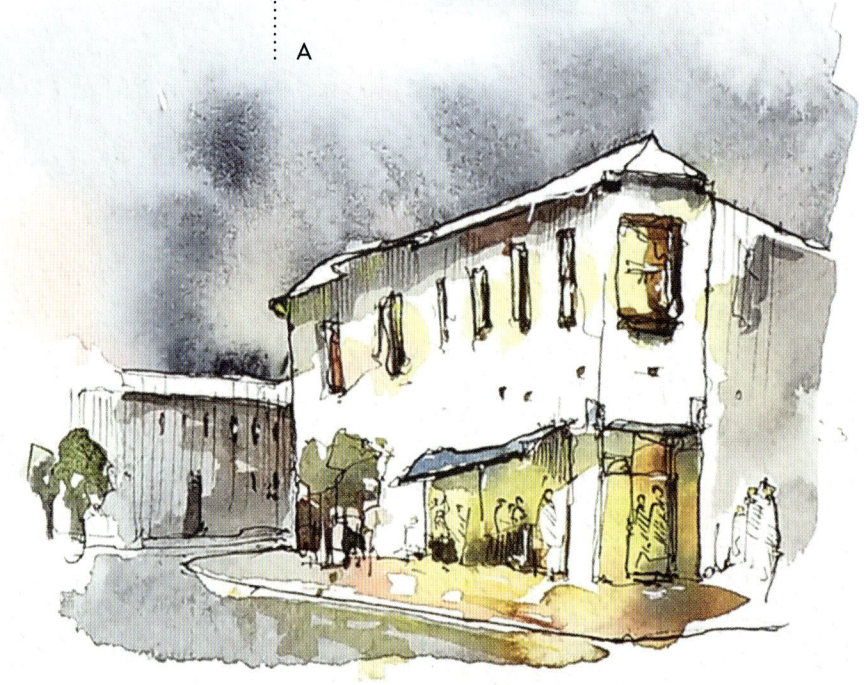

B

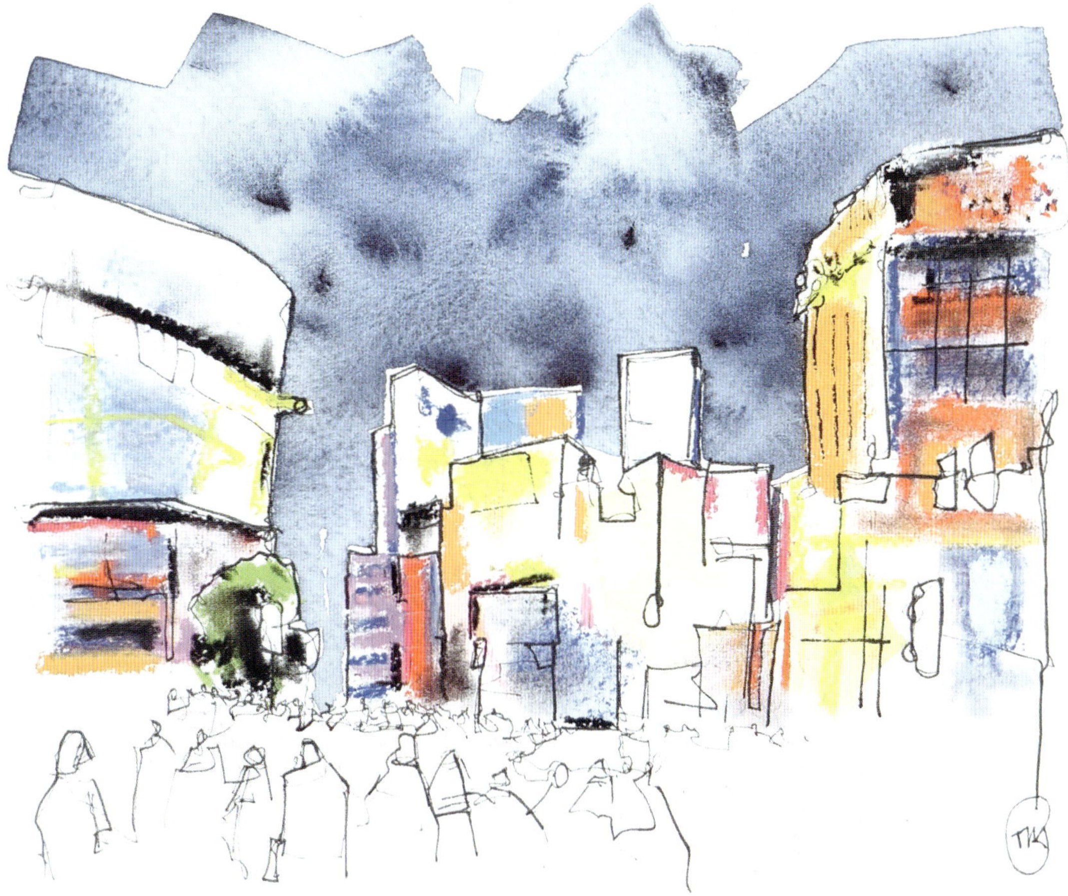

In contrast, the atmosphere of the Shibuya Scramble in Tokyo (B) felt much harsher and more vivid, with intense contrasts between light and dark. To reflect this, I used a different approach. Watercolours were applied boldly to the sky, but sparingly below with just a soft initial wash on a couple of the buildings. For the harsh glow of countless street signs and advertisements, opaque media was used more extensively to create a bold, punchy effect. Soft pastels were layered and lightly blended to bring vibrancy and contrast to the scene, mirroring the frenetic energy of the place. It's tempting to get stuck into the specifics of the crowds, but leaving the people as simple shapes left a negative space that I felt provided a contrast to the busyness above.

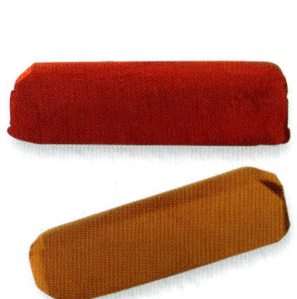

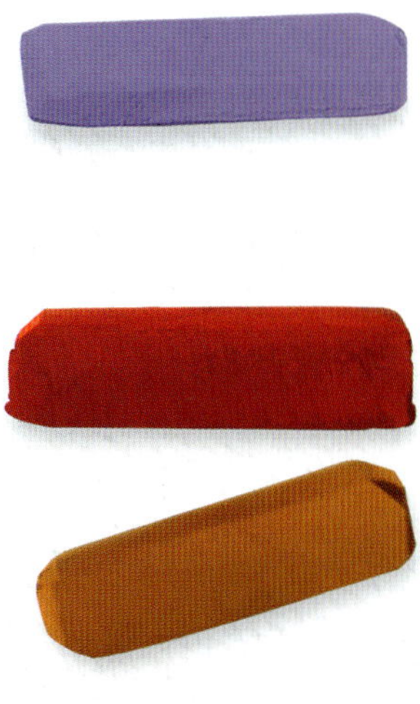

IMAGINARY CITYSCAPES

Sketching offers a wonderfully freeing way to immerse yourself in the creative process. With a slight mindset shift, we can turn our observational skills towards drawing from our imagination. Instead of fixating on a specific outcome, you can simply take your line for a wander, allowing textures, hints of detail, and playful shapes to emerge naturally on the page. Or you can build up shapes in intriguing ways before interpreting them – transforming simple forms into dramatic structures.

In the first scene (A), I started by letting my line wander freely, creating an interesting silhouette. This silhouette naturally felt like an industrial city, so I began filling in windows and buildings with blocks of ink. I like to tell myself a story as I build these pages – this one became a city under construction, with angular lines forming scaffolding, a crane cobbled together on the right, and even hints of underground plumbing beneath the road (perhaps). Repetition is key – repeating lines, shapes, and patterns ensures that the wandering process feels cohesive, while contrast through hatching and dark ink brings depth to the scene.

A

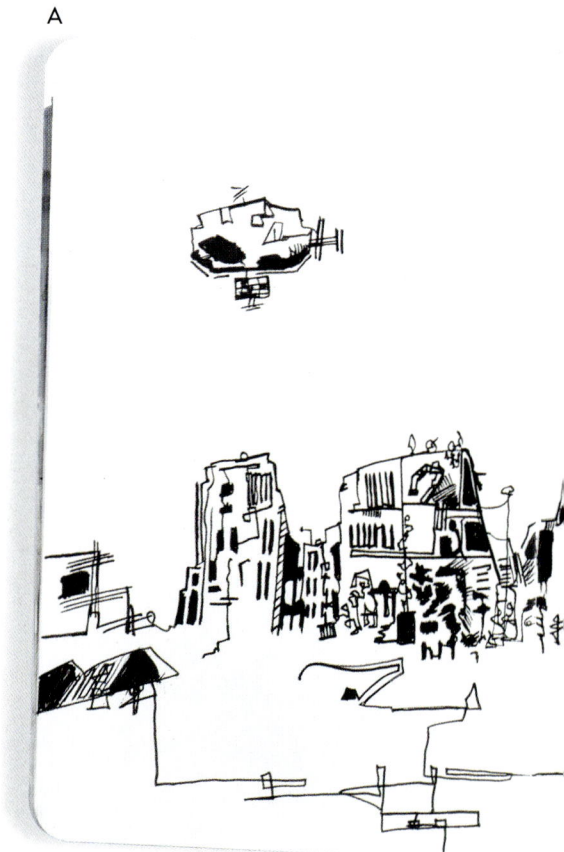

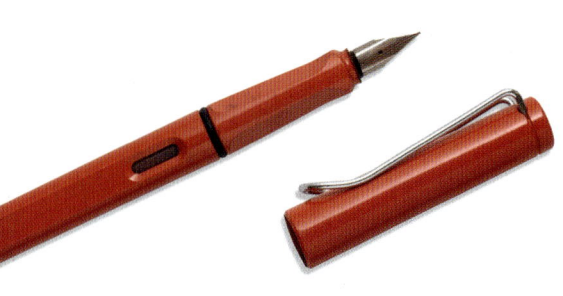

In the second scene (B), I took a different approach. Instead of letting my line wander first, I began with large, bold shapes – rectangles and a semi-circle stacked on either side. I used two ink colours, the first of which was a deep, rusty purple for the initial lines and textures, giving a layered richness to the composition. I allowed abstract elements to play a role – irregular hatching in the sky, both looped and straight lines, and patterns that hint at forms without strictly defining them. As the drawing evolved, semi-representational ideas emerged – statues lining the brim of the dome, traffic lights and road signs forming on the right. Finally, with the scene taking shape, I introduced black ink to solidify the composition, adding clarity and contrast to anchor the imaginative elements.

By allowing the process to remain open and exploratory, each cityscape develops its own character, formed by instinct, pattern, and the push and pull between structure and spontaneity. There is also a lot to interpret. I hand these sketchbook pages around to friends and family, and they each have a different take on what might be happening in the scene.

B

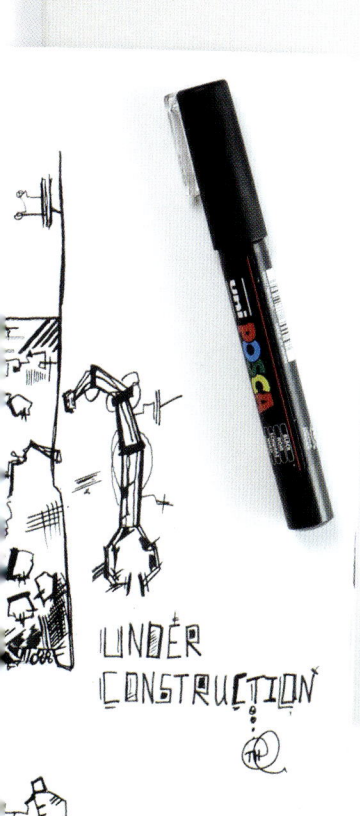

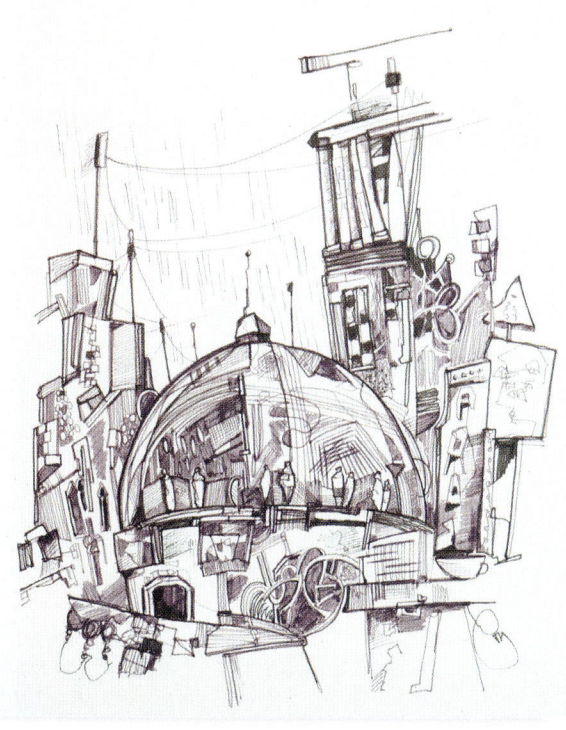

CONTROLLED CHAOS – ONE-LINE SKETCHING

One-line, or continuous line, sketching is one of my favourite ways to sketch. We have already explored the technique a little in the First Projects chapter, but it's worth revisiting to show its versatility. It forces you to observe, but also to simplify. It forces you to make decisions, deal with inevitable mistakes and inaccuracies, and learn to find joy in them. Whether capturing a simple still life, a quirky street, or an iconic landmark, the approach remains the same – let the line guide you and enjoy the process.

In this first sketch (A), I used just a single fineliner and a wandering line to pick up the key shapes and details of my trainers. When approaching a scene with a continuous line, we needn't confine ourselves to 'only using one line'. Instead, I strive to base the sketch on continuous lines. This allows me to pick my pen up, restate key lines, take breaks, and add extra textures and hatching without feeling like I've failed. The result is something fun, semi-abstract but also recognisable.

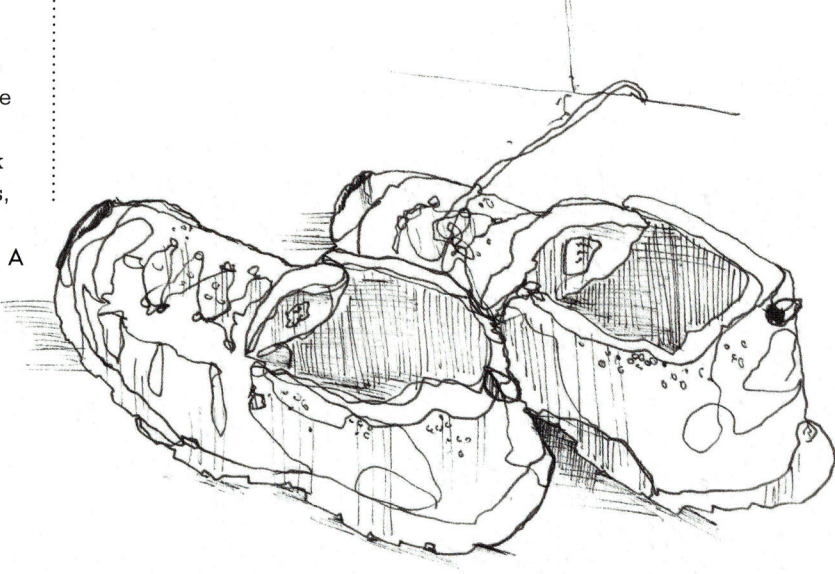

A

This sketch of a local butcher's and high street (B) demonstrates the same technique. I completed this sketch in around five minutes while out on a wintery walk. I didn't feel like standing for too long – a continuous line sketch gives me something fun on the page, and fast. Broad, sweeping lines outline the key structures, before I continued my line, finding small shapes to capture loose details.

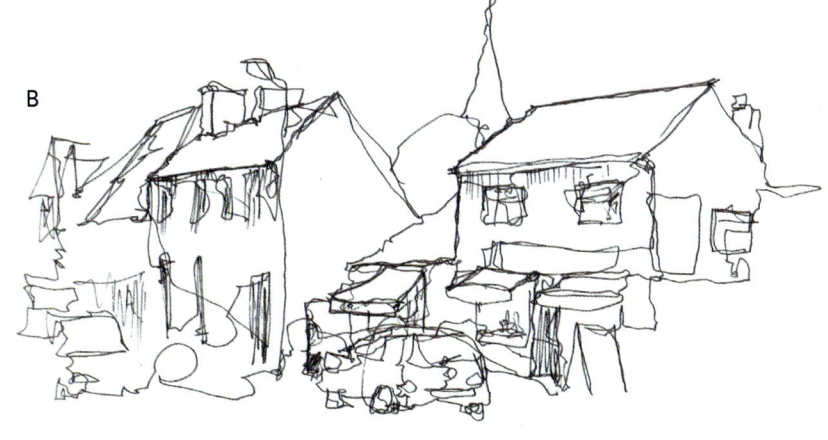

B

The third sketch is something more complex (C). As with One-Line Skyline (in the First Projects chapter), I started by inking the silhouette before resolving more details through the scene. I then restated a few key lines but was also playful with wet-on-wet colours, building up depth and texture. Taking this loose approach is actually rather confidence boosting and freeing when faced with complexity – after all, how can it be 'accurate' if you've completed it all in one line?

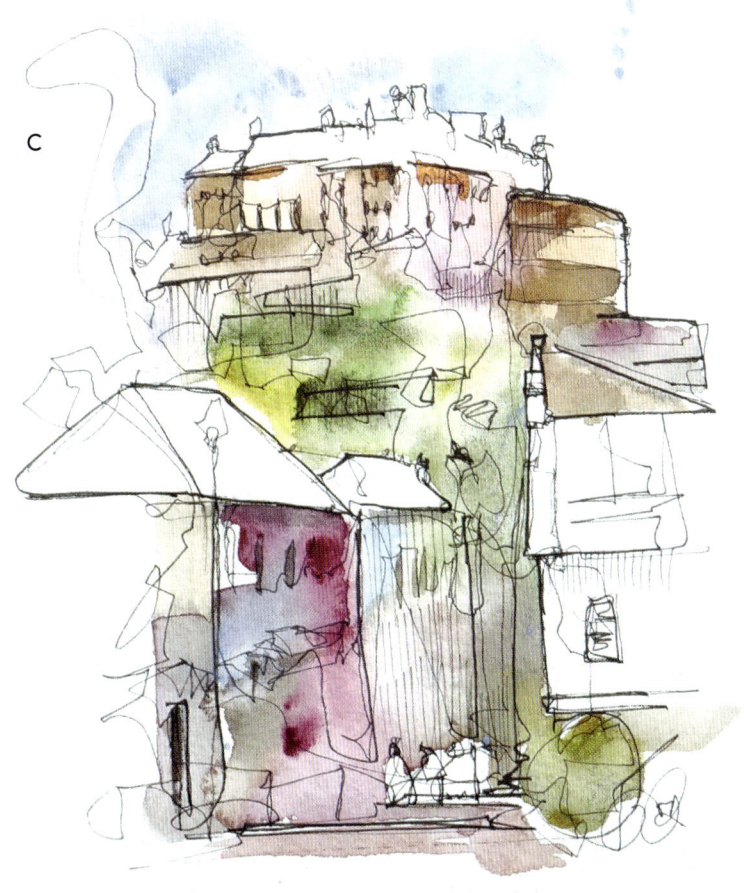

C

URBAN EATS

Food is an endlessly inspiring subject for sketching, with vibrant colours, varied textures, and intricate details. Food also offers a unique way to connect with your surroundings, capturing the culture and atmosphere of a place. Keeping a visual diary allows you to preserve memories and sharpen your observational skills, all while celebrating the simple joys of everyday life.

Sketching food can feel overwhelming due to the amount of detail in our close-up view. But simplifying the process, as with this bowl of ramen (A), makes it more achievable while also allowing us to find ways to represent those details. In this scene, I started with very light lines to map out the largest shapes, like the curves of the bowl and the position of my hand. Then I was able to consider what details were most important – the angle of the chopsticks, and the most intriguing and colourful details, like the eggs and toppings. Layered colours, as in our normal processes, gradually built up rich colours, before bold pen lines and simple hatching brought clarity and contrast.

A

B

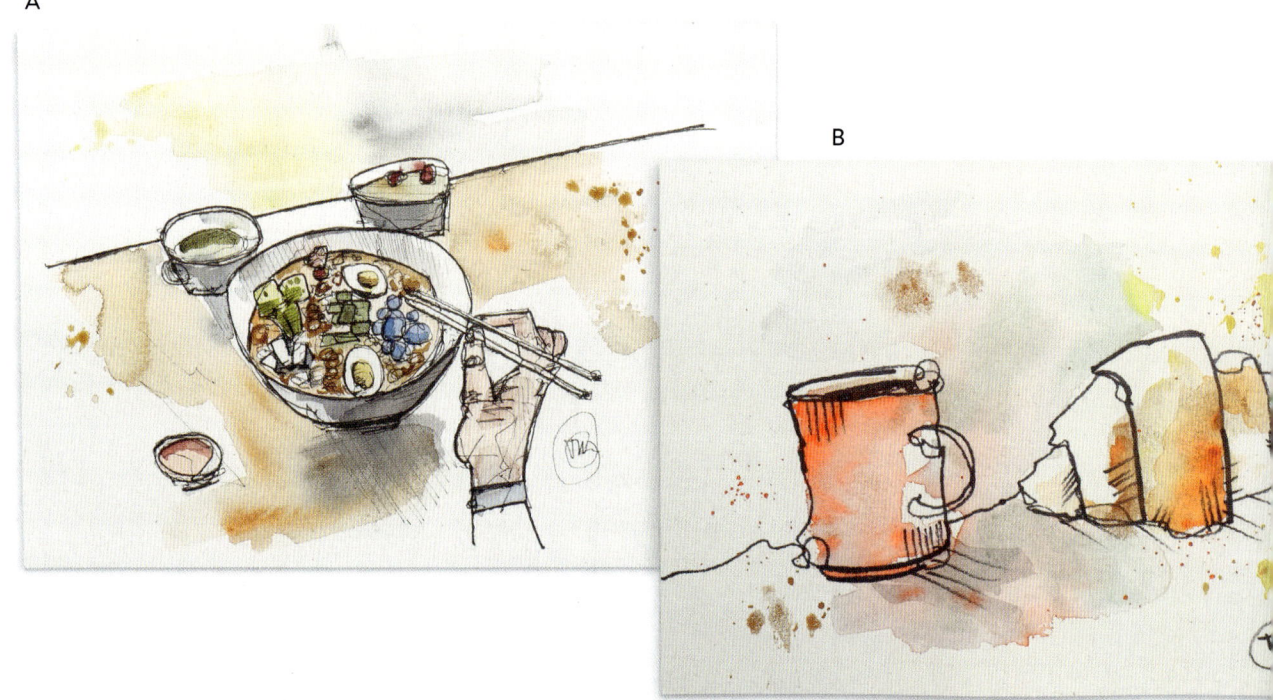

With these ideas of simplicity in mind, one of my favourite pastimes is heading into town with my pen and watercolours, enjoying a coffee and croissant, and sketching (B). Often, the coffee and croissant themselves become my subjects. Using a permanent marker and plenty of water, I transform these simple moments into enjoyable, creative sketches that capture the charm of a quiet café moment.

On a relaxing afternoon or weekend, a trip to the park or countryside offers the perfect setting for eating al fresco (C). Popping my fizzy drink on our camping table, I used quick, painterly strokes made with marker pens to bring the scene to life. This loose and dynamic approach captures the essence of a leisurely day outdoors, focusing on mood and simplicity.

When I'm stuck for inspiration but feel the urge to create, raiding the kitchen cupboards is my go-to activity (D). Everyday objects of varying sizes, textures, and shapes become fascinating subjects. Arranging them haphazardly allows for playful exploration of their relationships, resulting in dynamic and intriguing sketches.

D

C

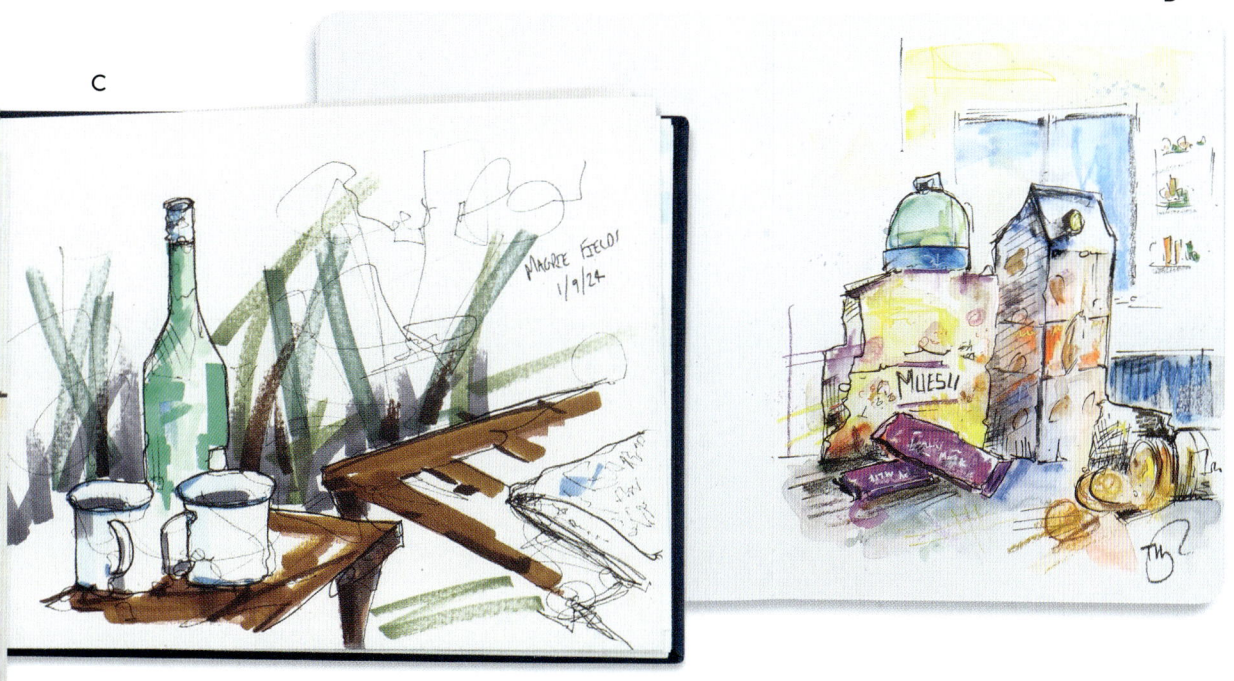

SKETCHING THE SEASONS

The change of season brings about some of the biggest changes in our cities – to the intensity of light and shadow, the colours, and even silhouettes. The feel of a place will change too. Exploring the same scene through different seasons, either visiting it throughout the year or imagining how it might change, is a great source of inspiration as there's always something different to look at.

To capture the same urban scene across the four seasons, I like to see all the sketches side by side. I started by creating a simple, clear sketch of the scene, focusing on shapes that are easy to replicate. Once the initial sketch was complete, it can be repeated for each season.

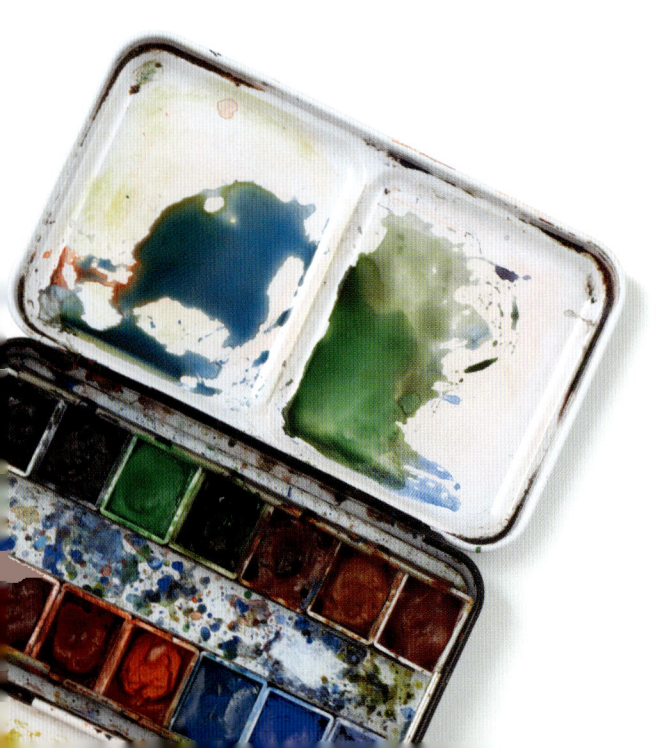

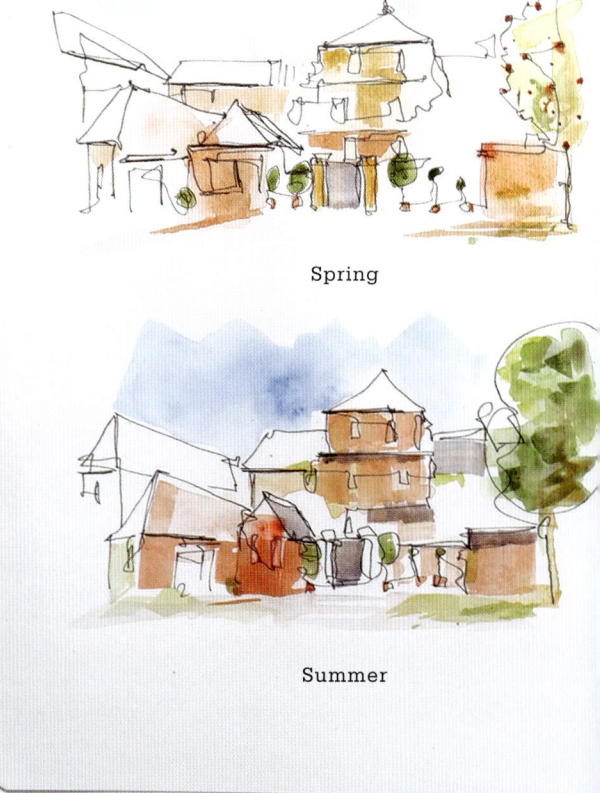

Spring

Summer

The aim of this technique is to keep the sketches consistent, but there will always be unintentional differences alongside intentional ones, such as bare trees in winter or fuller foliage in spring. These subtle changes help bring the sketches to life.

Think about the seasonal differences in colour and light. In spring and summer, the skies are vibrant shades of blue, while autumn (fall) often has a golden warmth, and winter feels more subdued and neutral. Trees are an obvious point of variation, but the quality and intensity of light at different times of the year can also inspire different interpretations of the buildings. Layering the colour, starting with a light wash, will help reflect these ideas.

For spring and summer, focus on warmer tones, with reds and oranges appearing stronger due to the intensity of sunlight, and they can help suggest blossom in the trees and plants growing. The later seasons, on the other hand, call for cooler, muted tones. Shadows become less defined, and touches of blue can suggest frost or snow in winter.

Once the colour layers are complete, I went back and restated bold lines and details, like contrasting windows, to tie all the sketches together. Finally, I added a few splatters to emphasize the differences in each scene – orange splatters to suggest falling leaves, or vibrant blue splashes in the summer sky to evoke its richness.

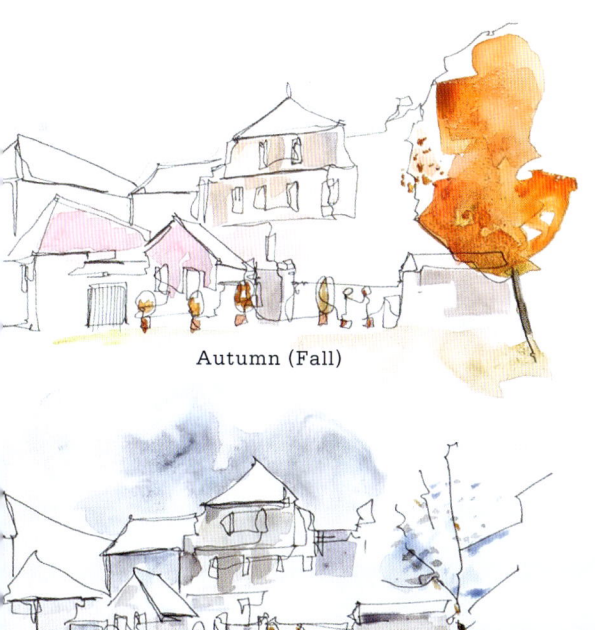

Autumn (Fall)

Winter

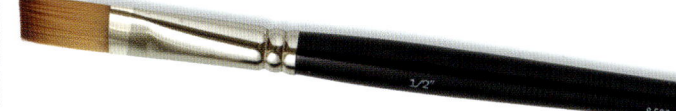

MIXING MEDIA

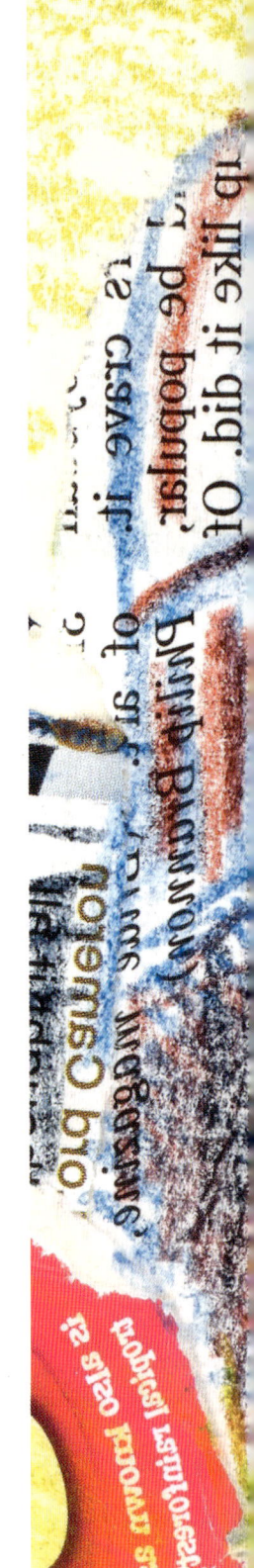

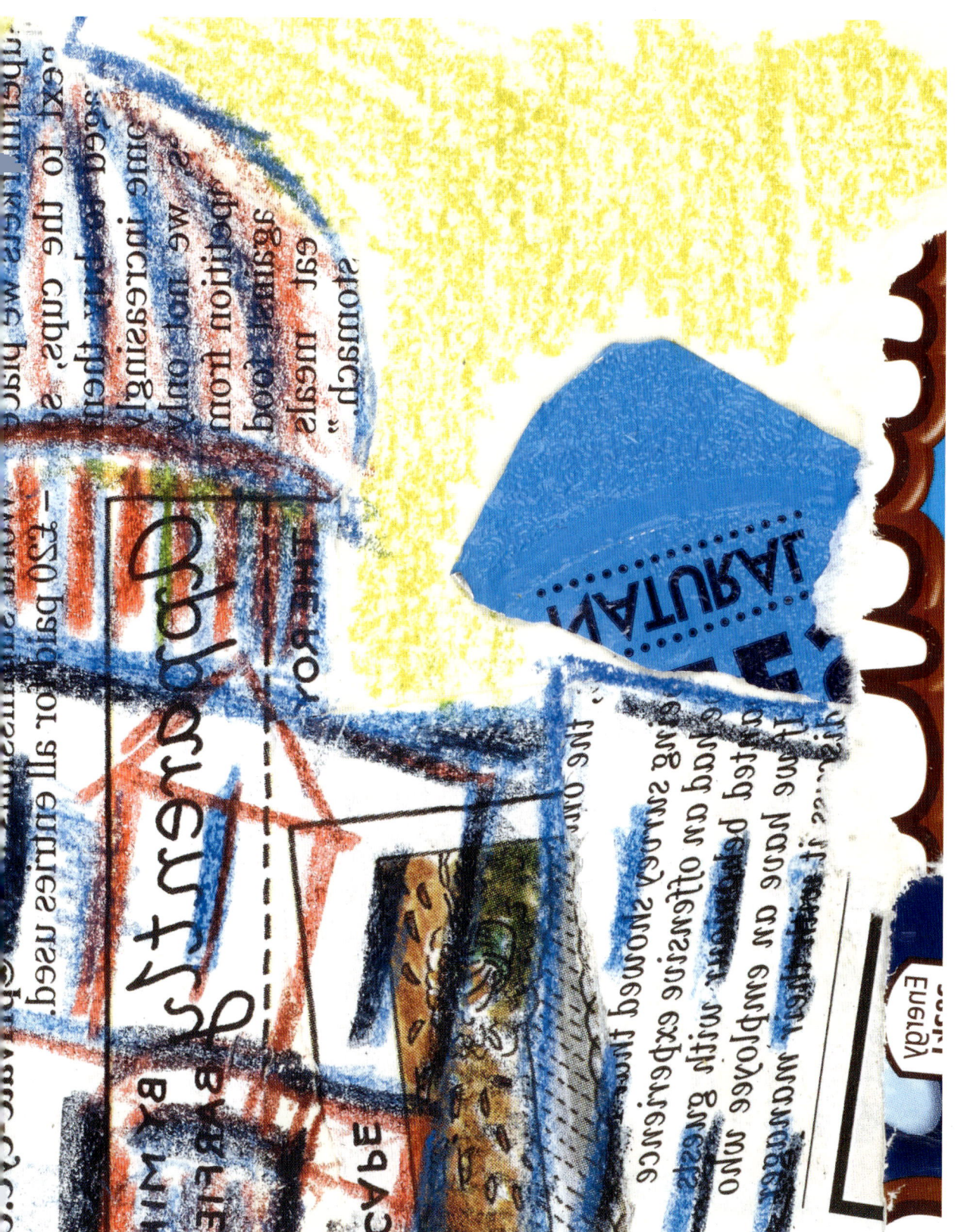

SUPPLIES

Mixed media sketchbook
or cold pressed
watercolour paper
....
Pencil
....
Scraps of newspaper and
sweet (candy) wrappers
....
Bold-coloured
watercolour pencils
....
Scissors
....
Glue stick
....

COLLAGING LITTER

Litter is an unfortunate fact of city life,
but does grant abstract creative possibilities.
Creating a full scene from collage alone
is, of course, a possibility – but combining
collage and sketching creates a quick, dynamic,
and intriguingly scene in our sketchbooks.

1 You may wish to create
a simple pencil sketch
of your scene as an outline
to work to for this first
step. Tear the newspaper
into pieces. Lay them in
an approximate plan of
the scene to map out the
largest shapes. Colourful
scraps can then be added
on top, ripped or cut to
suggest other objects.

2 When you feel your scene
is ready to stick down,
apply glue on the materials,
not the paper, to avoid
damaging the sketching
surface for the next steps.

3 Using bold-coloured
watercolour pencils, map
out structural lines, and a
few details such as windows
and shadows as well.

4 Block out the sky and the
foreground with some
lightly textured shading and
suddenly your creation will
pop to the front of your page.

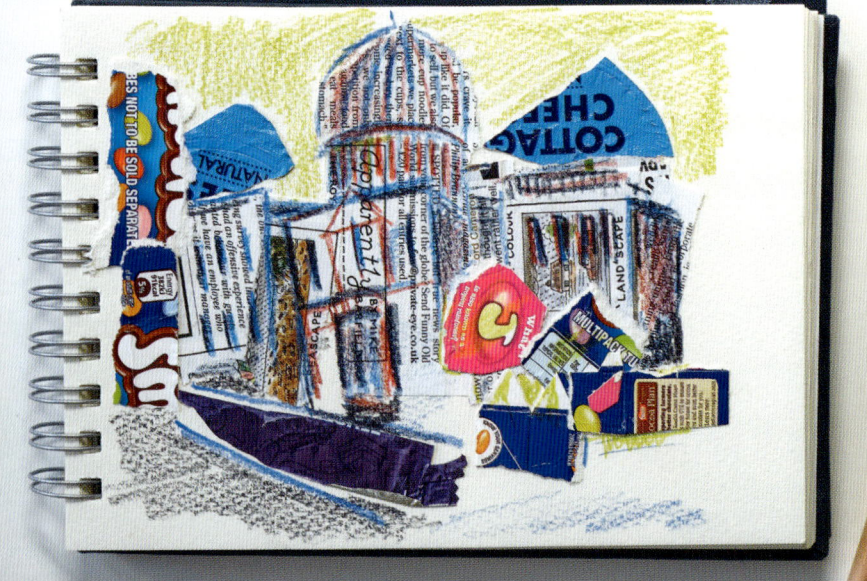

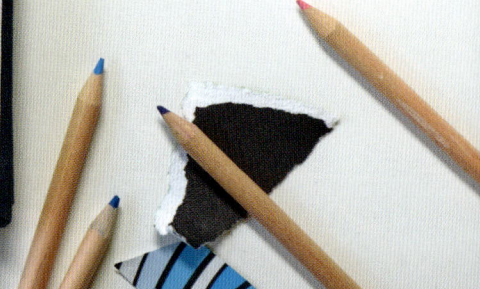

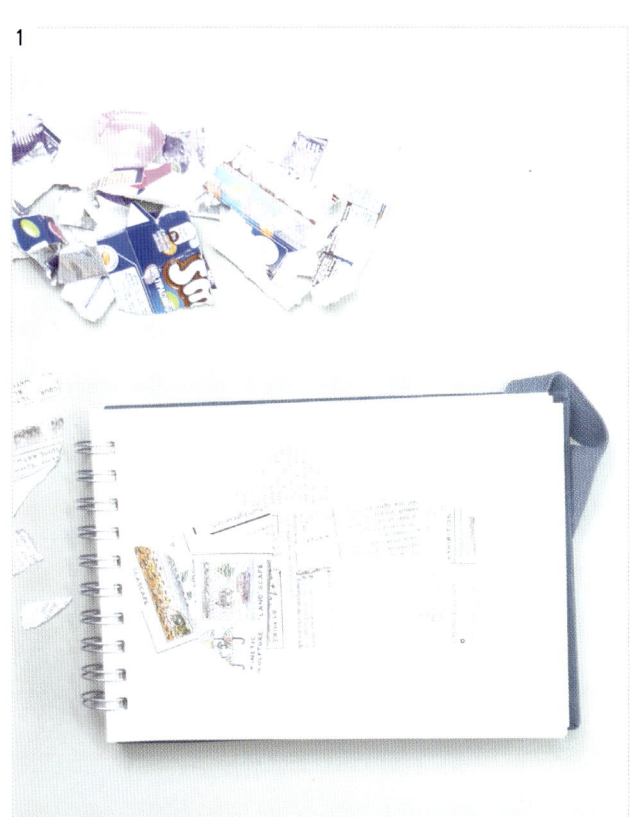

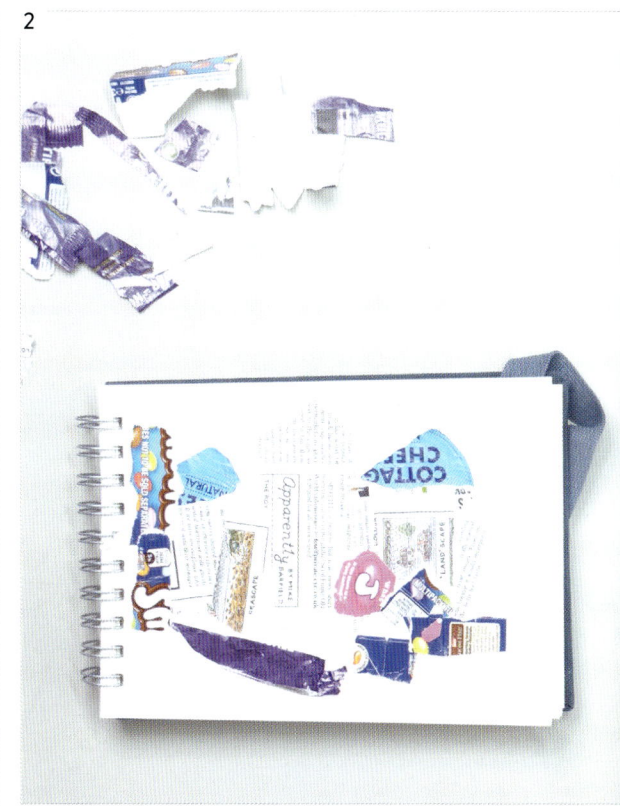

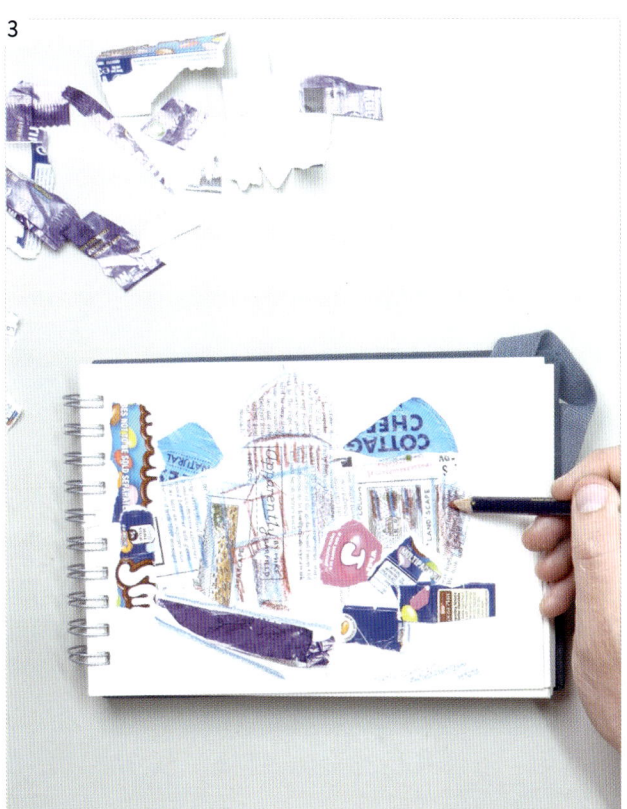

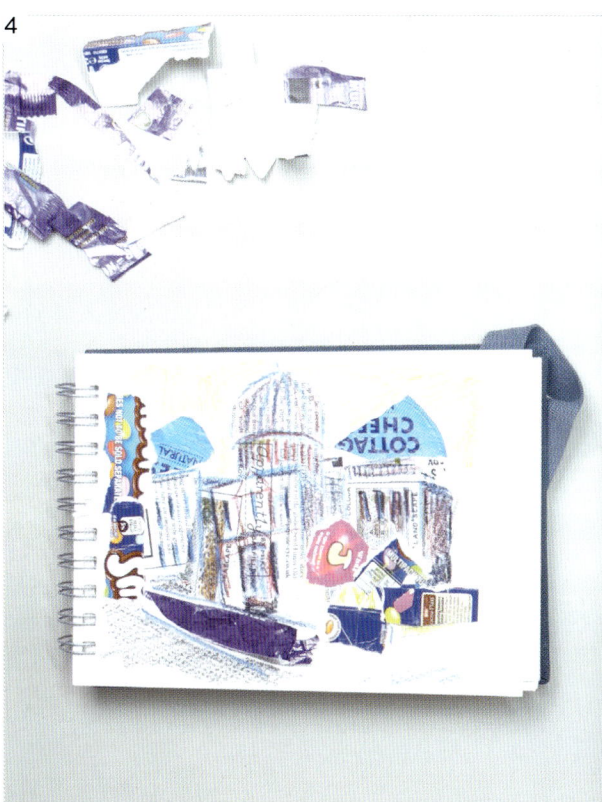

SUPPLIES

Cold pressed
watercolour paper
23 x 30.5cm (9 x 12in)
....
Round synthetic
brush (size 6)
....
Fineliners
....
Coffee of any kind, such
as espresso, or rich
instant coffee to create
the darkest tones
....
Spoon
....

COFFEE ART

Coffee is a fantastic pigment to use for
painting with. The soft warm tones of a
wash of coffee can enliven simple line work,
and it can be layered to create depth and
contrast to produce a range of values.

1 First make up a strong,
cup of black coffee and
allow it to go cold. Create
a simple sketch and then
tip some coffee directly
onto the image. Be brave!

2 Next, use a spoon to
move the splashed
coffee around the sketch to
create a random pattern.
Use a slightly damp brush to
manipulate the coffee further
until it meets the edges of
your sketch, but also spills
out beyond it in places.

3 When the sketch is dry,
use a fineliner to add more
ink detail, such as textures,
on top. You might also outline
the splashes and splatters
to bring them into the art.

4 Waterproof ink, it turns
out, is not waterproof if
you draw on top of coffee.
Apply a further layer of coffee
with a brush to soften that
ink and blend them together
to create fascinating tones
and shadows. Celebrate the
final sketch by 'stamping'
some coffee on your paper
using the base of the coffee
cup to finish off the piece.

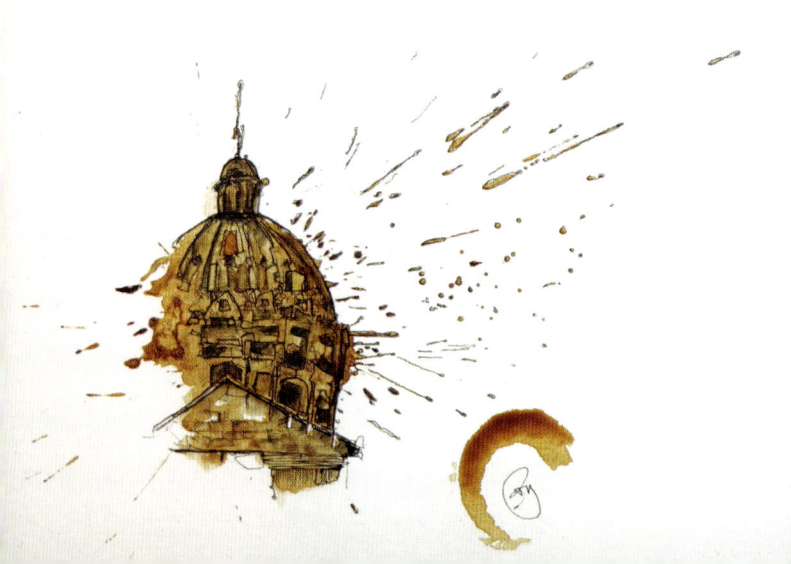

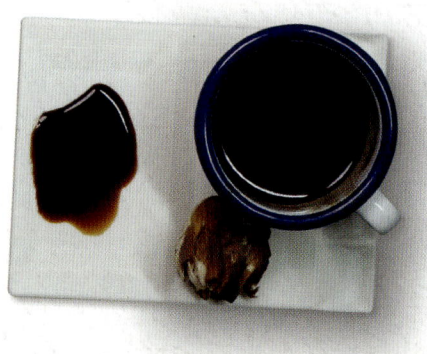

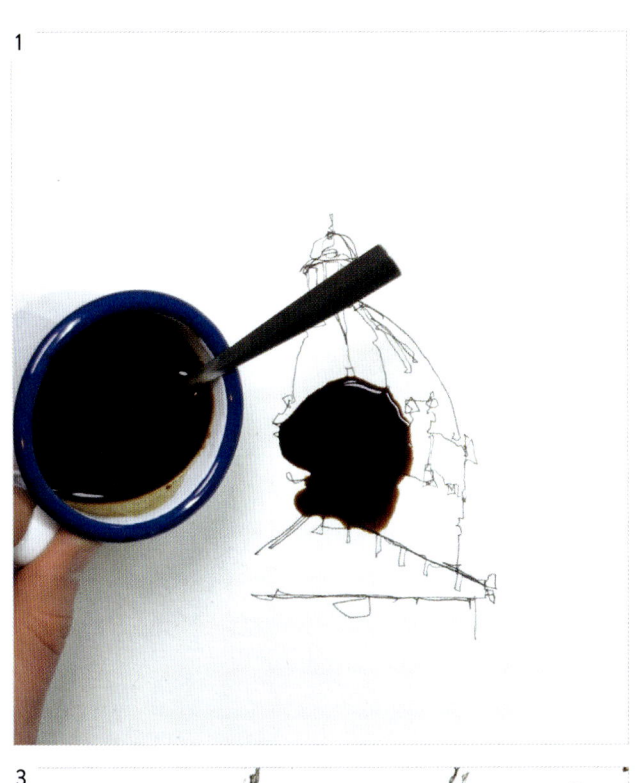

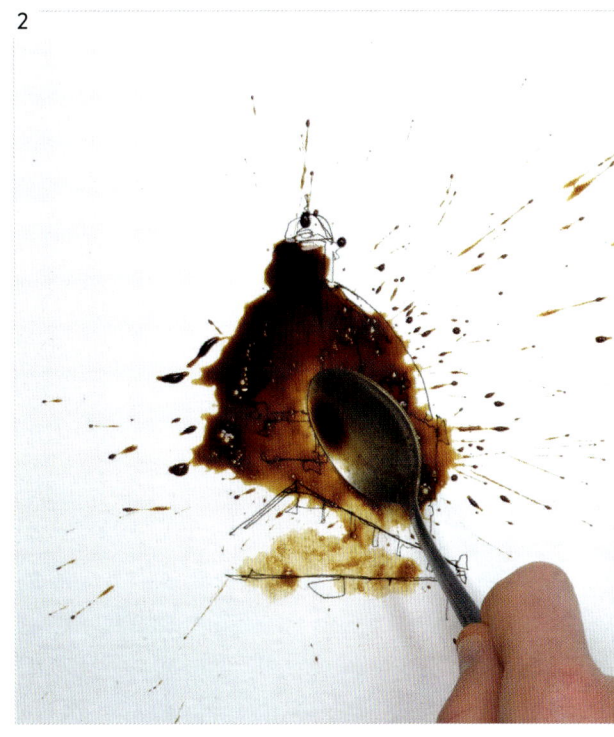

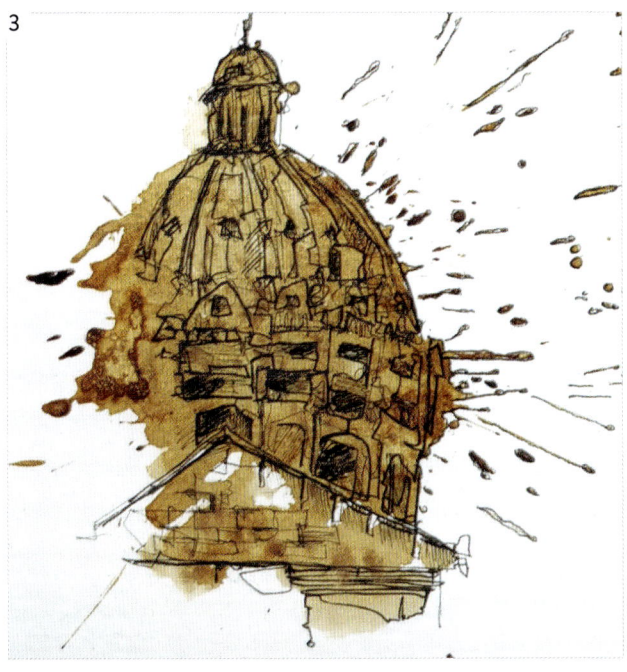

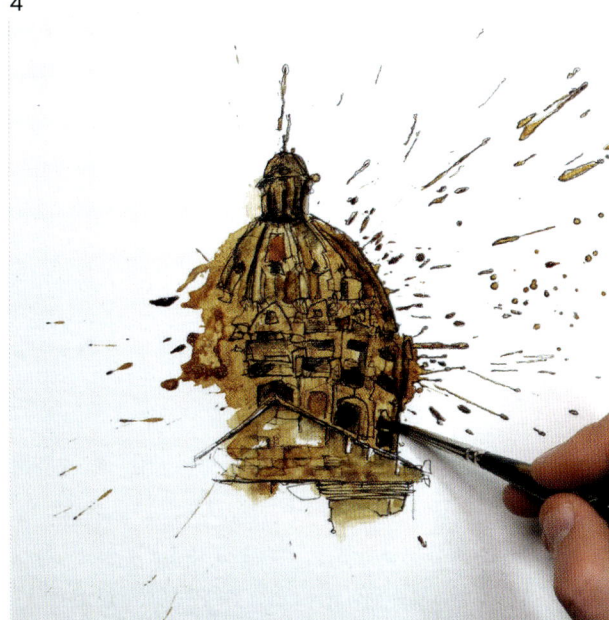

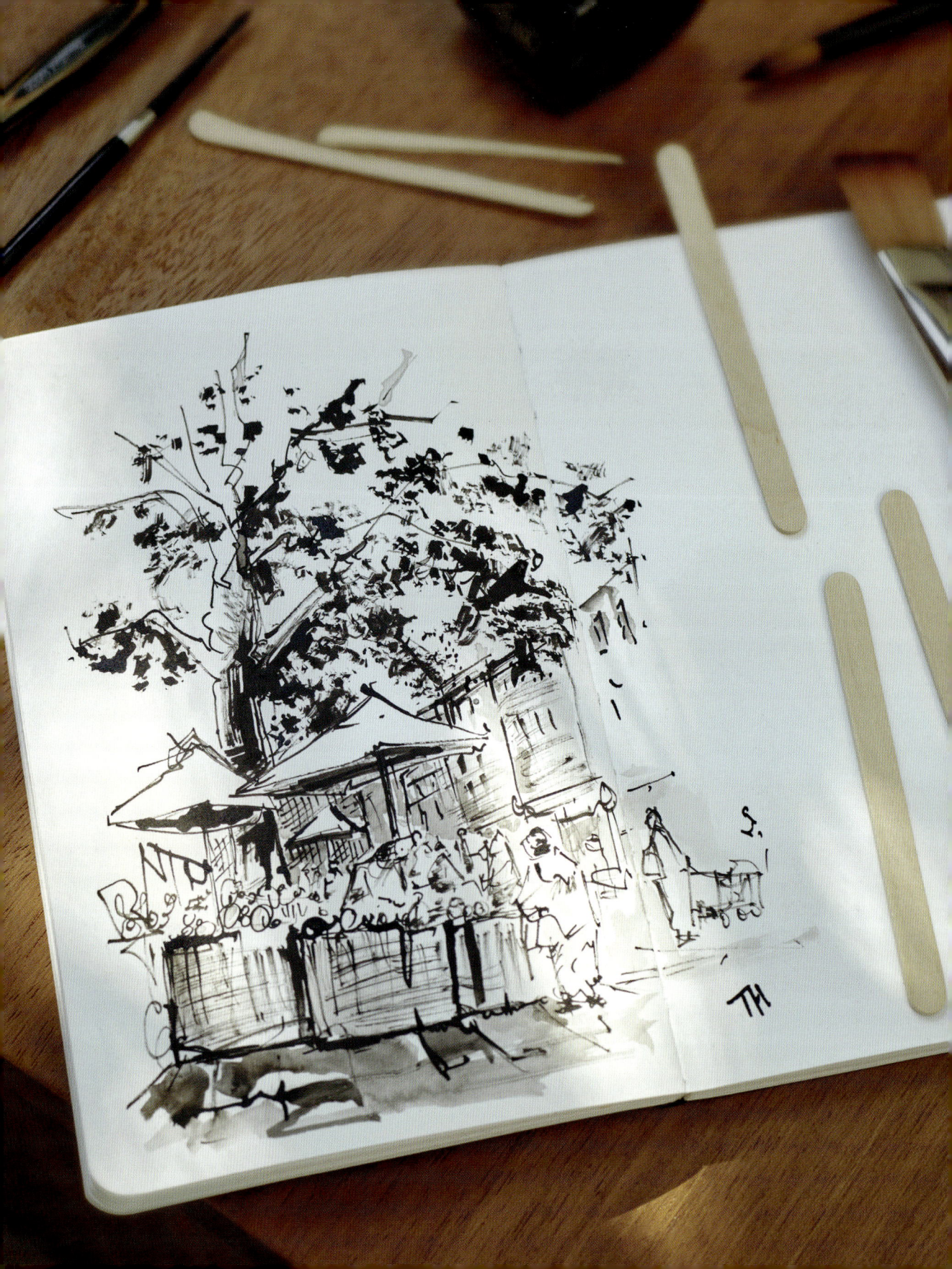

STICK AND INK

Exploring sketching with snapped or whittled lolly sticks offers a fresh and liberating approach to traditional Indian ink techniques. This method produces richly textured, contrast-filled sketches with a distinctive, impressionistic feel. Incorporating a waterbrush further enhances the range of textures and tones, adding depth and mood to your work.

SUPPLIES

Mixed media sketchbook
13 x 20cm (5 x 8in)
....
Lolly sticks
....
Black Indian ink
....
Medium waterbrush
....

1 Carefully snap and break lolly sticks (both across and vertically) into random shapes. This will give you a variety of 'nibs' to work with. Take time to experiment with the lines, marks, and textures you can create. Experiment with the waterbrush too. It's a lovely tool that can help wash the ink around while wet to create more mood and depth.

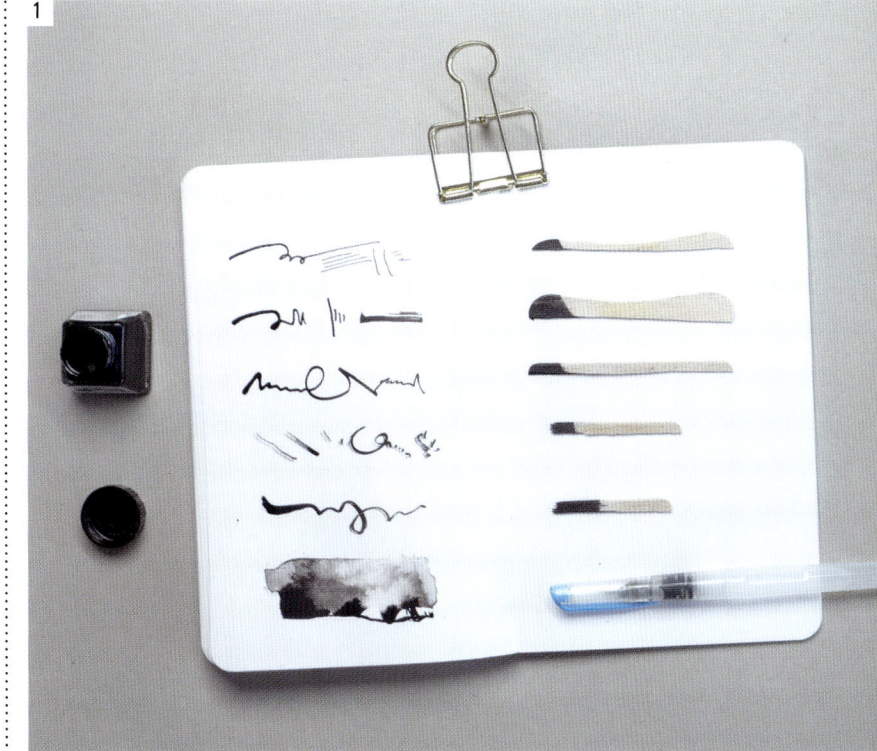

1

2 Next, use a stick that produces a clear, crisp mark to map out the main elements of your scene. As lolly sticks do not hold much ink, you will need to dip it frequently to maintain consistency in your lines. This natural pause between strokes can help keep your marks fresh and spontaneous.

3 Gradually build up the shapes using confident and gestural lines. Do not get stuck on fine details, as these will be hard to create with your homemade pens.

4 The roughness of the homemade nibs encourages a looser, more expressive style. For example, in my scene, a large tree was present and I found that one of my sticks produced a lovely 'double mark', which I used to suggest the texture of leaves.

5 Continue to build textures with hatching, scraping, and scuffing marks throughout the image. Enhancing the sketch with texture and abstraction can make your work even more dynamic. Draw inspiration from the marks this technique creates. Experiment with different angles, pressures, and overlaps to introduce unexpected textures.

6 Move onto using your sticks that create the broadest marks. This allows you to add crisp and impressive shadows. Use broader marks to introduce strong, dramatic contrasts but take care not to overdo it. Placing the boldest marks strategically in areas where you want to draw the viewer's eye helps maintain balance and focus within the composition.

7 To further refine the piece, manipulate wet ink using a waterbrush. Softening certain lines and blending areas establishes a mid-tone background, creating a greater range between deep blacks and the untouched white of the page. This interplay between sharp lines and washes adds richness and depth.

8 Once the ink is fully dry, it becomes waterproof, preserving the textures and marks. As a finishing touch, use a finer stick to sign or initial your expressive and character-filled sketch.

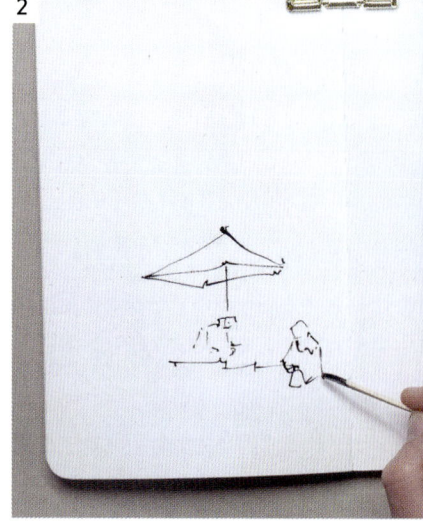

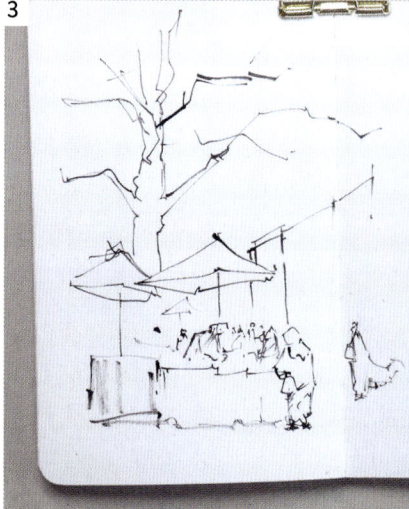

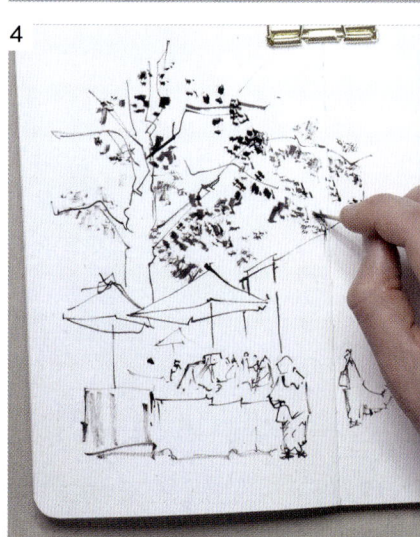

5

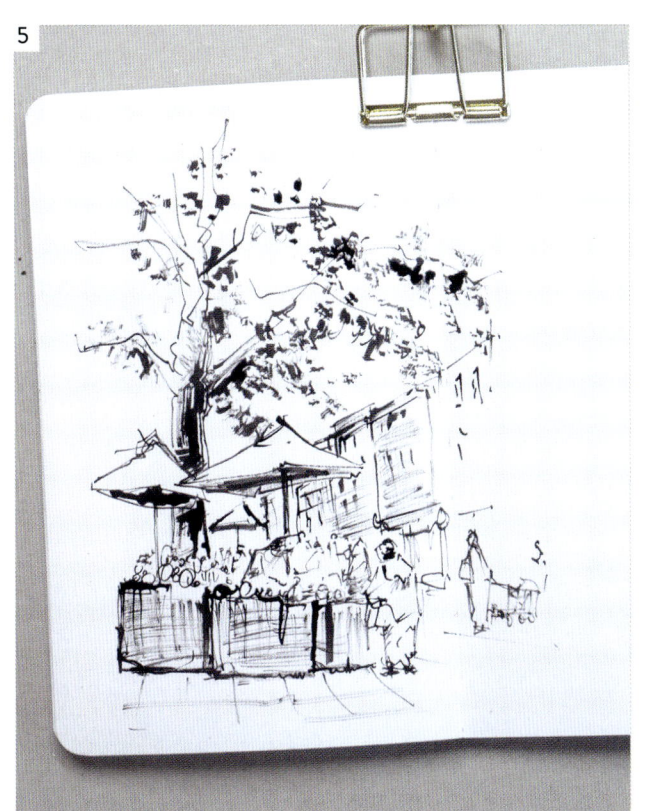

6

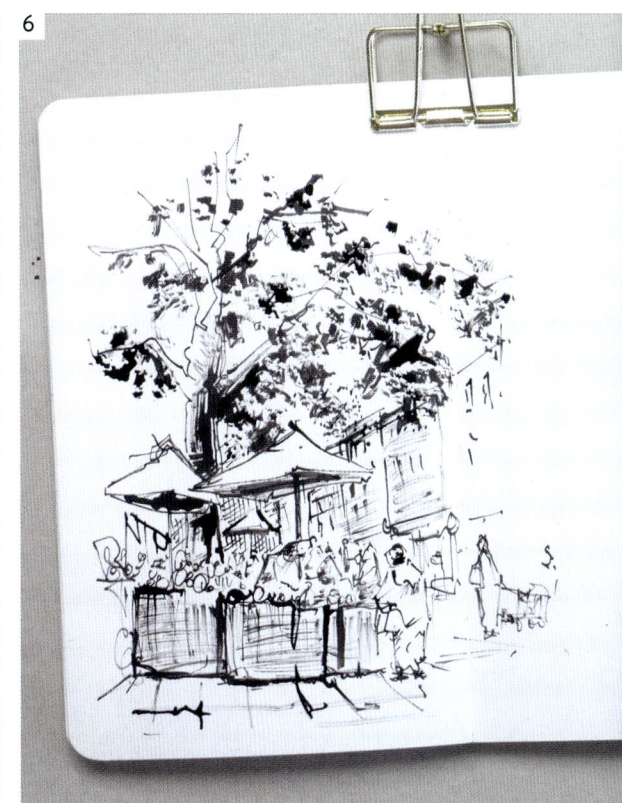

7

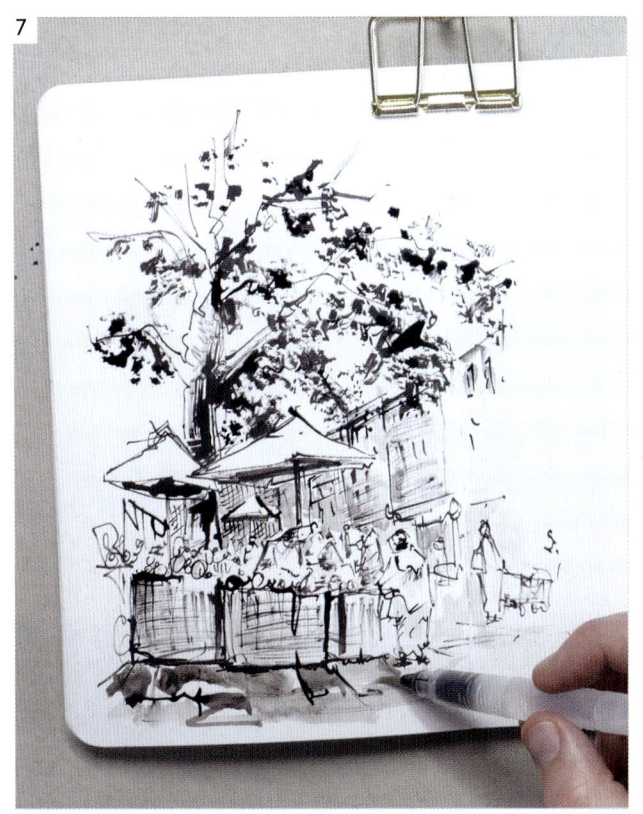

8

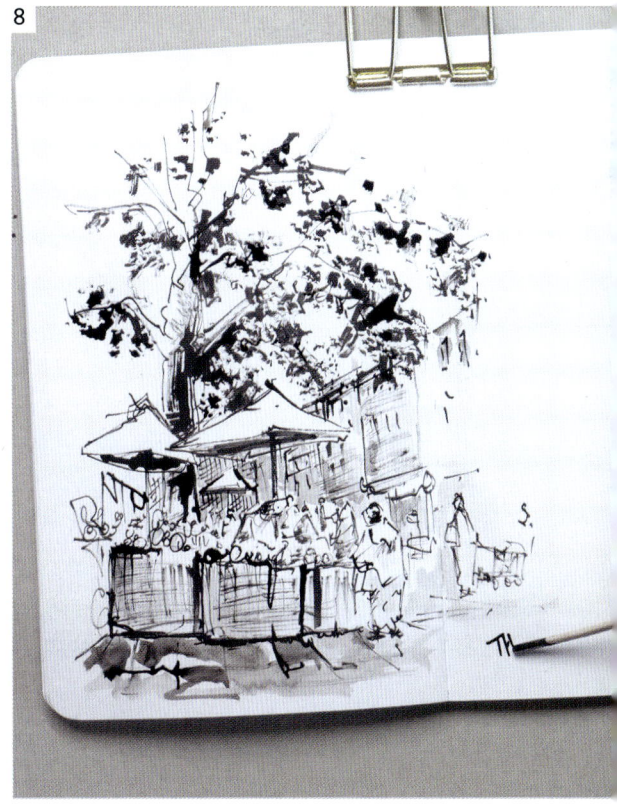

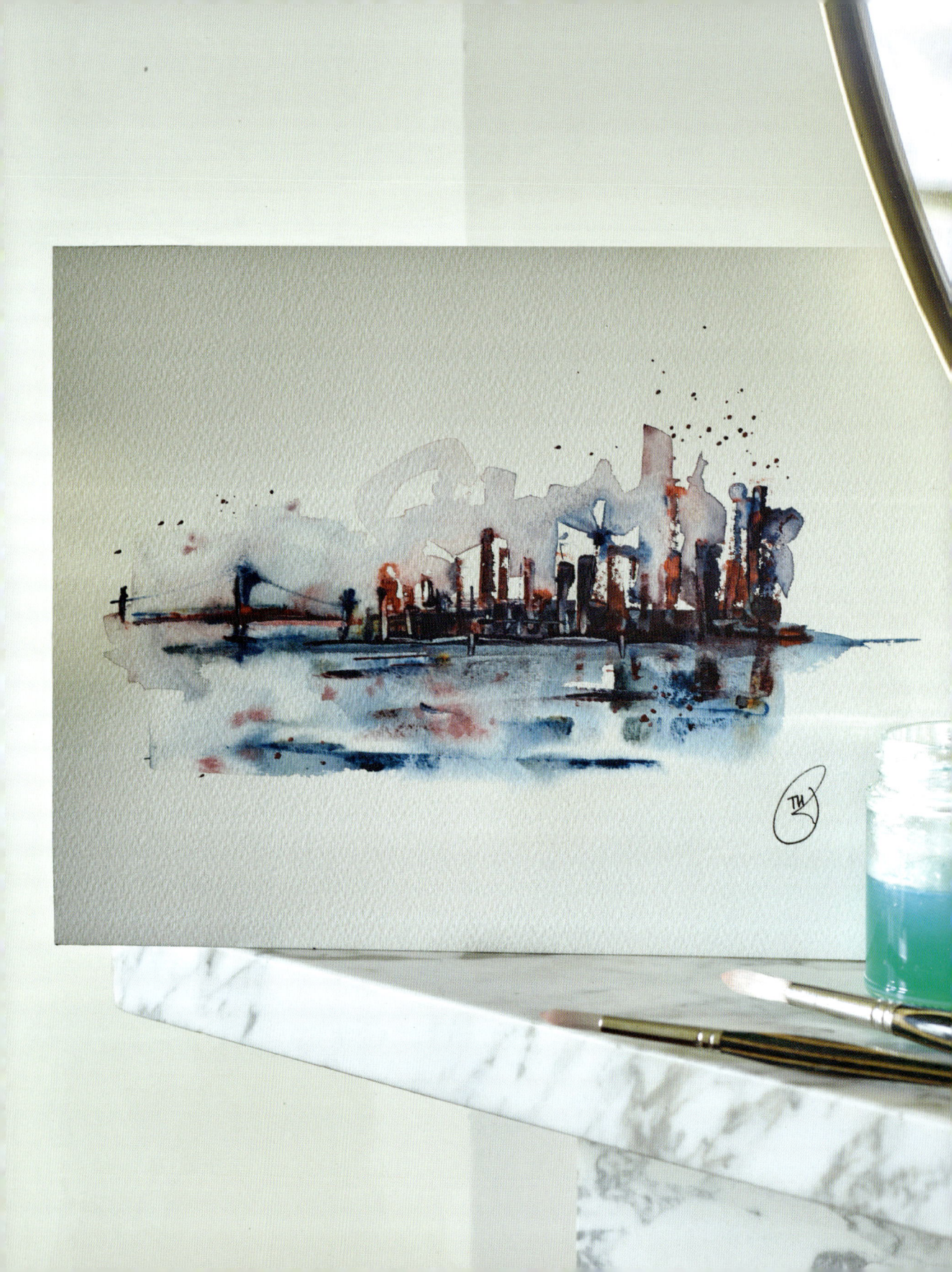

CREDIT CARD PALETTE KNIFE

Sketching with a palette knife is a familiar technique, but using an old credit card – whole or cut into shapes – offers a unique, abstract approach. This method creates bold, painterly marks that build up quickly, perfect for imaginary scenes or vibrant cityscapes.

SUPPLIES

Cold pressed watercolour paper 23 x 30.5cm (9 x 12in)

Flat synthetic brushes (sizes ½in and 1in)

Watercolour paint – cerulean blue, ultramarine, burnt umber, organic vermilion

A ceramic plate or palette

An old credit card or similarly shaped piece of plastic

Paper towel

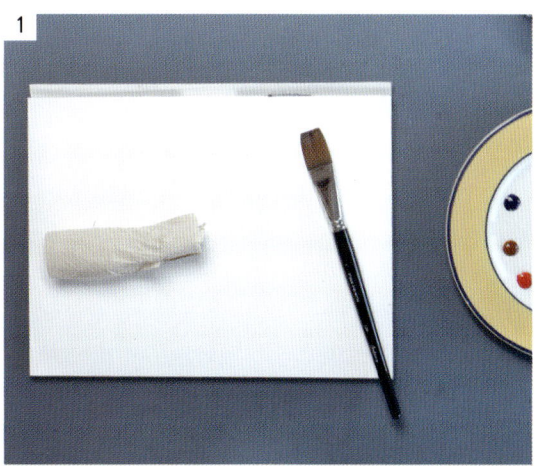

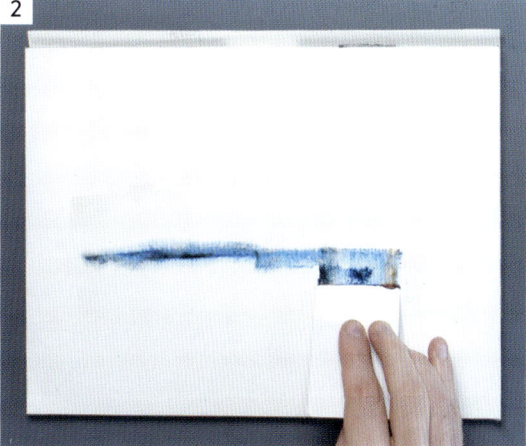

1 For this painting style, you'll need a larger palette than a traditional metal tin. The easiest option is to use a simple ceramic plate. Squeeze a small amount of your paints onto the plate to give yourself a large mixing area. Have some paper towel on hand to blot water and watercolours on the page, as well as to clean your card when needed.

2 Pre-wet the page across the horizon line, and use a mix of blues and complementary brown on your card. A simple line scraped across the page will soften and already produce a rather lovely effect.

3 Add a few more painterly marks in the foreground to start to suggest reflections and ripples of water.

4 Turn the card 90 degrees so you can mark in the structure of the city. Add some warmer red to the existing mix to make it feel distinct from the under-painting.

5 Experiment with different corners, edges, pressures, and angles to produce an array of different marks. You can use the very tip of the corner to scrape the paint already on the page to lift it and leave an area of white.

6 Try blotting the paint with some paper towel. It will lift both water and pigment, creating more variety and textures within the scene.

7 Use a wet brush to allow the pigments to flow more, which creates abstract watercolour effects.

8 As things dry, you can add a few more controlled touches, scrape out some highlights with the card, and splatter with a brush into the sky to complete an abstract, dreamy representation of a city skyline.

3

4

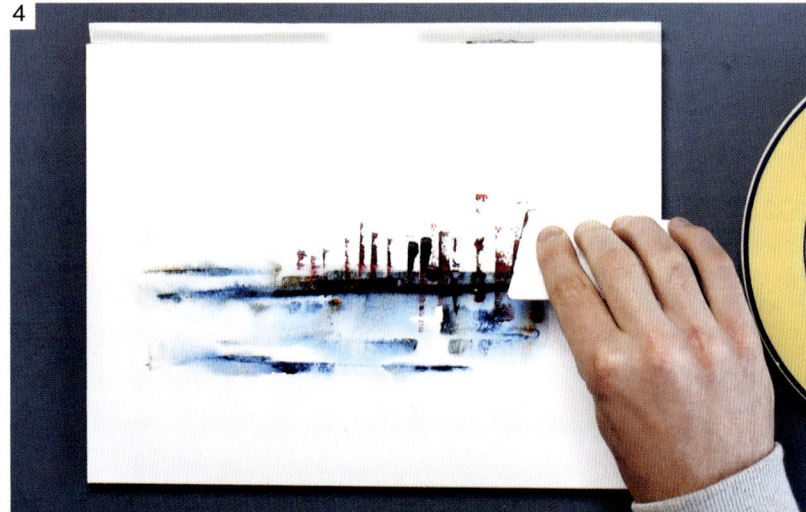

5

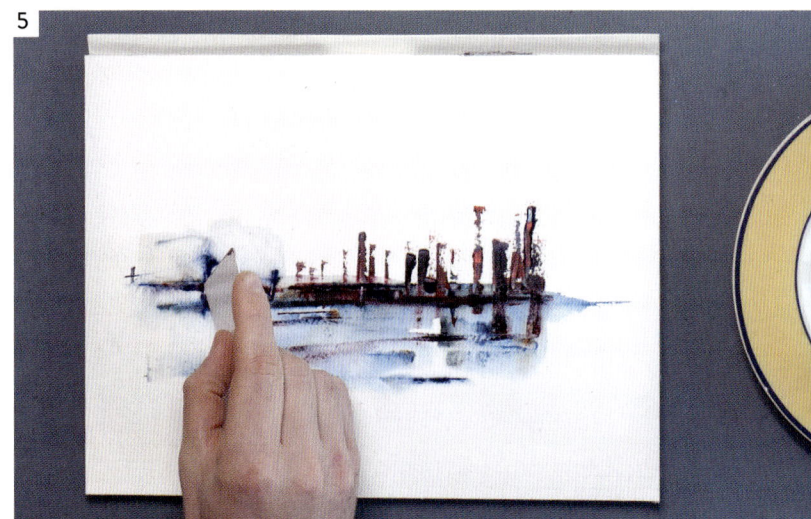

6

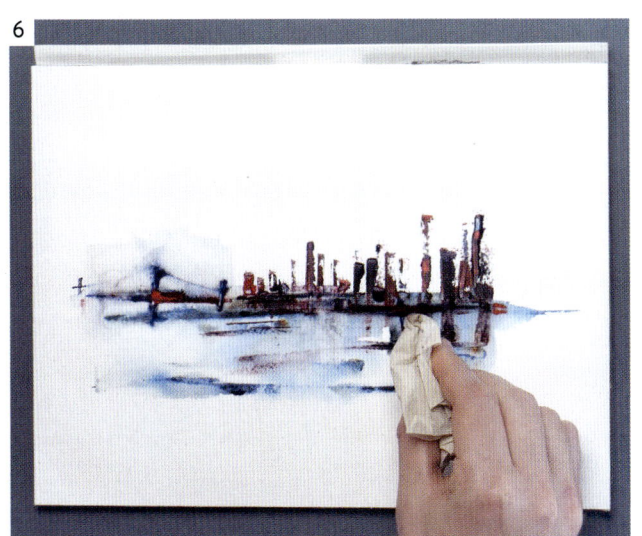

7

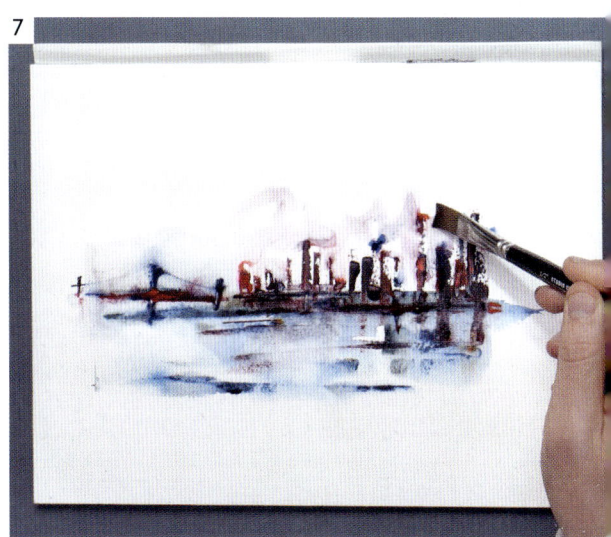

8

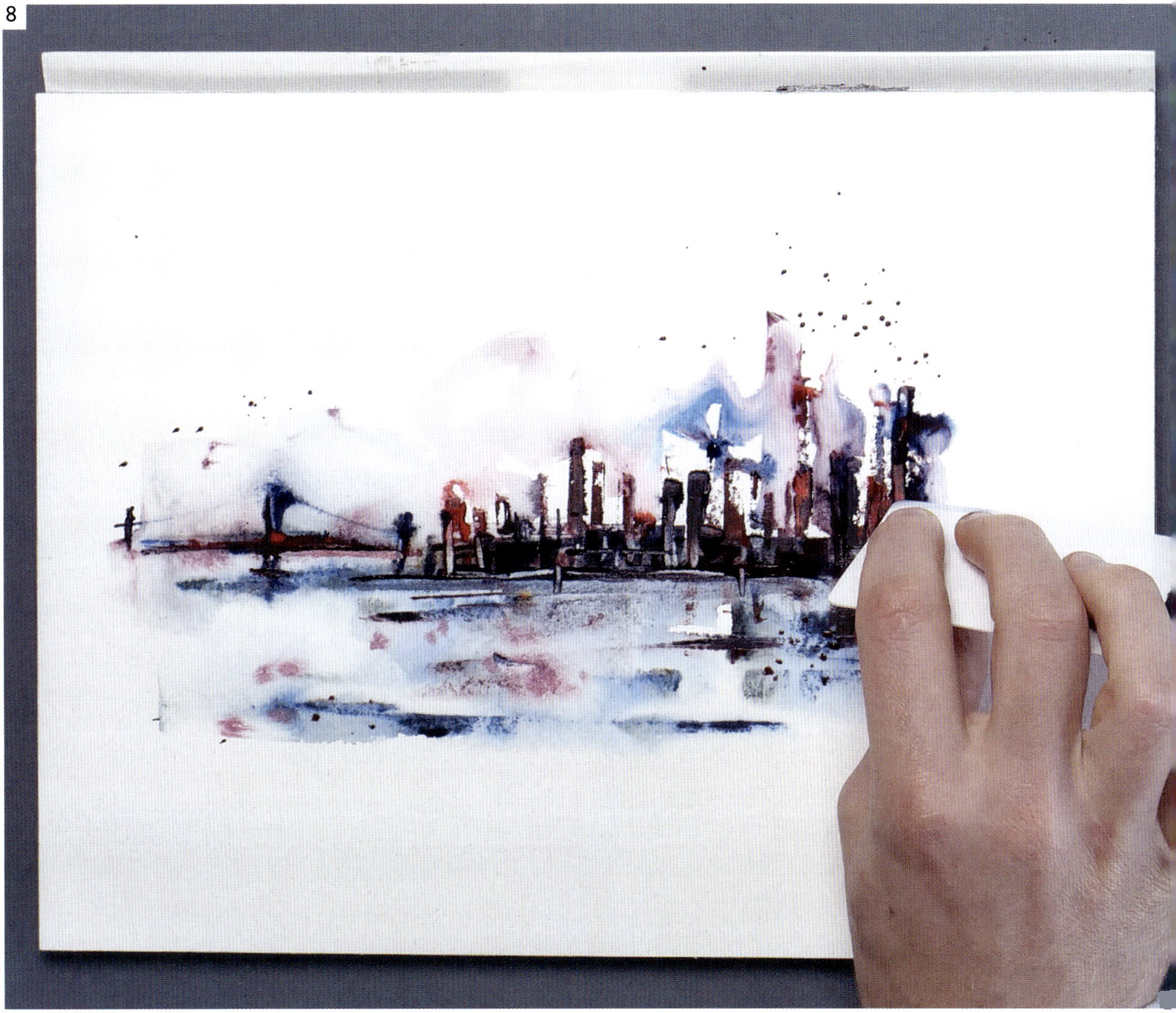

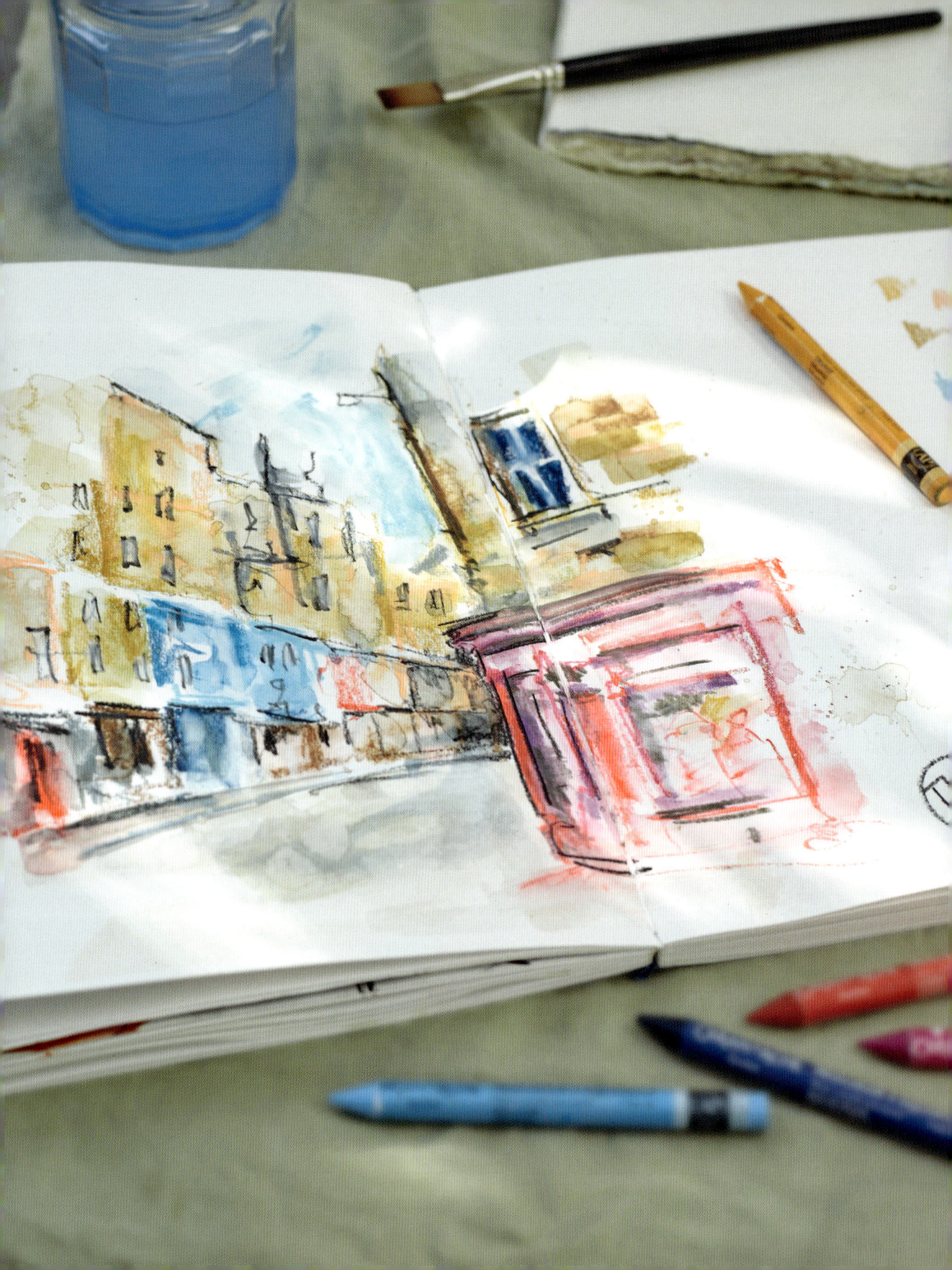

WATER-SOLUBLE CRAYONS

Crayons have made a comeback with the rise of artist-quality brands. Their vibrancy, immediacy, opacity, and blendability make them fantastic for creating bold, textured scenes. Whether working on fine details or loose, expressive strokes, they were perfect for capturing the colourful shopfronts of Edinburgh's city centre.

SUPPLIES

Mixed media sketchbook
20 x 25cm (8 x 10in)

Flat synthetic brushes
(sizes ½in and 1in)

Water-soluble crayons
and pastels

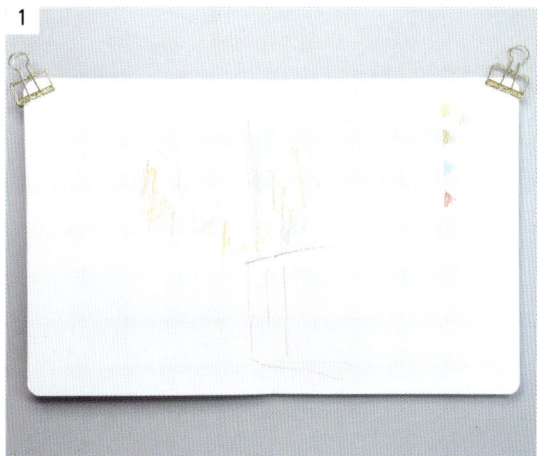

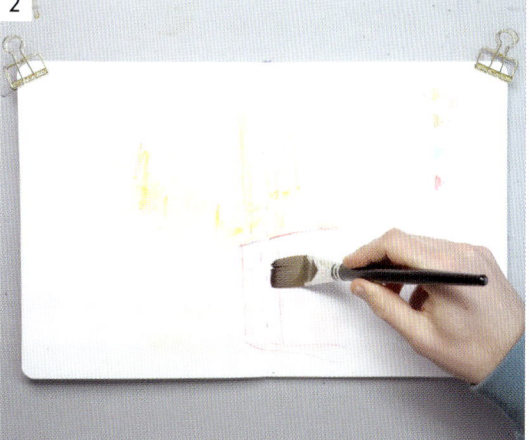

1 Start by sketching your scene out using lighter-hued crayons and quick marks. When using new or vibrant media, it can be useful to use the exercise as a test page, so utilise the edge of your sketchbook to check each crayon's colour before applying it to your page.

2 With water-soluble crayons, you can use a large brush to wash over the colours straight away. This immediately fills the page with tone and softens your lines.

3 Continue to work in sections to build up bolder tones, higher values, and more vibrant colours.

4 At each step, allow yourself to move the colours around a little (or a lot) with a brush and water.

5 Once you've worked your way around the sketch, start to consider what specific details you want to add in. Think about interesting shapes and colours for bricks in the foreground, or maybe certain shop window details.

6 Continue to add more details through the addition of dark marks drawn with deep blue, brown, and black crayons.

7 Blending white and light blue in the sky creates a more gentle effect than if just blue hues are used alone. This is important because the rest of painting is very busy, and an excessively bold sky might detract from the overall feel.

8 Finally, add a few more considered dark lines to bring just a little bit of structure to your scene and to frame the foreground with its punchy colours.

3

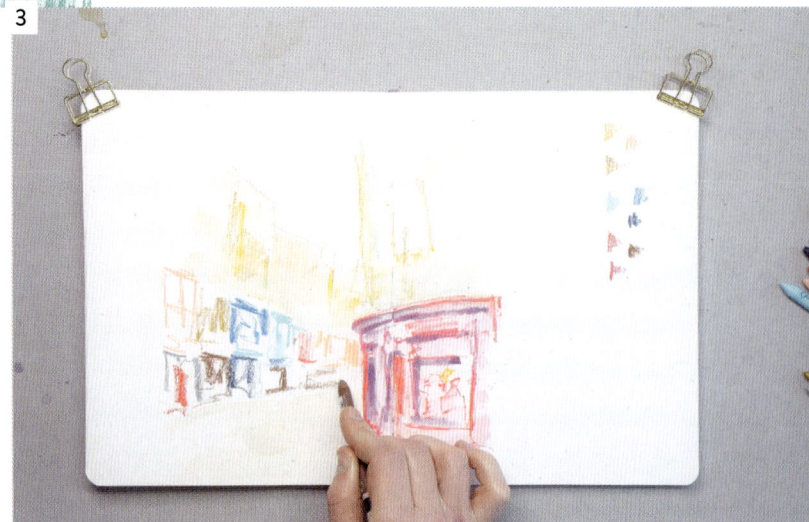

4

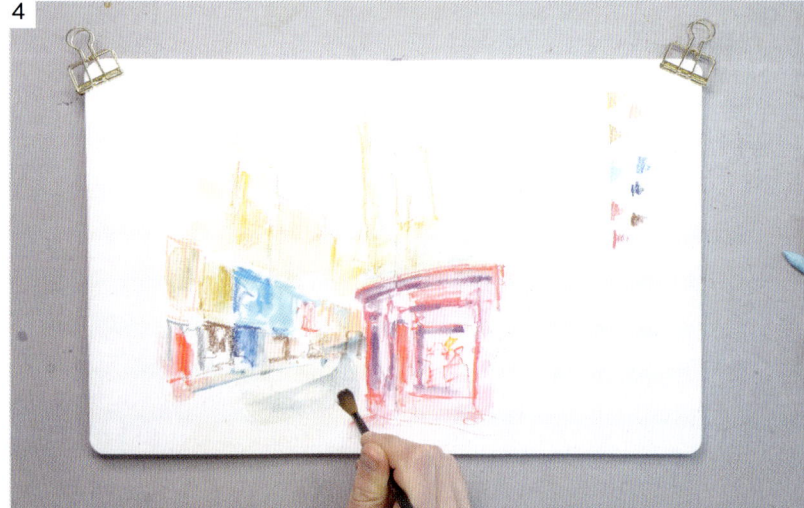

5

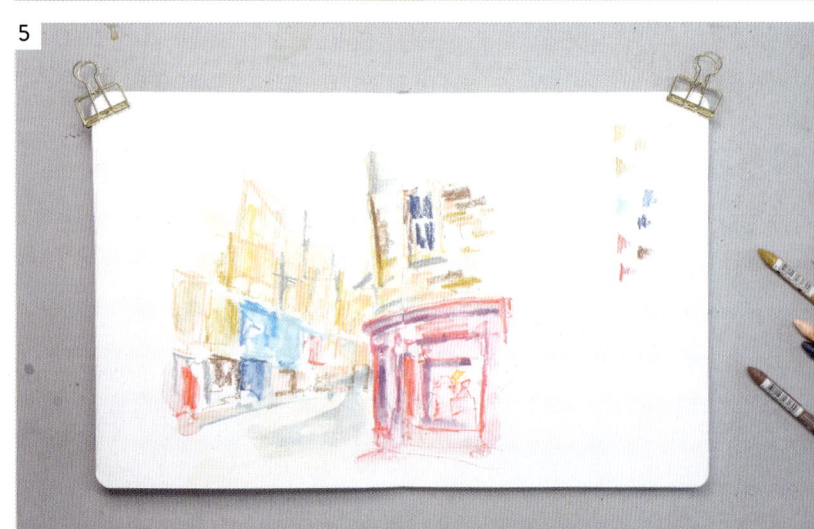

6

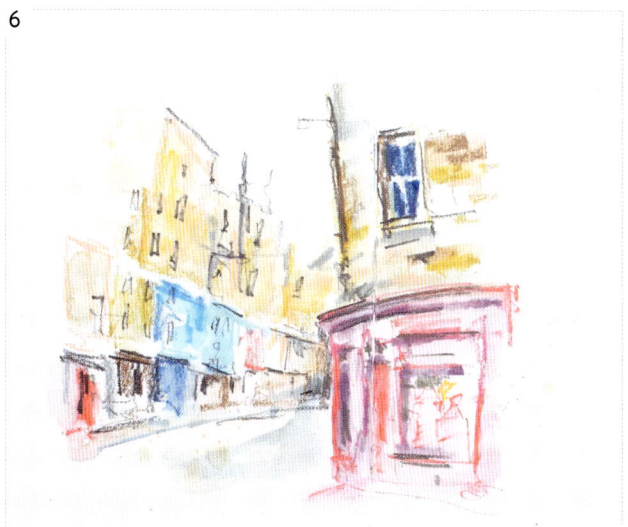

7

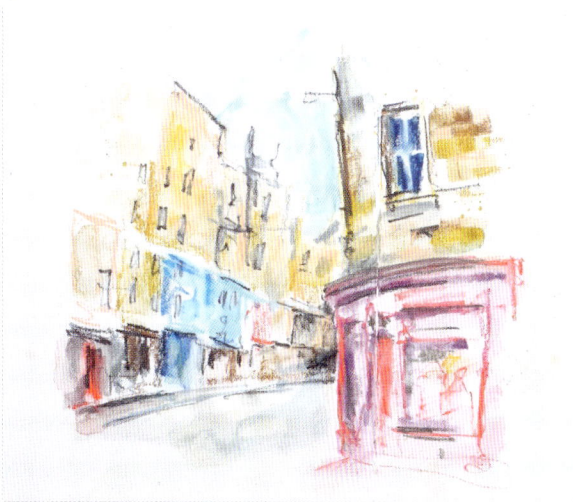

8

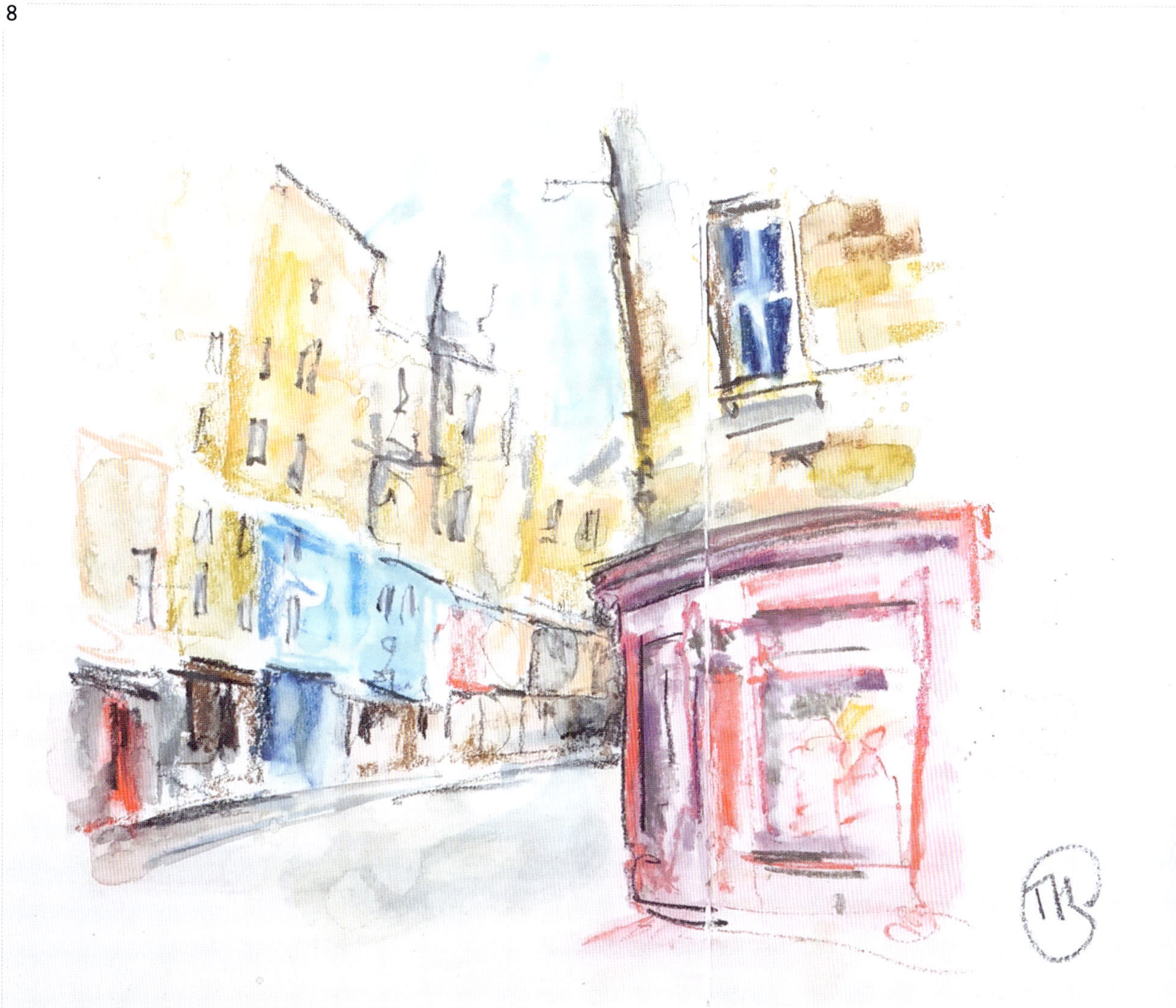

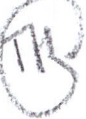

FURTHER
STUDIES

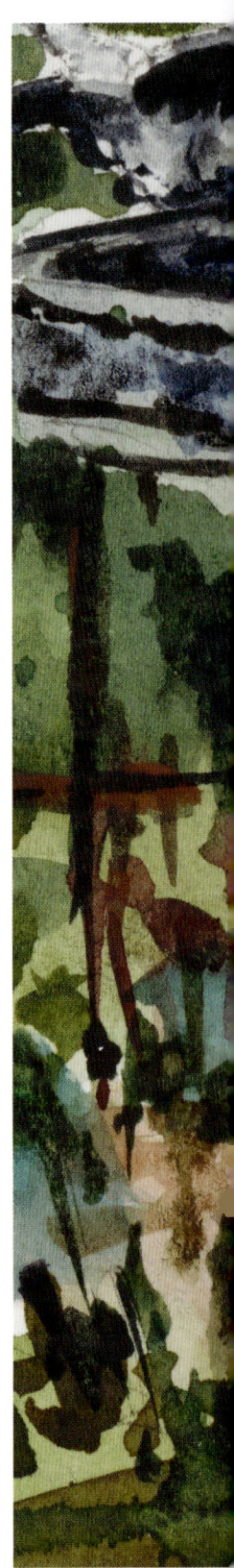

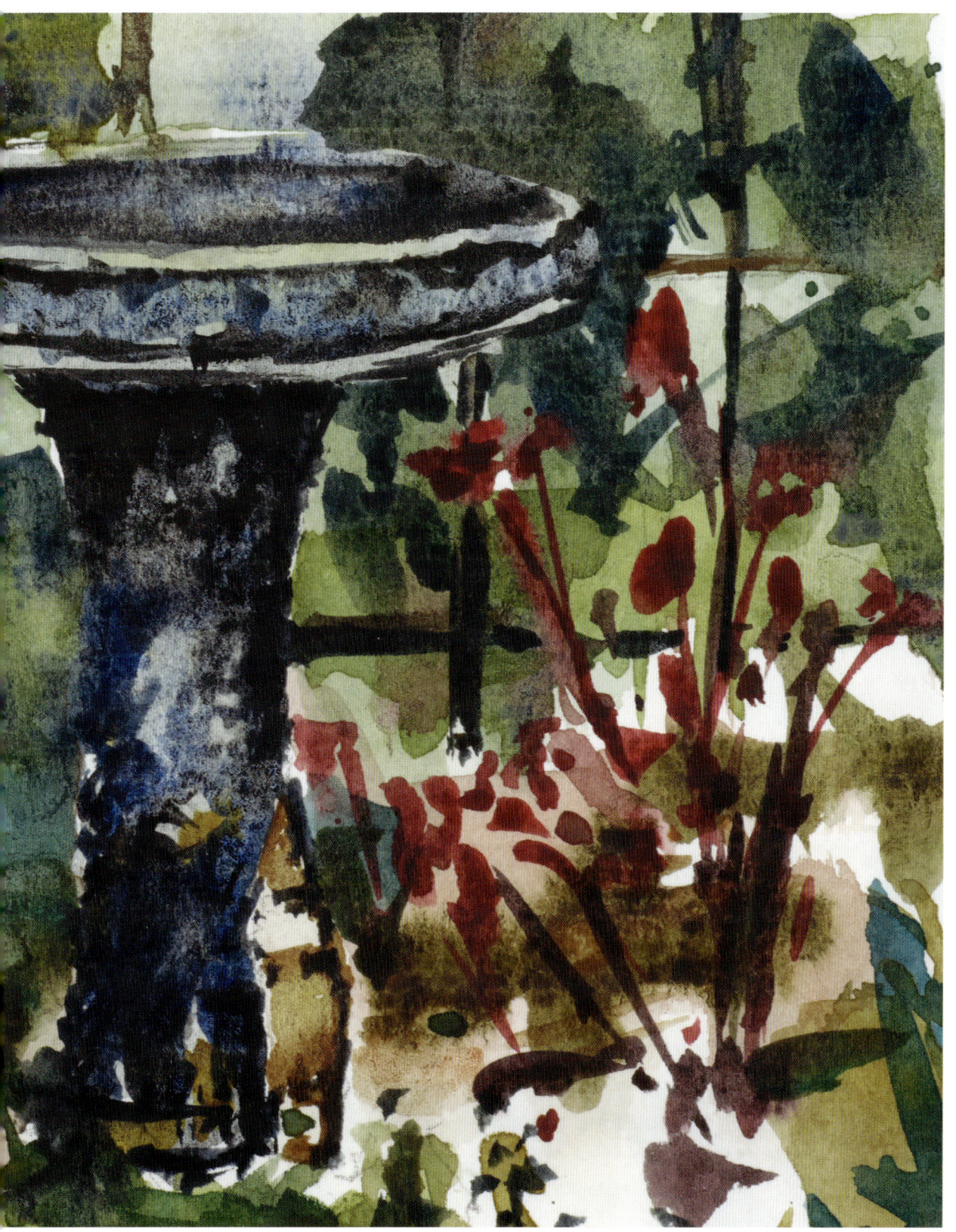

EXPRESSIVE COLOURS

Colours in art are not bound by the constraints of reality – they can be as expressive and abstract as you dare to make them. Beyond simply representing a scene, colours add texture and evoke emotion, transforming a sketch into something captivating. Whether through splashes of watercolour, the smooth opacity of crayon, or the bold strokes of brush markers, expressive colours are an exploration of both the medium and the subject.

SKETCH 1

In this first sketch, inspired by what was rather a gloomy tower in Bucharest, expressive use of pinks and yellows throughout the architectural elements adds a bit of fun. I used opaque greens to then pick out a few details, including signs and people's heads, to complete a very non-literal quirky scene.

1

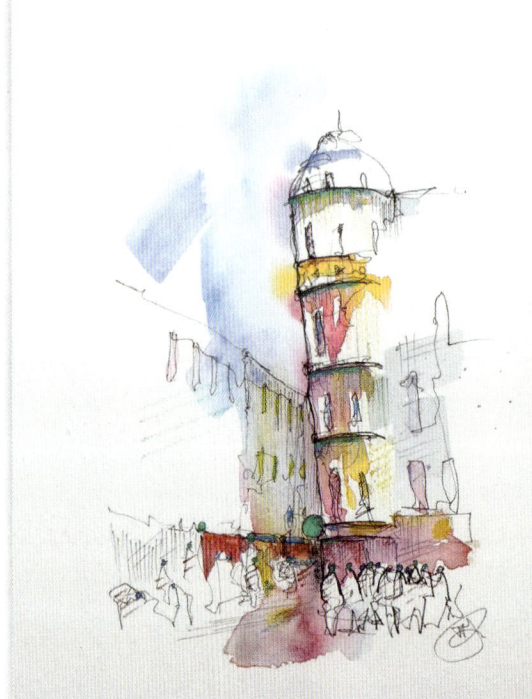

2

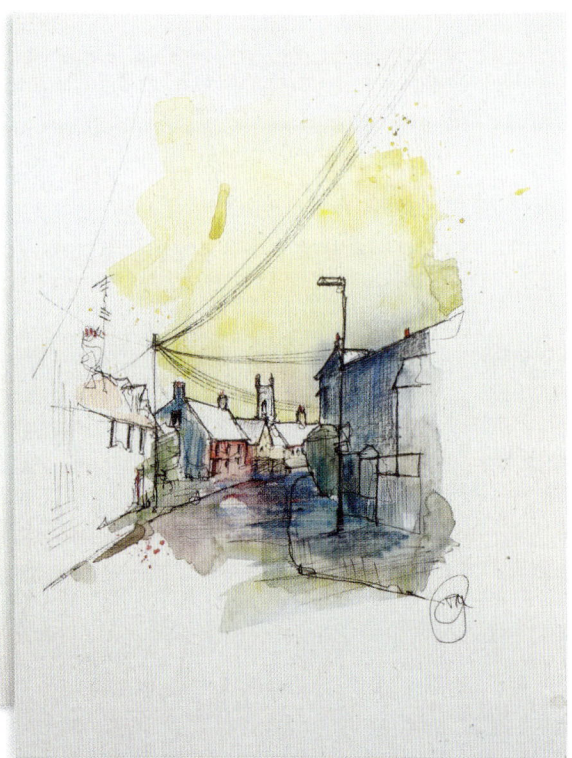

SKETCH 2

Inspired by the evening skies of my hometown, this scene plays with contrast. The soft, glowing yellows of the watercolour sky evoke a sense of warmth and calm, while the foreground's murky, opaque shadows, created with water-soluble pencil, add drama and weight. The juxtaposition of light and dark creates a compelling narrative within the scene.

SKETCH 3

Watercolour brush markers provide a flat, illustrative aesthetic that contrasts sharply with traditional watercolour techniques. The bold, bright colours of the brush markers are strikingly mobile in water, creating smooth, ungranulated washes. This approach to colour captures the vibrant energy of Chile's Puerto Natales in a way that feels fresh and contemporary.

SKETCH 4

This quirky interpretation of Ramsgate, UK, was created entirely with water-soluble crayons. Their vibrant, opaque colours lend a playful quality to the scene, while the solid textures in the foreground ground the composition. The medium transforms a simple sketch into a vivid, textured exploration of the seaside town.

3

4

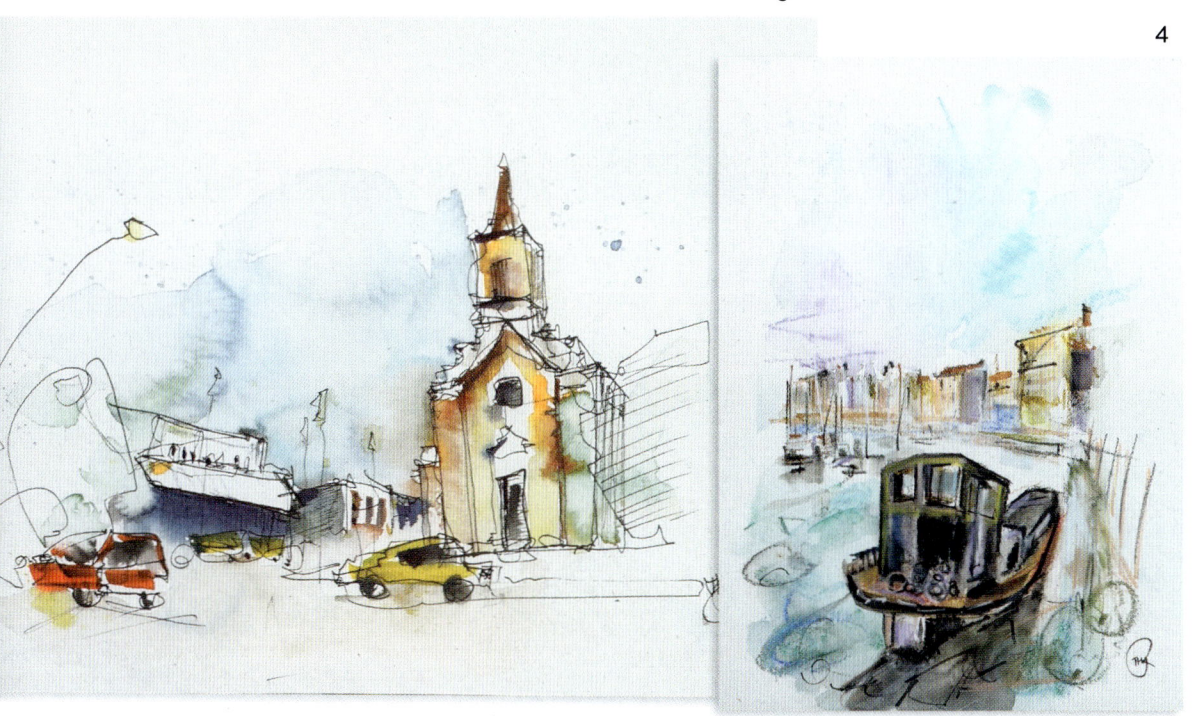

PARKS AND GARDENS

Cities aren't just moody streets and towering architecture – they are also home to green parks and vibrant gardens. These spaces offer a very different challenge. By focusing on the natural elements, we can create sketches that celebrate the softer, quieter side of urban life.

SKETCH 1

This doorway is framed by rather fascinating foliage in the form of a climbing plant. The ink work, which naturally feels more geometric and certain, is focussed around the structure of the building. A mixed-media approach with watercolours, pastels, and acrylics provides a lovely contrast in the flowers.

1

2

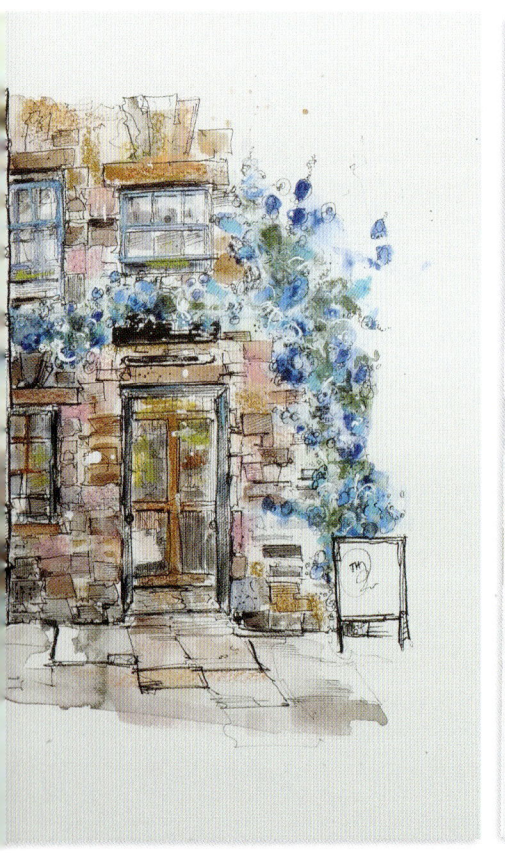

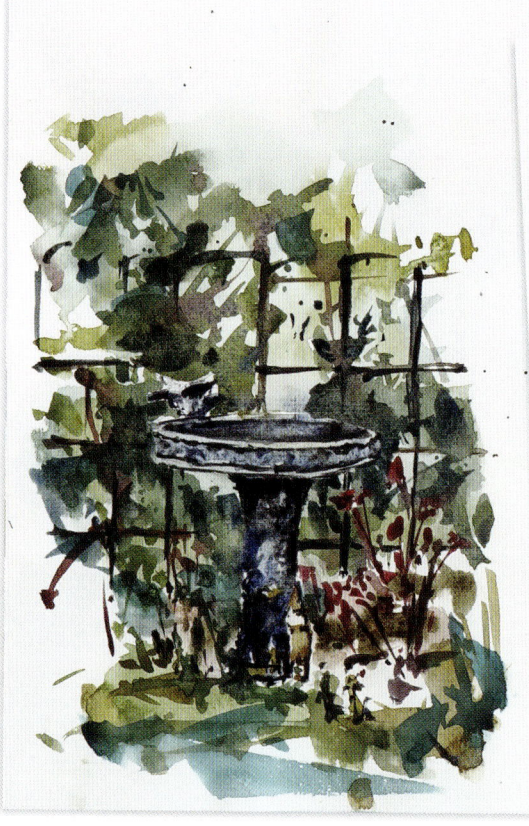

SKETCH 2

Here is the bird bath that I grew up with, nestled in my mum's garden – a place always green and full of life. Using a watercolour-only approach captures the vibrant and overlapping greens, creating a sense of the garden's lively, layered textures.

SKETCH 3

Using abstraction is a fascinating way to explore a more natural scene. This is my take on a botanical garden I wandered into in Japan. Wet-on-wet colours combine with a simple structure to create something loose and only semi-representative of the scene it's inspired by.

SKETCH 4

Another staple of many a city are riverside parks and boats. In this scene, alcohol markers have been used to bring out the vibrant colours of the sky, water, and greenery. The 'rag' paper used allows the normally smooth marker textures to become more rough and three dimensional.

3

4

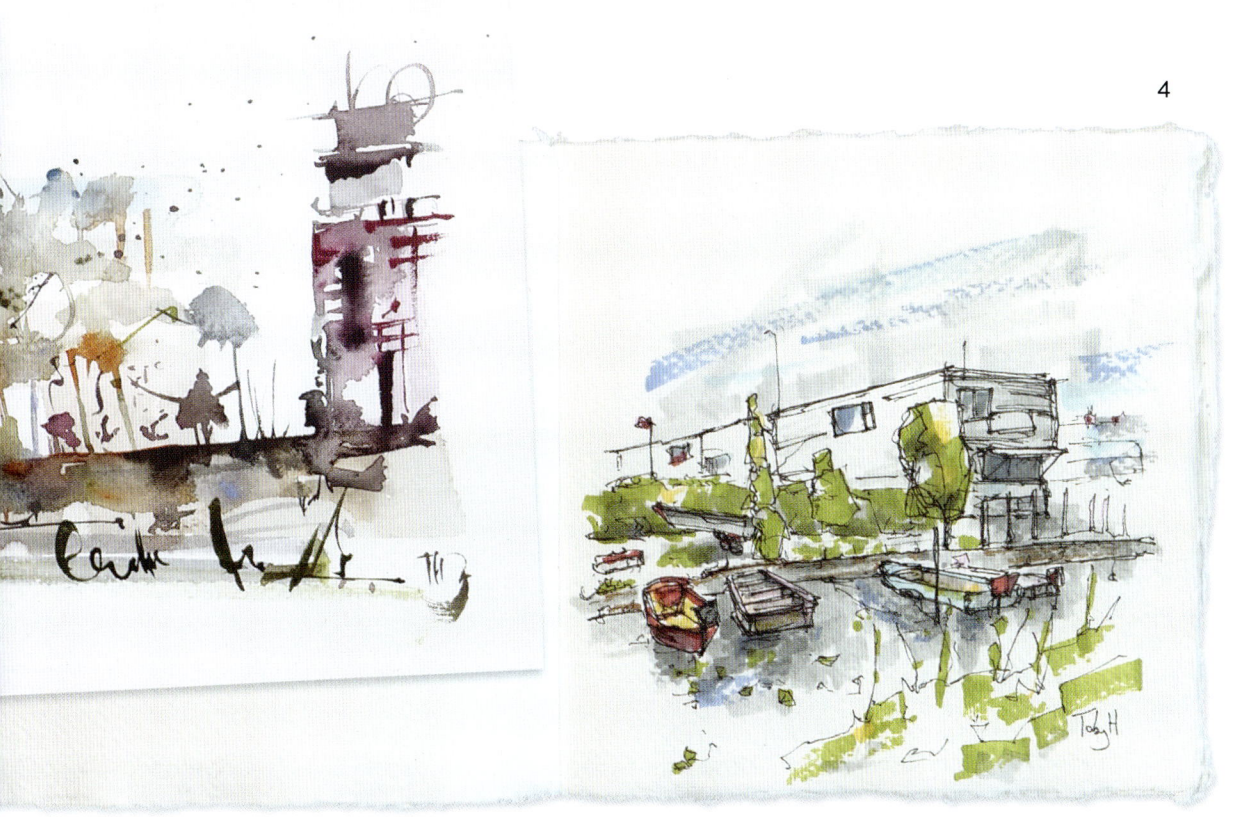

MONOCHROME INK

A major advantage of sketching is its speed and focus. These sketches were completed in just a couple of hours while exploring the city of Bath, UK, in the evening, using a fude pen for bold line work and a few alcohol ink markers for layered values. Quick sketches like these are perfect for outdoor sketching, filling sketchbook pages, or serving as studies and warm-ups for larger works.

SKETCH 1

Arriving late in Bath, I stopped to pick up dinner in a quiet burger bar. Capturing the perspective of the scene was a joy. The complex overlapping shapes give the scene depth, while offering a playful challenge. Adding small details to the menu on the left provided just enough context to tell the story, allowing the sketch to capture a fleeting yet vibrant moment.

SKETCH 2

I'm always drawn to scenes with intriguing perspectives and shapes, and this quirky narrow pub, framed by steeply angled streets on either side, was a perfect example. The irregularity of the architecture made it particularly challenging and fun to sketch, incorporating exaggerated perspective in the side streets.

1

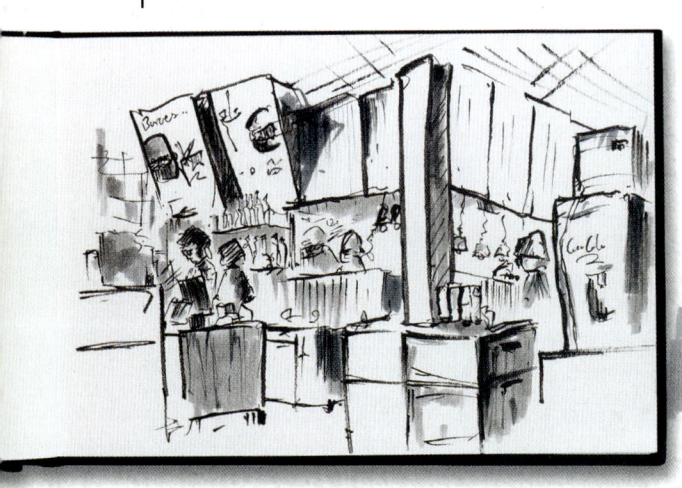

2

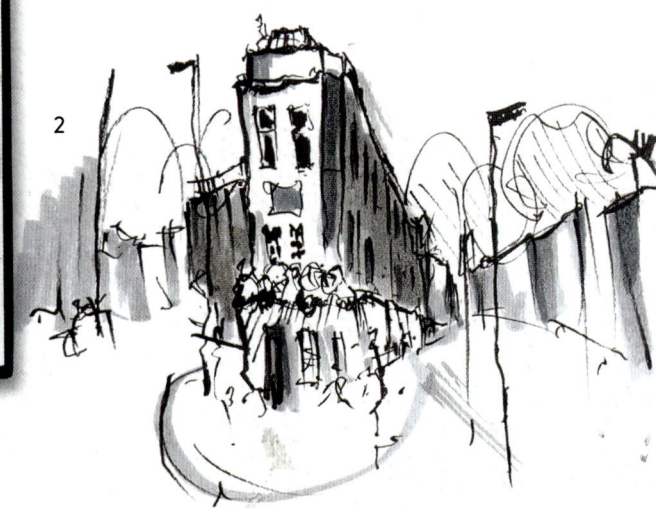

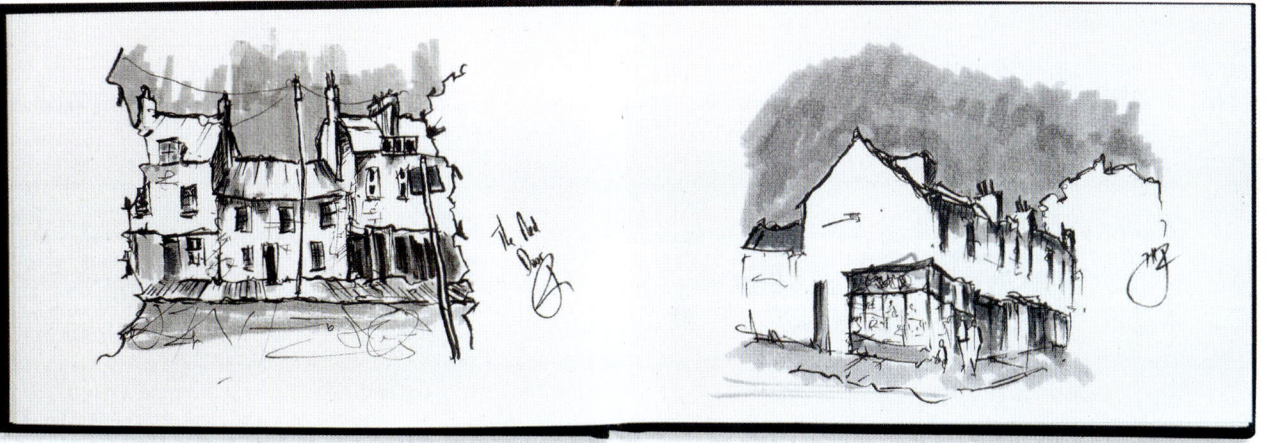

3   4

SKETCHES 3 AND 4

As evening set in, I came across a house with a striking red door. The vibrant colour immediately caught my eye, but it was the composition – framed by strong vertical lines on either side – that kept me sketching despite the cold. Later, on my way to the hotel, I paused for a few minutes to capture a cosy takeaway glowing against the night sky, another small but satisfying study of light and contrast.

SKETCH 5

These simple studies often serve as a foundation for more developed work. The cosy takeaway above was the inspiration for one of the scenes in The City Glows at Night in the Inspiration Finder chapter. The initial sketch of the house with the red door provided a loose and expressive base for a more detailed and colourful studio

version. Working from the on-location sketch, rather than just a photograph, allowed me to bring more energy and character into the final piece, keeping the spontaneous lines while

layering in richer colours and textures. That's the beauty of sketching on location – it documents a place, it deepens your connection to it, and enhances your memories as well as giving you a wealth of material to refine later.

5

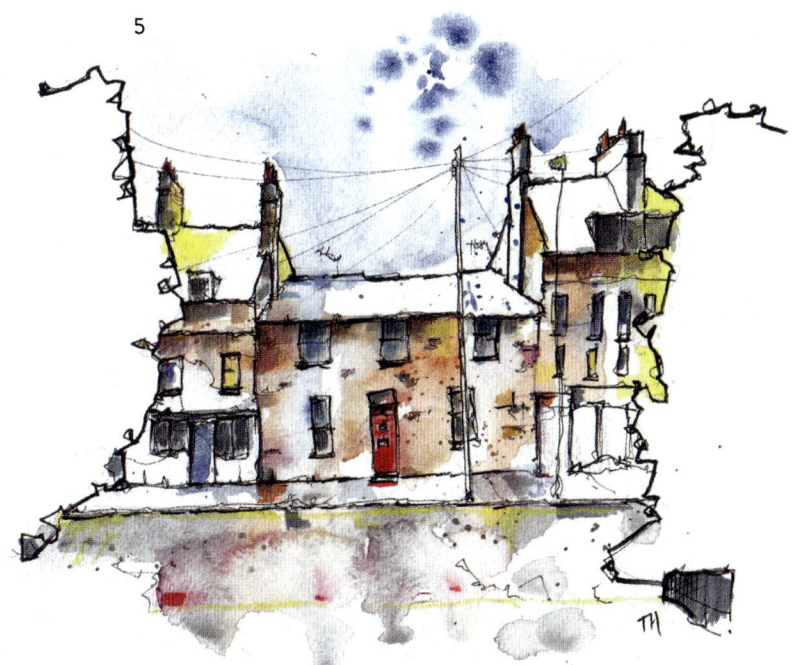

SAME SCENE, DIFFERENT TECHNIQUES

This is all about exploring how the same scene can take on different moods and personalities through varied techniques. By revisiting the same subject multiple times, we open ourselves up to fresh perspectives and creative discoveries. To demonstrate this, my good friend and fellow artist Colin Woodward and I sketched Bath Abbey using different approaches.

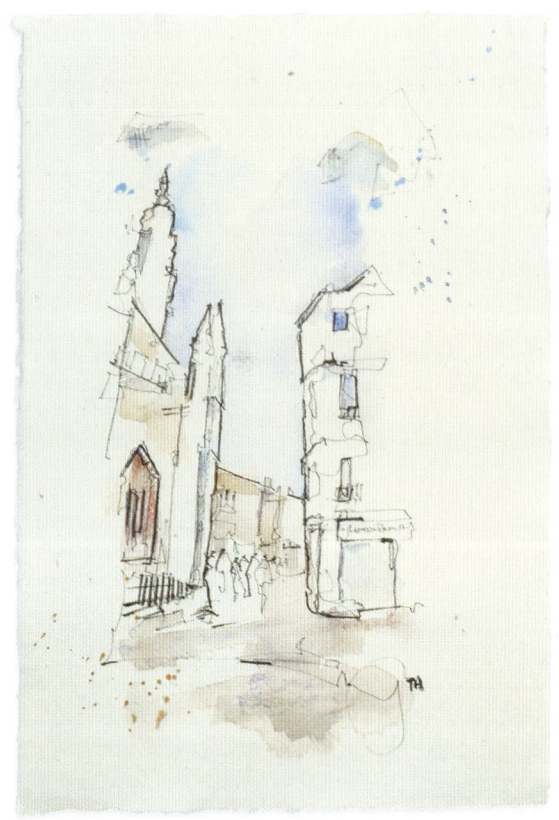

1

SKETCHES 1 AND 2

The first two sketches show how Colin and I typically work with ink and watercolour. Even with the same tools and the same subject, our personal styles shape the results.

I tend to use a wet-on-wet approach, letting colours blend freely on the page (1), while Colin layers his washes more deliberately, building depth with careful patience (2). The contrast between these techniques is fascinating – together they highlight the richness of artistic interpretation.

2

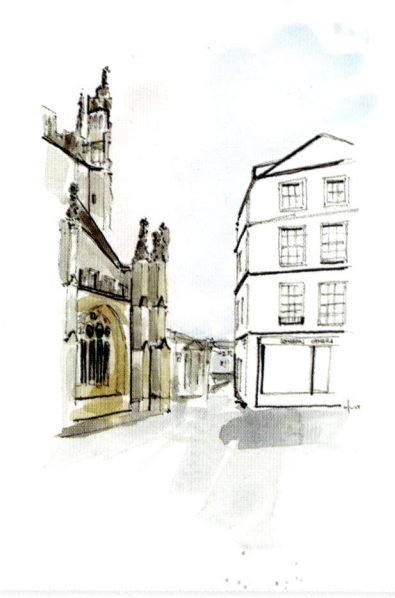

SKETCHES 3 AND 4

Next, we set ourselves a challenge: to step outside our usual methods and try something different.

I reached for water-soluble crayons, using a sepia crayon to define structure before softening and toning the scene with water (3). A few warm and cool colours were then added to lift the mood and introduce subtle vibrancy.

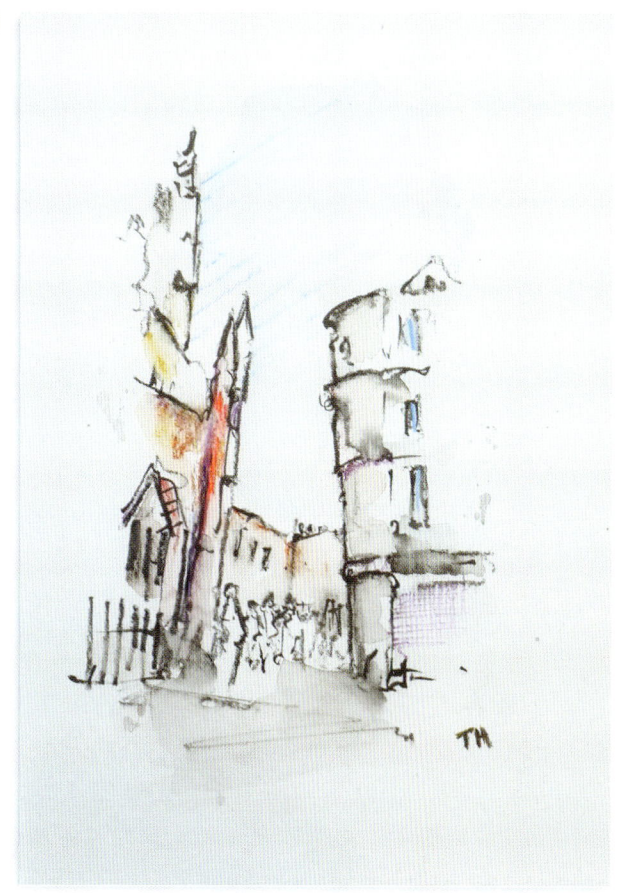

3

4

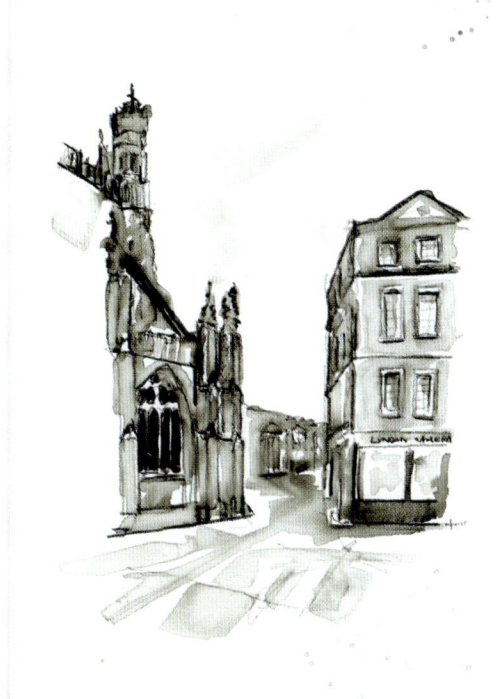

Colin created a striking, moody version of the Abbey using just a single indigo watercolour pencil (4). A crisp, confident line and a simple wash of colour were enough to bring the architecture to life in a bold yet minimalistic way.

PEOPLE SITTING DOWN

People sitting down can be uniquely challenging to sketch due to the complexities of the seated posture. However, it's also a great opportunity to capture relatively still subjects. Locations like cafés and trains are perfect for practicing, offering a steady stream of seated figures to observe and draw.

1

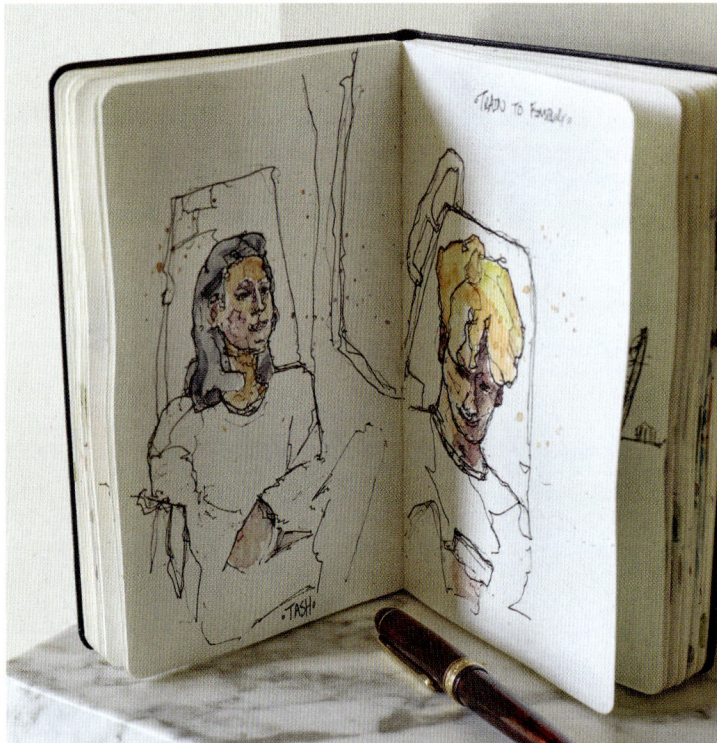

SKETCH 1

Here are two people sketched on a train journey through London. Capturing close-up portraits like these eliminates the challenge of the seated posture. Spending time getting the line work feeling right allows a limited and gentle set of colours to be more than enough to complete the sketch.

SKETCH 2

Home offers plenty of (usually) willing subjects, such as my wife sitting in our armchair. I enjoy using simple, abstract lines, often bypassing complexities like hands and feet. Despite this minimalist approach, the scene still includes enough detail to provide context and remain easily recognisable.

SKETCH 3

A view through a café can feel overwhelmingly complex. In this colourful scene, the line work is deceptively simple, mostly focussed on the crowd of heads. Abstract and expressive layered colours, including watercolours and alcohol markers, then make the image feel busy to represent that complexity.

2

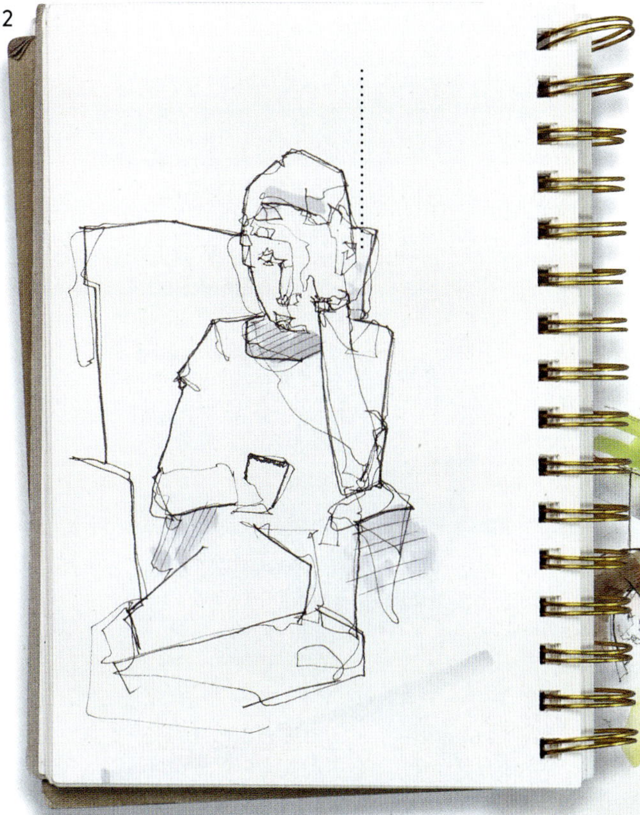

3

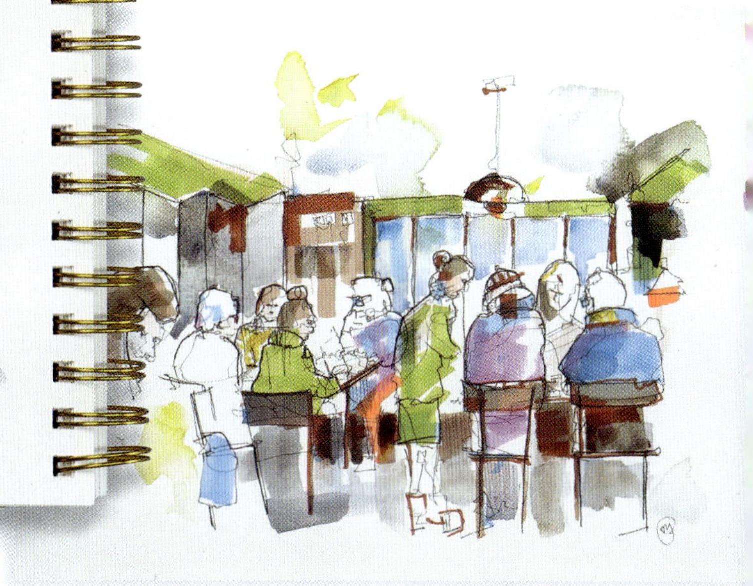

4

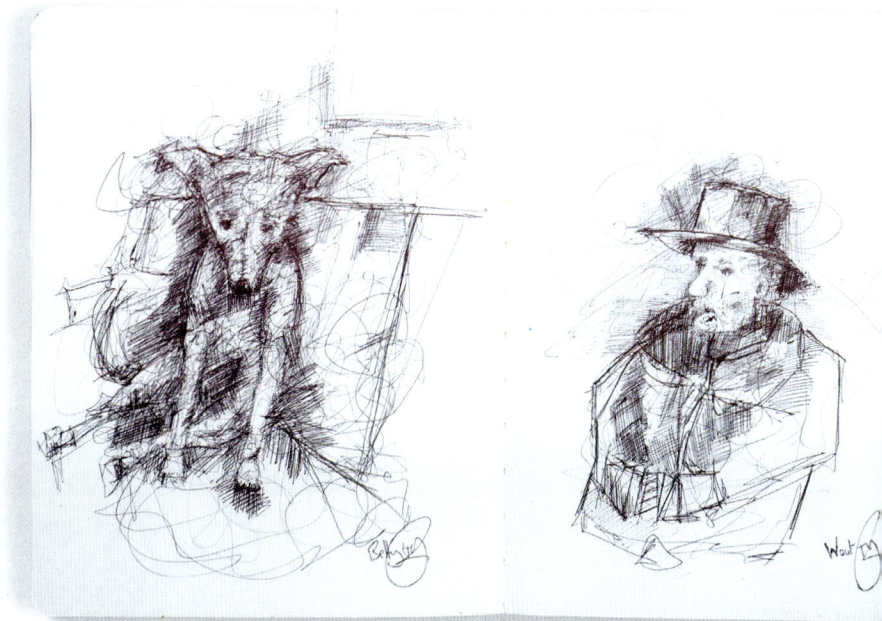

SKETCH 4

The humble ballpoint pen works beautifully for portraits, whether of people or animals. Rather than focusing on precise lines and contours, which can feel more illustrative, emphasizing values and shadows creates a moody, atmospheric effect.

JOURNALING

Keeping a sketchbook is a wonderful way to create art and document your journey. It serves as a visual journal, capturing your artistic growth, holiday memories, emotions, and more. Incorporating text, stamps, titles, or labels can enrich the pages, making them both a creative expression and a personal record of your experiences. These scenes are excerpts from my personal sketchbook, created during my honeymoon with my wonderful, beautiful, and very patient wife. They showcase how I cherish my memories through sketches that capture the moments, emotions, and places that mean the most to me.

SKETCH 1

This first spread from my sketchbook captures a memorable and elegant meal we enjoyed. The menu on the right and the labels scattered throughout the image provide just enough detail to vividly recall the experience. The addition of personal notes in the corner can add an extra layer of storytelling to prompt a memory.

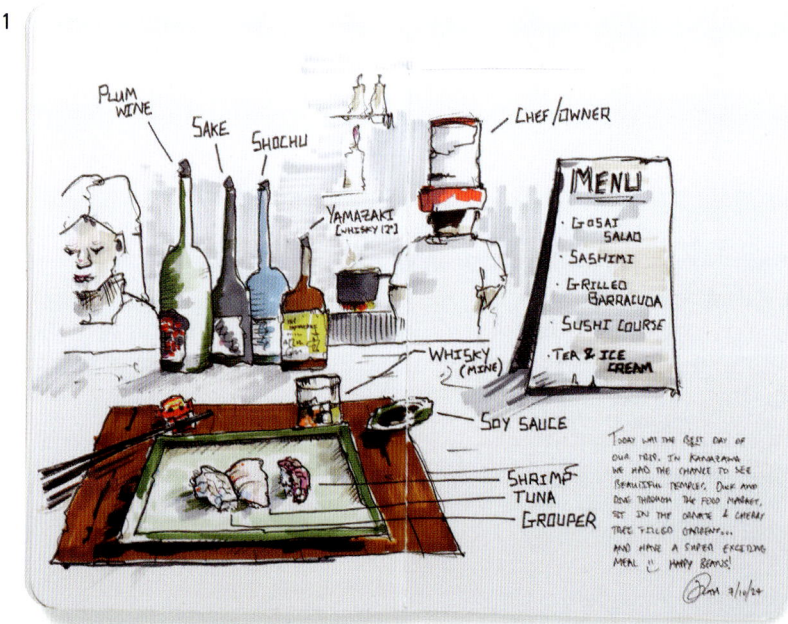

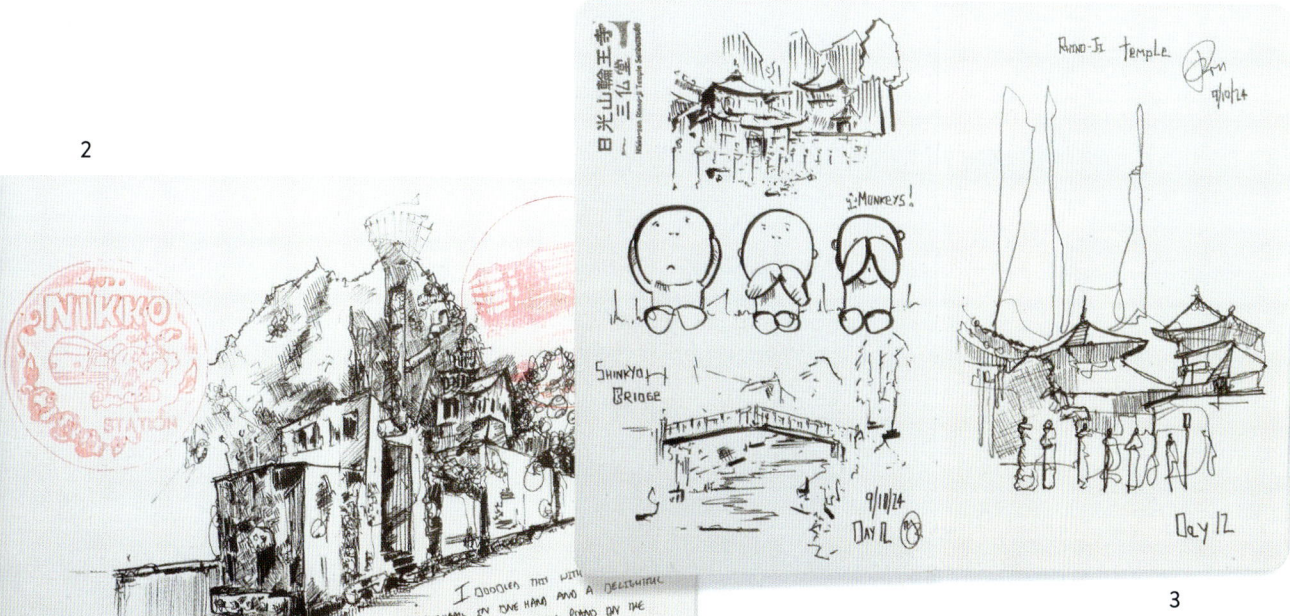

SKETCH 2

This is one of my favourite spreads from the entire trip. The text transports me back to a dimly lit bar in a mountainous town, sipping a whisky highball while sketching a captivating train from memory and imagination. The red-ink stamps on each page add a distinctive touch, weaving in more layers of memory and tying the experience together.

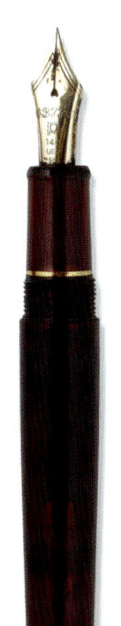

SKETCH 3

Holidays are often packed with sights, activities, and travel, leaving little time for intricate sketches. While my wife is patient, standing at each spot for hours to capture detailed scenes would have disrupted our day. Instead, a quick five-minute doodle of a key element (such as the origin of the famous 'hear no evil' monkeys) offers a perfect sketcher's approach to journaling experiences. It's fast, meaningful, and captures the essence of the moment.

ABOUT THE AUTHOR

Toby Haseler (aka Toby SketchLoose and Toby UrbanSketch) is an ink and watercolour sketcher who embraces simplicity, continuous lines, and the joy of the process. He believes that every sketch – mistakes and all – is a valuable part of the journey, and that mistakes can be positive experiences that help artists grow.

For Toby, sketching isn't about perfection. Instead, it's about capturing moments and exploring ideas. That's why he calls all his art sketching – a reminder that there's no need to fill the page, overwork a piece, or get stuck worrying about every detail. His approach is quick, expressive, and loose, blending continuous flowing ink lines with vibrant watercolours and the occasional mixed media.

Now, he shares this mindset with others, helping people break free from rigid expectations and rediscover the fun in sketching. Through his workshops, courses, and videos, he encourages artists to let go, loosen up, and find joy in every mark they make.

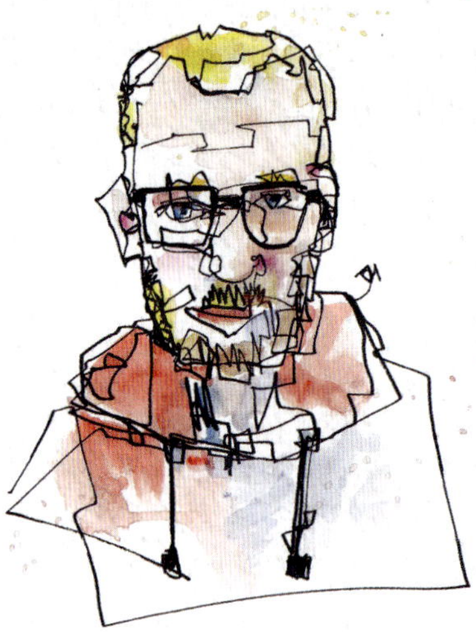

ACKNOWLEDGEMENTS

To Tash, my dear wife – thank you for your patience, your unwavering support, and for always lifting me up.

To Betty, for keeping me grounded, present, and always in the moment.

To Christine, for giving me the confidence to pursue my own path.

To my sketchbooks, for bearing the brunt of my experiments, mistakes, and providing me so much joy.

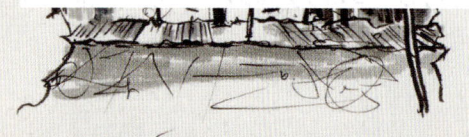

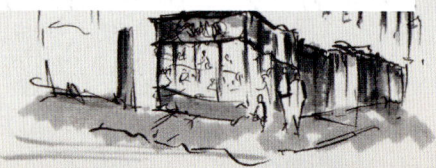

INDEX

This book has been printed on paper
from approved suppliers and made from
pulp from sustainable sources.

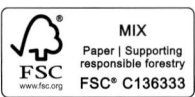

MIX
Paper | Supporting
responsible forestry
FSC® C136333

Printed in China through Asia Pacific Offset for:
David and Charles, Ltd
Suite A, Tourism House, Pynes Hill, Exeter, EX2 5WS

10 9 8 7 6 5 4 3 2 1

PUBLISHING DIRECTOR Ame Verso
SENIOR COMMISSIONING EDITOR Nigel Browning
PUBLISHING MANAGER Jeni Chown
DESK EDITOR Victoria Allen
COPY EDITOR Clare Ashton
LEAD DESIGNER Sam Staddon
DESIGNER Lucy Ridley
DESIGN, LAYOUT AND ART DIRECTION Wayne Blades
PHOTOGRAPHY Neal Grundy
PRE-PRESS DESIGNER Susan Reansbury
PRODUCTION MANAGER Beverley Richardson

David and Charles publishes high-quality
books on a wide range of subjects. For more
information visit www.davidandcharles.com.

Share your art with us on social media using
#dandcbooks and follow us on Facebook and
Instagram by searching for @dandcbooks.

Layout of the digital edition of this book may vary
depending on reader hardware and display settings.

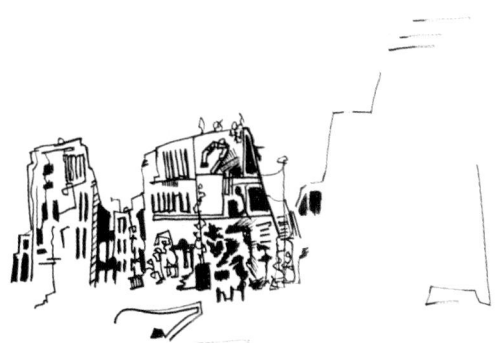